T0355199

On Marilyn Monroe

On Marilyn Monroe

An Opinionated Guide

RICHARD BARRIOS

OXFORD
UNIVERSITY PRESS

OXFORD
UNIVERSITY PRESS

Oxford University Press is a department of the University of Oxford. It furthers
the University's objective of excellence in research, scholarship, and education
by publishing worldwide. Oxford is a registered trade mark of Oxford University
Press in the UK and certain other countries.

Published in the United States of America by Oxford University Press
198 Madison Avenue, New York, NY 10016, United States of America.

Library of Congress Cataloging-in-Publication Data
Names: Barrios, Richard, author.
Title: On Marilyn Monroe : an opinionated guide / Richard Barrios.
Description: New York, NY : Oxford University Press, [2023] |
Includes bibliographical references, filmography, and index.
Identifiers: LCCN 2022049875 (print) | LCCN 2022049876 (ebook) |
ISBN 9780197636114 (hardback) | ISBN 9780197636145 | ISBN 9780197636121 |
ISBN 9780197636138 (epub)
Subjects: LCSH: Monroe, Marilyn, 1926-1962—Criticism and interpretation. |
Monroe, Marilyn, 1926-1962—Influence. | Motion picture actors and
actresses—United States—Biography.
Classification: LCC PN2287.M69 B347 2023 (print) | LCC PN2287.M69 (ebook) |
DDC 791.4302/8092 [B]—dc23/eng/20221223
LC record available at https://lccn.loc.gov/2022049875
LC ebook record available at https://lccn.loc.gov/2022049876

DOI: 10.1093/oso/9780197636114.001.0001

Printed and bound by CPI Group (UK) Ltd, Croydon, CR0 4YY

For
Joe Gallagher
Like MM, one of the High Holies
Truly

Contents

Acknowledgments

Few public figures have been so exhaustively chronicled as Marilyn Monroe. She has been the subject of biography, analysis, hypothesis, and, often enough, misunderstanding. As everyone knows, there has already been an enormous amount written about her and, as I write in chapter 16, a fair amount of it is (as Arthur Miller said of the *Let's Make Love* script) not worth the paper it was printed on. We all, I suppose, have our own agendas. Since in my writing I have seldom traveled the most established paths, I have to confess that I never envisioned that I would be adding a volume to so many shelves of work. (I may add, hopefully, that it might take its place among the more worthwhile occupants of those shelves.) Never, as we all know, say never, and thus I must say that it has been an absolute joy for me to have spent the past months refamiliarizing myself with Monroe and her achievements.

Everyone has an opinion about her work and, let's face it, her life, and thus I must extend a large thank you to those whose interest in Monroe and regard for her have led them to seek out the facts. Not the rumors or the speculations or, God help us, the conspiracy theories but the actual, provable truth. These biographers and scholars are cited in the bibliography and source notes, and their work has been indispensable to me. Special thanks to three gentlemen who shared memories with me: the late Miles White, the late Paul Valentine, and Don Murray, who is as friendly as he is talented. And highest praise and regards to those, the admirers as well as the archivists, who have made so many original documents pertaining to Monroe readily available. Call it the victory of truth over conjecture.

This current work is my sixth book—sixth and a half, really, if one counts the extensively revised second edition of the first entry in that sextet, *A Song in the Dark*. Over all that time, in all those books, I have never ceased to be amazed at the bifurcated nature of the processes of writing and research. Solitude, for much of it, is mandatory, even over and apart from pandemic-mandated isolation; I've even been known to eject feline intruders from my writing space. (This is especially advisable around the time they commence a jaunt across the keyboard.) The paradox is that there are so many people—I should put that in italics and capitals—who contribute so vastly to the work and to the well-being of the writer. The support and wisdom and kindness of my friends and associates has been as essential to this book as has the work of Monroe herself.

I must first thank my editor at Oxford University Press, Norman Hirschy. We first worked together on that second *Song in the Dark*, and from then to now, he has been a steady source of sense, enthusiasm, and discernment. For this project, he has given me leeway, guidance, and—most gratifyingly—full license to speak/write in my own voice. It would be boon enough just to be under the Oxford aegis, but Norm makes it a joy as well. So does project editor Zara Cannon-Mohammed, whose friendliness, knowledge, and efficiency are a boon to both this publisher and this author.

If this book were conceived as a multivolume work, I would have the space necessary to thank everyone whose care and help have enriched my writing and my existence. Alas, current space and paper requirements dictate something more concise, so my apology in advance to those who have been cited generally instead of specifically. I must, however, be completely specific about the contribution of Cynthia Robertson, whose help, encouragement, wisdom, and vision (literally as well as figuratively) have been more valuable than words could properly express. Thank you, Cindy, and my great thanks also to that other Robertson, Hal, even though he continues to plague me with references to *Paint Your Wagon*.

Amy Bent, Paul Bent, and Eliza Bent are my dear friends, caregivers, and cheerleaders, to whom many words of thanks are quite insufficient. Similarly, I extend sincere appreciation to Joann Carney, who has been a nurturing friend through thick and thin. So has Christopher Diehl, whose friendship has happily extended across the entire expanse of the continental United States, from California to New Jersey. And deep and abiding thanks to Pastor Anna Thomas and my entire family—for that is what and who you are—at Beverly Methodist Church and Meals of Love. You have sustained me beyond measure, and while I would like to cite everyone individually, please allow me a special mention of that remarkable nonagenarian Marjorie Joyce. Thank you as well to John and Beverly Haaf, Karen Van Hoy, Marsha Bancroft, and all the lovely folks in and around this small and caring community known as Beverly, New Jersey. I'm fairly certain that your friendship toward me and your interest in my work have meant more to me than you realize.

As always, my thanks to my family and friends in Louisiana, including my sister, Rev. Peggy Foreman, and all those I've known and loved for so long, including Keith Caillouet, Ned Pitre, Keith Matherne, and many others. My love and gratitude to my New York family as well: Roseann and John Forde, Edward Maguire, Rev. Amy Gregory and Bill Phillips, Moshe Bloxenheim, Marc Miller, Prof. Joe McElhaney, Craig Schreiber, Edward Walters, Edward Willinger, Jane Klain, Jeremey Stuart de Frishberg, Patty Maxwell and Kevin Kostyn, Larry Gallagher, Lawrence Maslon, Connie Coddington, Richard Skipper, Bob Gutowski, and many others. Elsewhere, Lou and Sue Sabini, Lawrence and Rosalind Bulk, Chip Reed and Christopher Fray, David Pierce, Marilee Bradford (sweetie!) and Jon Burlingame, Beverly Burt and family, my beloved Paul Brennan, Jonas Norden, Aureo Chiesse Brandão, Mark A. Vieira, Lee Tsiantis, Christopher Connelly and James Goodwynne, dear Karen Latham Duncan, Rob McKay, and William Grant and Patrick Lacey. (Thank you especially, Bill, for all your help in shaping my response to that gnarly work *The Misfits*.) There remains, besides these names, a huge cast of friends and advisers, who could be said to total several times the number of the participants in that massive CinemaScope finale to *There's No Business Like Show Business*. And that, folks, is a whole lot. *Merci beaucoup!*

It is always a major privilege for me to thank all those whose help and guidance have played such a great role in my work and my life. That privilege is made much larger, and more poignant, when I come to acknowledge and thank those who are now gone. Their presence, so essential and appreciated, has become absence. Fortunately and more happily, in a larger and finer way, they will always remain with me and with the many others whose lives they enriched. My late friend Henry Fera had a knowledge of film that was surpassed only by his enthusiasm, and Monroe occupied an honored niche in his pantheon of celluloid goddesses. Henry's skill as a pop-culture improviser was such that, out of nowhere, he could conjure up a full aria for Natasha Lytess to sing in some phantom Marilyn opera. He is loved and missed, and I am so glad I have such strong recollections of his spot-on imitations. Marty Kearns and Ken Richardson were special friends, a terrific California couple whose enthusiasm and helpfulness were extended to me and to many others as well. Thanks, guys. How fortunate I was to have met Judy DeVicaris near the end of her long and eventful life. We bonded immediately, and her glamour and zest for living will always remain among my happiest memories. Mary Maguire was my devoted NYC mom, a force for good, a leading advocate for great film, food, and opera, and an overall astonishment. How difficult it is to contemplate that she's no longer with us, and yet what a joy to note that she's with me now and always. Finally, there is Joe Gallagher. As I've said before, Joe, you were, and are, the best kind of best friend. This book is dedicated to you, and, although Zsa Zsa is mentioned only briefly, I hope you're pleased with it.

Again, to all of you, my humble and heartfelt appreciation and gratitude. You are all blessings, and my world is astoundingly better because, like MM, you've been part of it.

Beverly, New Jersey
September 2022

Introduction

Watching Her

She was born nearly a century ago and has been gone more than half that time. The body of work she left behind is of limited size and, in some cases, debatable quality. The environment in which she thrived, popular entertainment in the 1950s, is a distant memory, if that. Those are indisputable facts. Why is it, then, that they seem so immaterial? How is it that the phenomenon continues unabated, that the iconography and mythology only seem to increase? Why all the interest and speculation and merchandising, and why all the documentaries and miniseries about her? Plus, to cut a little closer, all those shelves of books?

With Marilyn Monroe, there is never one single answer. To start with one of the most obvious: some of it has to do with the element of tragedy, the special kind that crashes in when a life of magnetic achievement and renown is cut short with miserable suddenness. Alexander the Great, Joan of Arc, Byron and Keats, Valentino, Hank Williams, James Dean, the Kennedys, Malcolm X, Dr. King, Joplin and Hendrix and Morrison, Elvis, Princess Diana, Michael Jackson. How natural to mourn, how easy to speculate on what could have been. Monroe offers unusually ripe territory for this, with her blatant, rapid-fire explosion into the world's consciousness, the tumult and visibility of her private and professional paths, and the sharply cut-off way she died, overlaid with just enough ambiguity to cause some people to wonder about the circumstances. From there, eventually and alas, to an unseemly franchise based on conjecture about that death, with most of the ruminations drenched in paranoia and personal agendas.

So yes, she died young, but, paradoxically enough, that is only the beginning. The truth is that she was that consequential, that earth-shakingly famous for the last decade-plus of her life. This fame came suddenly, around 1951, and never abated. It does not require hindsight to gauge her effect, as a look at her press coverage makes plain. There was something about her that caused a major sensation that, at first, was oddly out of proportion with the small film roles she was playing. Billy Wilder, her most insightful director, coined the term "flesh impact" to describe the peculiar radiance of her photographed presence. Perhaps it was that glow, more than those early small parts, that attracted people. Naturally, this attraction was immediately connected with the notion of sex and sex appeal. She posed endlessly for pinup photos, and not the rather sterile kind that most movie starlets did. She projected a sexuality as tangible as it was unavoidable. It was hardly a coincidence, too, that her fame took a quantum leap upward when it was revealed that she had been the model for a sensationally popular nude calendar. Then there was the whole "Poor Cinderella" myth she propagated so skillfully and her romance with, and eventual marriage to, baseball legend Joe DiMaggio. (At first, his celebrity may have exceeded hers. That eventually changed.) By the middle of 1953, the fame was complete. It never subsided for the rest of her life, and if anything, it has grown exponentially ever since.

The life she had, the one off the screen, was an odd and unsettled mix of the glorious and the pathetic that took place in both personal and public domains. Always astute where her own fame was involved, Monroe was completely aware that the masses watched her life with as much interest as, or more than, they paid to see her portray Lorelei Lee or the Girl Upstairs. It may be that her life, as viewed by the public, was her greatest role, for from first to last, and through all the interference and distraction and misery, she was an artist. Acting—*performance*—was her avocation, and everything she did publicly, from 1946 to 1962, was geared to that end. Whenever she faced the world, she was playing a role: kittenish starlet, audacious and sometimes garish up-and-comer, devastating and witty star, committed actress, loving wife, ailing and gallant institution. In none of these public personas was there any insincerity: she always *meant* the effects she was creating. She loved the attention—at least, in its more benevolent forms—and she was immensely, genuinely grateful to the millions whose devotion and interest had done so much to put her on top. An instinctively bright person, she always remained conscious of the creation of effect. She knew what she was doing, and she never stopped doing her damnedest to control the image. Not just on the screen but also in public and in photographs. If the concept of "control" later became a mantra with such performers as Janet Jackson and Madonna (perhaps MM's most determined latter-day emulator), it was Monroe who led the way, and with a style and effect that put the later practitioners in the shade.

So which was it with Marilyn Monroe? Was her art her life, or was her life her art? The answer might be, simply, yes. Where the life is concerned, nearly everyone ever associated with her (save DiMaggio) shared their thoughts and memories and hypotheses. The contradictions they offer can be quite clamorous, which is one way to account for the endless biographies and unremitting mythology. About the actual trade she practiced, the work she did with such success, there is not nearly as much. We hear and read much about the life and less about the performances she created with such dedication. And surely, it's not surprising. Just look at how much more compelling it can be, for some, to read about her association with the Kennedy family—whatever it was—than it is to give a thoughtful look into something as unprepossessing as *Let's Make Love*.[1] That, however, falls into the trap of disrespect as well as disregard. Whatever messes may have come in her personal life, Monroe was proud of her professional identity as a successful working actor, even as she seldom felt that she was given good material. "I want to be an artist," she said frequently; whether or not she felt she succeeded is another matter entirely. Insecure person that she was, she went to her grave doubting that she'd gone the distance, to the point where she asked her final interviewer not to make her look like a joke. Yet, even with her massive network of uncertainties, part of her may have known that, on some level, she had succeeded. Her legacy, tangible and accessible as it is, shows the extent to which she did realize that goal.

This book, then, measures Monroe from the perspective of her work, in terms of her stated and treasured identity as a performing artist whose achievements were and are, at best, fully realized. Through the lens of the work, as through the lens of the movie camera, it is possible to observe and gauge what she intended as her most permanent gift to posterity. If it might not be completely possible to assess all of her techniques—she was famous for studying her roles with unusual thoroughness and intensity—the unshakable evidence of her achievement comes with the fact that she worked in an art form that is, by most measures, permanent. We can see what she did, we can see in some cases how she did it, and we can form opinions about how successfully she realized her ambitions.

To state the obvious, the opinions many hold about Monroe's work vary wildly. During her lifetime and afterward, condescending and critical

---

[1] Perhaps it's unfair to lead off with a mention of what may be Monroe's least effective starring film, one of several where the off-screen drama eclipsed anything put on film. Remember, then, that even the most worthy of artists can occasionally wind up mired in uninviting dross. Sometimes they can rise above the circumstances. In this case, the liftoff occurred only fleetingly, and an actor's achievements need to be measured by toxicity as much as by glory.

assessments were as plentiful about her acting as about her conduct. "Both charming and embarrassing" was the verdict of Pauline Kael, which seems particularly snide considering that she was discussing what is likely Monroe's greatest performance in her greatest film, *Some Like It Hot*. For many critics, the flashpoint nature of her early work, with its conscious turn-on-the-heat sexuality and air of genial artifice, canceled out any discussion of there being someone there who was creating and deploying these effects with skill as well as cunning. The eternal fact of the matter is that Monroe's performances have been perpetually undervalued and underrated. Given the quality of some of the films she appeared in, this is not altogether surprising; nor can it be denied that at times, on screen, she can be seen reaching for effects and emotions she does not entirely grasp. The paradox there—to be discussed in these pages—comes largely in the way her instinctive gifts are sometimes undermined by her own personal needs. And often by inappropriate training; it is quite evident, for example, that the instruction coming from one of her prime mentors, drama coach Natasha Lytess, could be a very mixed blessing.

For some, it can be somewhat trying to access the gifted actor who lay at (or near) the core of Monroe. The glare, after all, can be daunting, as are all the layers of tragedy, innuendo, patronizing, and even sainthood. Her biography, miserable as much of it is, is so compelling that it constantly threatens to overtake what she was doing and why she was doing it. And for some, the projection of sexuality is so intensive that it threatens to obscure the actual performance. As inviting as Monroe seems to be on the screen, she offers constant challenge. It takes some dedicated effort to receive her gifts in the same spirit in which they are being offered. There are mannerisms to get past, sometimes her concentration seems off or opaque, and those overenunciated line readings taught to her by Lytess can pose some difficulty. Then there's a reverse problem connected with a kind of ingratitude: when she's soaring delightfully, as in *Gentlemen Prefer Blondes*, she can be so dazzling that it isn't always obvious that this is something she created, rather than an intrinsic thing photographed by the camera.

Monroe's problem, as an actor, has always lain in that troubled coordination between the exterior and the interior—that sensational appearance versus the mechanics that sought constantly to assemble a performance. The resulting tension is always there, and the additional overlay comes with her own need for approval, which was eternally coupled with an insecurity that can fairly be termed both exhaustive and exhausting. It was this insecurity that lay at the root of her legendary penchant for lateness, which habitually undermined whatever professionalism she could summon. The recorded memories of her coworkers seldom stray from recalling the hours spent waiting for her to show up on the set—usually adding that upon arrival, when her stars were properly aligned, she would be devastating. The cost to her psyche was high, and her own personal drive for perfection did not always tally with the needs of a still-flourishing big-studio system in its final glory years. It's also worth mentioning that she was shockingly underpaid for some of her most successful films, and what a small wonder that she rapidly became unhappy with the roles offered to her by her studio. Try taking on bupkis material and doing nose-to-grindstone work to build something meaningful out of it. Then, having done your best, you read reviews that focus on your derrière. This is both corrosive and draining.

Thus, it takes some methodology to direct one's gaze to Monroe's work in a way that is both insightful and fair. When that effort is made, with some awareness and contextualization, there is often immense bounty to be found. Certainly, she could be an unusually generous performer, with spectators if not always with other actors. With insight and intuition, plus all that hard work, she produced a range and variety that were often ignored at the time but that, quite often, can now be seen as astounding. As with other performers— actors of color come immediately to mind—who were hemmed in by odious stereotypes, she had to manage her effects stealthily in order to transcend written words which verge on the cringeworthy. Usually, she is able to manage it in a way that none of her emulators can touch. Even in nothing roles—say, the lusciously incompetent secretary in *Monkey Business*—she is working to build something more substantial than the meager scraps offered to her by the script. Look hard, and you can almost see the wheels turning. *What sort of backstory does this person have?* she's thinking. *And how might she move and sound?* If her resources often had to emerge from a private chaos, she was still able to deploy them as a surprisingly well-realized actor, even before her much-touted sojourn at the Actors Studio. With her intense preparation and constant drive to improve, she can, in some significant ways, be viewed as the avatar of a new kind of postwar acting, one that overlapped with the Method while retaining its own contours.

The material could be shoddy and the directors clueless or unsympathetic, even hostile; even the coaches she was so dependent upon could fail her. She herself, as will occasionally be noted, was not immune to overreach or miscalculation. Yet, on the screen, she remained unusually capable of transcending junk and rising above demeaning circumstances. Far from the "amateur" tag it received during her lifetime and afterward, her acting was a complicated thing, what with her rigorous study, acute instincts, and intrepid (if oddly inconsistent) training. It's worth noting, too, that she quickly became an astute judge of scripts, which served to heighten her dissatisfaction with the roles Twentieth Century-Fox tried to assign her. The instinct could come to the fore especially at the frequent times when her roles had both predictable and unsuspected elements of autobiography, as with her hatcheck-girl-turned-Broadway-diva in *There's No Business Like Show Business*.[2] By the time she gets to *Some Like It Hot*, she has assembled all the pieces in a masterful fashion. The difficulty she had in creating that performance and the problems others had with her are so well known as to be folklore. Those, it should be said, were the issues of a long-ago past, specifically 1958. The film's the thing, and it's permanent. That, as she knew, was what mattered. Her films allow us to watch the way she builds, formulates, calculates, and achieves. When we do so, when we observe and study her performances, we confront and comprehend the artist, and the person, in a fashion that is both fair and respectful. Rewarding, too, and necessary.

This is the real Marilyn Monroe. Not the person named Norma Jeane who came from a fragmented background, from a family with a lengthy history of mental illness, who struggled against horrific odds and ultimately succumbed to them. It's Marilyn, or MM, the created and ultimately joyful being forged from great gifts and honest effort, whose work continues to dazzle and fascinate the world. When Peter Lawford introduced her at Madison Square Garden, he noted, "In the history of show business, perhaps there has been no one female who meant so much, who has done more . . ." The only error in that statement is the word "female," which is the way people like Lawford said things in 1962. Work of this quality—uneven at times, ultimately transcendent—is not limited to gender or time or even context. To many, when she was alive, it seemed temporal. They were hugely wrong. It's eternal.

---

[2] That film, rather a stopgap entry in her filmography, doesn't give Monroe much in the way of worthy opportunities, but the role has some striking reminiscences of her own life and rise to fame. It doesn't appear in the movie that she's entirely aware of this fact—but then those instincts of hers could operate in pretty remarkable ways. *We* can see it, even if she consciously doesn't.

Chronology

A Life in Days

From day one in 1926 to the end in 1962, the events of Marilyn Monroe's life have been chronicled in so detailed a fashion as to shame the likes of, say, de Tocqueville or Pliny the Elder. The research has been impressive, the detail staggering, and the layers of extrapolation and speculation are frequently in hailing distance of infinity. As an exercise in triumph and tragedy, her life has acquired an almost Shakespearean air, with a mercurial comet of a central figure supported by a suitably formidable cast of participants: Monroe's sad, mad mother, Gladys Baker; her saintly mother-substitute, Ana Lower; her nice first husband, Jim Dougherty; the intense, needy, equivocal Natasha Lytess; the tragic star builder Johnny Hyde; the savvy yet uncomprehending mogul Darryl Zanuck; her superstar husbands Joe DiMaggio and Arthur Miller; the godlike acting guru Lee Strasberg and his less-revered partner, Paula; and, of course, the real and imagined presence of the Kennedy family. These, and many others, had an impact on Monroe's personal and professional lives in a panorama of ways; driven and determined as she was, Monroe was immensely reactive to, and exhaustively interdependent upon, those in her orbit.

This chronology, primarily focused on Monroe's professional life, is intended to provide as accurate a framework as possible for the progression of her career as an actor. Yet, since her existence was never less than filled with spillovers between the private and the public, a number of personal associations and events must be considered as well. On the professional front, note the events of 1951–1952, when she was focused on her career, the buildup began to accelerate, and one film after another charted a quick ascent. This somewhat gives the lie to the notion that Monroe languished in apprenticeship before Twentieth Century-Fox noticed her, although paying attention and giving worthwhile assignments are two different things. There were points when she seemed to be working nonstop; later on, the gaps and down periods grew, for a variety of reasons, far larger. While her rocket-like rise might seem inevitable in hindsight, the arc of her biography shows both a steady progression and a series of detours and lurches. The moments of unparalleled victory were intermingled, especially in the latter stages, with all manner of downsides, including illness, uncertainty, questionable choices, and too many trips to the pharmacy. Thirty-six years, when lived this intensively, can seem far, far longer.

1926

June 1   Norma Jeane Mortenson is born at Los Angeles General Hospital at 9:30 a.m. Her mother is Gladys Monroe Baker, a cutter at Consolidated Film Industries. The father's name given on the birth certificate is Edward Mortenson, Gladys's estranged second husband; in truth, the baby is illegitimate. (MM, and many biographers, believed the real father to be C. Stanley Gifford, who worked with Gladys at Consolidated.)

June 13   Norma Jeane is taken to live in Hawthorne, California, with a foster family, the Bolenders. She will remain there for seven years; initially, her mother visits frequently.

1933

August 23   Gladys Baker makes a down payment on a house near the Hollywood Bowl. For the only time in their lives, she and Norma Jeane live together for an extended period.

1935

January 15 Gladys Baker, who has been experiencing episodes of instability over the past year, is declared insane (paranoid schizophrenia) and committed to a state mental institution. Her closest friend, Grace McKee, applies to become Norma Jeane's legal guardian. As part of this process, it is deemed necessary for Norma Jeane to be placed in an orphanage.

September 13 Norma Jeane, who has been living in a series of foster homes since her mother's commitment, is placed in the Los Angeles Orphan's Home.

1937

June 7   Norma Jeane leaves the Orphan's Home. A further succession of foster homes follows. Among them are those of

Grace McKee and Grace's aunt, Ana Lower, with whom Norma Jeane forms a strong bond.

1942

June 19   Norma Jeane, who has not yet completed tenth grade, marries James (Jim) Dougherty, whom she has dated casually over the past year. The marriage has been viewed—by MM, among others—exclusively as one of convenience, arranged in order to give Norma Jeane a more stable home life. Dougherty, for his part, later asserted that the union was a happy one that ended only because of Norma Jeane's professional aspirations and burgeoning modeling career.

1944

April   Jim Dougherty, now a Merchant Marine, is shipped out to the South Pacific. Norma Jeane begins work at the Radioplane Company, which manufactures drone aircraft used in target training.

December   Norma Jeane is photographed at Radioplane as part of an "attractive women doing military work" photo project. The photographer, David Conover, suggests that she might consider a modeling career.

1945

Spring   Norma Jeane leaves Radioplane and begins to seek modeling jobs. By summer, she has signed with Blue Book Modeling Agency and is soon sent on a number of assignments. Photographers find her hardworking and cooperative. It is rapidly apparent that her husband, still serving in the military, is not happy with her new avocation.

1946

March   Beginning to consider a film career, Norma Jeane signs with the Helen Ainsworth Agency for representation; her agent is Harry Lipton. Her first interview, at Paramount Pictures, is unsuccessful.

July 24   Norma Jean (having dropped the final e professionally) meets with Twentieth Century-Fox head of talent and former film actor Ben Lyon. Having already seen some of her modeling photos, Lyon has her read lines from the film *Winged Victory* and decides to give her a screen test. (Many biographies of MM give the date for this crucial meeting as July 17. However, one of her most reliable chroniclers asserts that on July 17, she was still in Nevada, where she had gone to file for divorce from Jim Dougherty.)

July 25   Ben Lyon sends a memo to studio attorney George Wasson stating that Norma Jean will be given a screen test and, if it is deemed successful, will be signed to a six-month contract.

August 14   Norma Jean is screen-tested, at Fox. Apparently, there are two tests. One, in black-and-white, is a short scene opposite contract actor Robert Cornell. The other, in Technicolor, is silent, made to see how Norma Jean photographs and moves; she walks, sits down, lights and extinguishes a cigarette, and exits. Various biographies of MM have reported, unverifiably, that this second test was shot by cinematographer Leon Shamroy and directed by Walter Lang, possibly on the set of *Mother Wore Tights*.

August 24   Norma Jeane Dougherty (her legal name) is given a six-month contract with Twentieth Century-Fox. She signs the contract two days later.

December 3   An internal Fox memo advises that Norma Jean's professional name is now Marilyn Monroe. The first name was suggested by Ben Lyon and possibly his wife, Bebe Daniels. Lyon had worked with, and reportedly had been romantically involved with, Broadway and film star Marilyn Miller. Norma Jean supplies her mother's maiden name, Monroe.

1947
February   After months of posing for photos and other in-studio duties, MM is cast in her first (known) film. From late February to early May, *Scudda Hoo! Scudda Hay!* is shot both at the Fox studio and on location. MM is cast in the infinitesimal role of Betty, although most of her footage will be cut from the completed film.

February 24   MM appears on the nationally broadcast *Lux Radio Theatre* on the CBS network. In a short scripted interview with host

	William Keighley, she plugs both Lux Soap and the current Fox release *The Shocking Miss Pilgrim*.
February 26	MM's Fox contract is renewed for another six months.
Spring	MM begins classes at the Actors' Laboratory Theatre in Hollywood. Commonly known as the Actors' Lab, it is based in part on the teachings of Konstantin Stanislavski and is seen as a West Coast extension of the Group Theatre in New York. Like the Group Theatre, it includes members who will eventually be blacklisted.
Summer	MM is believed to have appeared as an extra in a square-dance scene in Fox's *Green Grass of Wyoming*.
Late June	For a salary of $125, MM works for a week in a low-budget Fox drama about juvenile delinquency, *Dangerous Years*. She plays Evie, a waitress, and is given multiple lines of dialogue and on-screen billing.
July 26	One month before her contract is due for renewal, MM is informed that it will not be renewed. She receives her final check from the studio on August 31.
August	While continuing to seek modeling jobs, MM works as a "starlet caddie" at several celebrity golf tournaments. On August 17, she caddies for actor John Carroll. Carroll and his wife, MGM talent scout Lucille Ryman, take an interest in her career and eventually sign her to a personal management contract.
October 12	At the Bliss-Hayden Miniature Theatre in Beverly Hills, MM appears in the second lead of a comedy called *Glamour Preferred*. Written by Florence Ryerson and Colin Clements, the play had had a brief Broadway run in 1940. MM is cast as Lady Bonita Town, a role she alternates with actor Jane Weeks, and the play runs until November 2.
December 7	*Dangerous Years* is released. Although shot after *Scudda Hoo! Scudda Hay!* it is the first MM film to run in theaters.

1948

March 9	MM signs a six-month contract with Columbia Pictures, where her mother had worked as a film cutter in the early 1930s. The contract is a result of MM's close friendship

with Fox executive Joseph Schenck, who speaks on her behalf with Columbia studio head Harry Cohn. At Columbia, MM's hairline will be raised by electrolysis and its color lightened from ash to true blond.

ca. March 10   MM meets Columbia acting coach Natasha Lytess. This marks the beginning of an intense and often controversial seven-year association.

March 16   Though she is no longer under contract to Twentieth Century-Fox, MM appears in a variety show, *Strictly for Kicks*, on the Fox lot. Alongside Fox contract actors, she sings and dances in a number called "I Never Took a Lesson in My Life."

April   MM is considered for and ultimately cast in a low-budget Columbia musical, *Ladies of the Chorus*. Coached by Fred Karger of the studio music department, MM proves surprisingly able to do her own singing.

April 22   *Ladies of the Chorus* begins shooting, with MM in the second lead of Peggy Martin, a burlesque entertainer romanced by a wealthy young man. Shot with the speed endemic to B-pictures, the film wraps on May 3.

May   Having been told by Fred Karger that her front teeth protrude slightly, MM sees an orthodontist and is given a retainer. She wears it privately as much as possible over the coming months, which results in a more even smile.

August–
September   MM reportedly performs onstage in another Bliss-Hayden production, the George S. Kaufman/Edna Ferber play *Stage Door*.

September 9   MM's Columbia contract expires and is not renewed. It is later reported that this was due to her refusal to succumb to the advances of studio head Harry Cohn. For public consumption (at the very least), Cohn said, "The girl can't act."

December 31   It is apparently at a New Year's Eve party hosted by producer Sam Spiegel that MM meets Johnny Hyde. One of the film industry's most important talent agents, Hyde has represented Bob Hope, Lana Turner, Betty Hutton, and Esther Williams. He is immediately smitten with MM and becomes both her agent and her protector.

1949

February 10   *Ladies of the Chorus* is released and earns MM her first review, in the trade publication *Motion Picture Herald*: "One
of the brightest spots is Miss Monroe's singing. She is pretty
and, with her pleasing voice and style, shows promise."

March 2   MM signs with Johnny Hyde's company, the William Morris
Agency.

March (?)   Johnny Hyde's first professional coup for MM is a tiny
role opposite Groucho Marx in *Love Happy*. Although the
trouble-plagued project had been in production the previous summer, MM's scene is an add-on, shot in one afternoon on the RKO lot.

May   Johnny Hyde takes MM to a plastic surgeon. Eventually, she
will have work done to slightly reshape her nose and chin.

May 28   MM poses nude for photographer Tom Kelley. Two different shots from the two-hour session ("Golden Dreams"
and "A New Wrinkle") will be published on calendars.

June–July   Billed as the "Woo Woo Girl," MM does a five-week tour
to publicize *Love Happy*. The tour starts and ends in
New York City, with other stops including Chicago, Detroit,
Milwaukee, and, for a "pre-premiere," Rockford, Illinois.
It is indicative of the film's chaotic history that its actual
premiere will not occur until October 12, 1949, in San
Francisco, and its general release will be in March 1950.

August   MM returns to Twentieth Century-Fox to play a showgirl
in the Technicolor western *A Ticket to Tomahawk*. She joins
the rest of the cast in Durango, Colorado, for an extended
location shoot.

October 10   *Life* magazine publishes a photo layout, shot by Philippe
Halsman, titled "Eight Girls Try Out Mixed Emotions."
The feature consists of shots of eight young film actresses
portraying various emotions. MM is called on to demon-
strate "seeing a monster," "hearing a joke," "embracing a
lover," and "tasting a drink." Others in the shoot include
Cathy Downs (*My Darling Clementine*), Laurette Luez
(*Prehistoric Women*), Lois Maxwell (later James Bond's Miss
Moneypenny), and Enrica "Ricki" Soma (who would marry
John Huston the following year).

November   After intensive lobbying by both Johnny Hyde and Lucille Ryman, MM is cast as Angela Phinlay in John Huston's crime drama *The Asphalt Jungle*. The MGM production is MM's best opportunity to date, and she prepares extensively for the role with Natasha Lytess. Lytess accompanies her to the set and, from a prominent position off-camera, gestures silently to indicate how well MM does in each take.

1950

January   MM appears in *The Fireball*, a low-budget independent vehicle for Mickey Rooney. As Polly, an elegant habitué of roller derbies, she is seen briefly (if prominently) in several scenes. MM had complained to Johnny Hyde that the role was short on lines; in the completed film, she has exactly four.

February   Playing an even smaller (and this time, unbilled) role than she had in *The Fireball*, MM has five short lines in MGM's *Right Cross*. As the exotically named Dusky Ledue, she appears opposite Dick Powell in a restaurant scene.

February (?)   *Home Town Story* (working title *The Headline Story*) is filming at Hal Roach Studios. Financed by General Motors, it is a kind of advertisement (without product plugs) for "can't we all get along?" industry–public camaraderie. Eventually, it will be acquired by MGM and released commercially. Dressed in a series of tight sweaters, MM plays Iris Martin, secretary in a small-town newspaper office.

March (?)   MM shoots her only known television commercial: an ad for Royal Triton motor oil, manufactured by the Union Oil Company of California.

March 27   In another coup by Johnny Hyde, possibly with an assist from Joseph Schenck, MM is cast as Claudia Caswell, "A Graduate of the Copacabana School of Dramatic Art," in Joseph L. Mankiewicz's *All about Eve*. The film will be shot in less than two months, starting on April 15. MM is included in the location filming at the Curran Theatre in San Francisco.

May 11	MM signs a one-year contract with the Twentieth Century-Fox Film Corporation. The salary will be $500 per week for forty weeks (i.e., one year including twelve weeks of layoff).
May 12	*The Asphalt Jungle* is released. Although MM is not billed in the opening credits, she is listed in the final cast crawl and is mentioned favorably in a number of reviews.
June (?)	Wearing the same sweater dress already seen in *The Fireball*, *Home Town Story*, and even *All about Eve*, MM shoots a screen test for a Fox crime drama titled *Cold Shoulder*, playing opposite Richard Conte. Fox eventually opts not to make the film.
Fall	Now between pictures, MM enrolls in a ten-week course in world literature at UCLA.
October 7	*The Fireball* is released; MM receives passing mention.
October 13	*All about Eve* premieres in New York City. Although the rapturous reviews seldom mention MM, this is the kind of triumph that lifts up all participants.
December 14	MM does wardrobe fittings and tests for her first role under her Fox contract: Harriet, a secretary, in the comedy *As Young as You Feel*. The film begins shooting the following day.
December 18	After a massive heart attack suffered the day before, Johnny Hyde dies in Los Angeles. By all accounts, MM is inconsolable.

1951

January 1	In a *Life* magazine spread titled "Apprentice Goddesses," MM is presented as one of a dozen up-and-comers. Others include Debbie Reynolds, June Haver, Jean Hagen, and Eleanor Parker. The color photo features MM in an extremely low-cut gown and bears the caption "Busty Bernhardt."
January	As the filming of *As Young as You Feel* continues, MM meets Arthur Miller for the first time. She is already acquainted with his associate Elia Kazan.
March 29	In her only appearance at an Academy Awards ceremony, MM presents the Oscar for Best Sound Recording to the

Twentieth Century-Fox Sound Department for *All about Eve*. Thomas T. Moulton of Fox accepts the award.

Spring   Concerned about a possible stall in her career momentum, MM engineers some self-promotion. Barefoot and clad in a thin negligee, she takes an attention-grabbing six-block walk from Fox's wardrobe department to its photo studio. Shortly afterward, as one of the Fox actors directed to attend an exhibitor's luncheon at the studio commissary, she arrives an hour and a half late and is immediately inundated with questions about her next project. By way of an answer, she offers the coy "You'll have to ask Mr. Zanuck." Spyros Skouras, the president of Fox, gets the message immediately.

April 11   MM signs a new contract, now for seven years, with Twentieth Century-Fox, effective May 11. Starting salary, once again, is $500 per week.

April–May   Cast an ex-WAC named Bobbie, MM shoots the Fox comedy *Love Nest*.

May–June   Another Fox comedy, *Let's Make It Legal*, casts MM as a scheming gold digger.

June 15   *As Young as You Feel* is released. *New York Times* critic Bosley Crowther calls MM's performance "superb."

July 18   *The Home Town Story* is released. MM receives some critical mention.

August 11   Twentieth Century-Fox agrees to lend MM to Wald-Krasna Productions at RKO for the role of Peggy in *Clash by Night*.

September 8   "The 1951 Model Blonde," the first major article about MM in a national publication, is published in *Collier's*.

Fall   MM begins acting classes with Michael Chekhov, author of *To the Actor*.

October– December *Clash by Night* is shot on the RKO lot and on location in Monterey, California.

October 31   *Let's Make It Legal* is released.

November 14   *Love Nest* is released. As with *Let's Make It Legal*, the reviews mention MM mainly in terms of her physical impact.

December   MM begins work on *Don't Bother to Knock* at Fox. The role of the disturbed Nell Forbes is by far her most extensive professional opportunity to date.

1952

January   MM shoots segments in two multistory Fox films: the comedy *We're Not Married* and the compilation *O. Henry's Full House*. In the latter, she plays a streetwalker in "The Cop and the Anthem."

January 14   Shooting concludes on *Don't Bother to Knock*.

January 26   MM receives her first significant award: the Henrietta Award, presented by the International Press Club, as "Best Young Box Office Personality."

February–
April   Cast again as a secretary, MM films *Monkey Business*, directed by Howard Hawks.

March 8   MM has her first date, arranged by mutual friends, with Joe DiMaggio.

March 13   United Press reporter Aline Mosby publishes a story under the headline "Mystery Cleared! Nude Calendar Beauty at Last Is Identified. Marilyn Monroe Admits She Posed for It When Broke Three Years Ago." Contrary to the fears of MM's studio, the public's response to the revelation is overwhelmingly favorable and sympathetic.

April 6   Performing before an audience of ten thousand marines at Camp Pendleton, MM sings "Do It Again" and "Somebody Loves Me."

April 7   The cover of *Life* magazine is emblazoned with a portrait of MM and the words "Marilyn Monroe: The Talk of Hollywood." The article inside, titled "Shooting Marilyn," features both text and photos by Philippe Halsman.

April 28   More headlines result when MM's appendix is removed at Cedars of Lebanon Hospital. Prior to the surgery, she taped notes to her abdomen entreating the doctor to do as little cutting as possible. When the operation is over, she is photographed in her hospital bed wearing full makeup.

May 3   Issuing a statement to the *Los Angeles Daily News*, MM confirms the rumors that she was not an orphan, as was once believed. She gives a carefully worded account of her mother's mental illness and her own life in various foster homes.

May 21	MM makes wardrobe tests for her next film role, the faithless Rose Loomis in *Niagara*.
June 1	On her twenty-sixth birthday, MM learns that she will be cast as Lorelei Lee in Fox's *Gentlemen Prefer Blondes*.
June 2	Location shooting begins on *Niagara*, in and around both the American and Canadian sides of the falls. Along with the crew and remaining cast, MM stays at the General Brock (now Crowne Plaza) Hotel, adjacent to several of the shoot's main locations. On some weekends, she flies to New York City to visit Joe DiMaggio.
June 16	*Clash by Night* is released, earning MM good reviews.
June–July	*Niagara* continues shooting at the Fox studio.
July 23	*We're Not Married* is released.
July 30	*Don't Bother to Knock* is released. MM's reviews run the gamut from highly critical to laudatory.
August 29	MM attends the world premiere of *Monkey Business* in Atlantic City. Over the next few days, she makes a series of personal appearances and, wearing a dress with a deeply plunging neckline, serves as grand marshal for the parade kicking off the Miss America pageant.
August 31	A prerecorded broadcast of *Statement in Full* on NBC's *Hollywood Star Playhouse* marks MM's only dramatic appearance on radio. Continuing her *Niagara* femme fatale persona, she plays June Cordell, a murderess attempting to cover up her crime. This marks the program's second airing of this particular play; in January 1951, the role had been taken by Joan Crawford.
September 5	*Monkey Business* is released and receives generally good reviews.
September 18	*O. Henry's Full House* is released. Despite the brevity of her role, MM receives billing equal to all the other cast members.
October–November	MM's preparation work for *Gentlemen Prefer Blondes* includes wardrobe fittings and tests, script conferences, musical coaching, and dance rehearsals, for which she and

costar Jane Russell work alongside choreographer Jack Cole and his assistant, Gwen Verdon.

November 17   Shooting begins on *Gentlemen Prefer Blondes*.

December 3   MM attends an auction and buys a large collection of notebooks and annotated materials by famed director Max Reinhardt. The following month, she sells the collection to Reinhardt's son, Gottfried, who in turn will sell them to what is now the State University of New York at Binghamton. Although some mock MM's role in this as a publicity stunt, she had long heard about Reinhardt from Natasha Lytess and was genuinely interested in his work.

1953

January 7   MM records "Kiss" (from *Niagara*) and "Do It Again." The recording will not be issued until after her death.

January 21   *Niagara* opens at the Roxy Theatre in New York City, marking the beginning of MM's career as a star. Columbia's reissue of *Ladies of the Chorus*—now billing MM over the title—opens for a brief run (as the top feature of a double bill) in various Loews theaters in Manhattan and Brooklyn. The ads bill MM as "America's Calendar Girl."

January 28   *Niagara* is given an "official" premiere simultaneously in Niagara Falls, New York, and Niagara Falls, Ontario. MM is still working on *Gentlemen Prefer Blondes*, so Fox sends Debra Paget and Dale Robertson to attend the dual event.

February   More awards: on February 9, MM receives the New Star Award from *Photoplay* magazine, and on February 25, *Redbook* gives her its Silver Cup for "Best Young Box Office Personality" of 1952. Her appearance at the *Photoplay* function, wearing a skin-tight gold dress from *Gentlemen Prefer Blondes*, draws both attention and, from Joan Crawford, pointed criticism.

March   Upon the recommendation of Michael Chekhov, MM begins studying movement with mime, dancer, and teacher Lotte Goslar.

March 6   Shooting ends on *Gentlemen Prefer Blondes*.

March 9	Shooting begins on *How to Marry a Millionaire*. It is filmed in the new widescreen process CinemaScope, as is *The Robe*, produced concurrently.
March 13	*Millionaire* costar Lauren Bacall presents MM with the *Look* Achievement Award as "Best Feminine Newcomer of 1952."
April	MM tests two costumes for the fashion show sequence in *How to Marry a Millionaire*. One outfit, called "Double Frozen Daiquiris," is obviously not to her liking, as she poses for the test photo with her hand over her face. The dress will be worn by another model in the scene, and MM will appear in a diamond-studded swimsuit, which she tests on April 9.
April 13	Jean Negulesco is the latest of MM's directors to become exasperated with her on-the-set reliance on coach Natasha Lytess and has Lytess banned from the set of *How to Marry a Millionaire*.
April 14	Citing bronchitis, MM does not report for work on *Millionaire*. Her representative, agent-producer Charles Feldman, advises Fox that she cannot perform without Lytess, so the coach is reinstated (with a raise in salary), and work continues until the production ends late in the month.
June 8	MM makes wardrobe tests for her next film, *River of No Return*. She does not like the script and focuses instead on the four musical numbers.
June 26	Enacting one of film's essential rites, MM and Jane Russell place their hand- and footprints in the forecourt of Grauman's Chinese Theatre.
July 1	*Gentlemen Prefer Blondes* premieres in Atlantic City. MM does not attend. The film is a huge success, and most of the reviews are outstanding. To counter rumors that she did not do her own singing in the film, Darryl Zanuck issues a statement asserting that the voice was indeed that of MM.
July	MM is notified that after *River of No Return* is completed, she will star in a musical variously titled *Pink Tights* or *The Girl in Pink Tights*. Upon receiving a plot synopsis—the script is not yet completed—she decides that this is a film she does not wish to do.

July 28	*River of No Return* begins a physically arduous shoot near Banff and Jasper, Alberta, in the Canadian Rockies.
August 8	After director Otto Preminger bans Natasha Lytess from the set, MM contacts Darryl Zanuck and has her reinstated.
August 20	MM sustains an on-the-set ankle injury and has her leg put in a temporary cast.
September 1	Still on crutches, MM returns to California to shoot the remainder of *River of No Return* at Fox.
September 13	MM is the guest star on *The Jack Benny Program*, broadcast live on the CBS television network. She appears with Benny in a sketch titled "Honolulu Trip," which includes her rendition of "Bye, Bye Baby."
October	MM signs a recording contract with RCA Victor. Milton Greene photographs MM for *Look* magazine. In the course of these sessions, they exchange thoughts about what directions her career might be, or should be, taking.
November 4	The world premiere of *How to Marry a Millionaire* is held at the Fox Wilshire (now Saban) Theater. MM, who attends the heavy-duty event alongside Lauren Bacall and Humphrey Bogart, murmurs to the radio microphones that "This is just about the happiest night of my life." Once again, she receives excellent reviews, and the film, the second released in CinemaScope, is a smash hit.
November 17	MM begins shooting retakes on *River of No Return* at Fox. These are under the direction of Jean Negulesco, with whom she has a far better rapport than she had with Otto Preminger. The retakes cause the start date for *Pink Tights* to be moved to December 15. *Tights* is to be produced by Sol C. Siegel and directed by Henry Koster.
December 5	MM is notified that rehearsals for *Pink Tights* will begin in two days. While terrified of being suspended for noncooperation, she decides that she will not accede to the studio's demands. In addition to her objections to the material, she is also unhappy about her salary and various other terms of her contract, plus her discovery that she will not be considered for the role of Nefer in the upcoming Fox epic *The Egyptian*.

December 11	MM returns to Fox, not for *Pink Tights* but for additional work on *River of No Return*. Charles Feldman warns Darryl Zanuck about pressuring her with the *Tights* situation and soon drafts a list of demands to be submitted to Fox: more money; fewer films; and approval of director, script, and cinematographer on all her films.
December 23 ca.	MM finishes work on *River of No Return*.
December 28	MM, now in San Francisco with Joe DiMaggio and his family, is notified that *Pink Tights* will begin production on January 4.

1954

January 4	Still in San Francisco, MM does not report to Fox for *Pink Tights* and is suspended without pay.
January 14	In a three-minute ceremony at City Hall in San Francisco, MM is married to Joe DiMaggio.
January 16	Acceding to the tumultuous press coverage surrounding her wedding, Fox rescinds MM's suspension and orders her to return to the studio to begin *Pink Tights*. She has already been informed that following *Pink Tights*, she will appear in another musical, *There's No Business Like Show Business*.
January 24	MM and Joe DiMaggio return to Los Angeles after their honeymoon. She is finally sent a *Pink Tights* script and once again declines to do the film.
January 26	Fox suspends MM for the second time.
February 1	MM and Joe DiMaggio leave for a trip to Tokyo, where DiMaggio will be helping to celebrate and publicize the start of Japan's baseball season. The reception given to them in Japan is tumultuous nearly to the point of riot, and MM receives an invitation from General John E. Hull, chief of the Far East Command, to entertain the troops stationed in Korea. Despite DiMaggio's objections, she accepts.
February 16–19	MM gives ten performances at various army bases in Korea, entertaining more than one hundred thousand troops. She will later refer to the tour as "the highlight of my life."

February 24	MM (recovering from a short bout of pneumonia) and DiMaggio return to the United States.
March 8	MM receives the *Photoplay* magazine Gold Medal as "The Most Popular Actress of 1953."
March 15	Meeting with Charles Feldman, MM is notified that *Pink Tights* is being officially canceled. She will be paid more money for her services, and Fox agrees that she may do only two films per year. (She later learns that her demands for script, director, and cinematographer approval are denied.) Feldman also informs her that he may be producing *The Seven Year Itch*, to be directed by Billy Wilder, for which she may be offered the lead.
April 13	Fox removes MM from suspension.
April 15	MM returns to Fox and holds a dressing-room press conference. She promptly begins preparing for *There's No Business Like Show Business* with vocal coach Hal Schaefer and dance director Jack Cole.
April 23	A review of *River of No Return* (which will premiere in Denver six days later) runs in the *Hollywood Reporter*. MM is devastated by the critic's contention that the film demonstrates her "inability to handle a heavy acting role."
May	Milton Greene and MM discuss the possibility of forming their own production company.
May 8	When Charles Feldman informs MM that he will be producing *The Seven Year Itch*, she furiously replies that where her Fox contract is concerned, he has not been operating in her best interests.
May 28	*There's No Business Like Show Business* begins shooting. MM's participation in the lengthy shoot is marred by illness, a lack of rapport with director Walter Lang, dissatisfaction over her role and Fox in general, and what seems to be an increasing reliance on medicinal assistance.
August	MM, her new Fox contract still unsigned, sets her sights on the role of Miss Adelaide in the upcoming Samuel Goldwyn production of *Guys and Dolls*.
August 23	With a new, shorter hairstyle, MM makes costume tests for *The Seven Year Itch*, which will commence production shortly after she completes *Show Business*.

August 27	Joe DiMaggio visits the set of *There's No Business Like Show Business* and watches as MM films her provocative "Heat Wave" number. His disapproval is apparent to many present.
September 8	MM arrives in New York for location work on *The Seven Year Itch*.
September 13	MM shoots her first scene for *The Seven Year Itch* while leaning out of the window of an apartment on East 61st Street.
September 15	Beginning just after midnight, MM and costar Tom Ewell are filmed on the sidewalk in front of the Trans-Lux 52nd Street Theatre (now demolished), near Lexington Avenue. With fans set up below the sidewalk grating, Billy Wilder shoots fifteen takes of the skirt-blowing scene. While the scene will largely be reshot in California, the publicity value is enormous. Joe DiMaggio is in attendance and is visibly not amused.
September 16	MM and DiMaggio return to California, and she soon learns that she will not be appearing in *Guys and Dolls*. Due to her illness and the unraveling of her marriage, the *Seven Year Itch* shooting schedule, originally planned for thirty-five days, is eventually extended to forty-eight.
October 5	MM sues for divorce from Joe DiMaggio.
November 4	Shooting ends on *The Seven Year Itch*. MM is informed that her next film for Fox will be *How to Be Very, Very Popular*, in which the studio hopes she will be reteamed with Jane Russell.
November	MM continues to discuss plans to form a production company with Milton Greene. They are both enthusiastic about her filming a biography of Jean Harlow.
November 22	Charles Feldman, unaware that MM has decided to drop him as her representative, suggests Terence Rattigan's play *The Sleeping Prince* as a possible project.
November 29	Milton Greene's attorneys inform Fox that due to its delay in renewing her contract, MM is no longer under any obligation to the studio.
December 10	MM records "You'd Be Surprised" for RCA.

December 13   Charles Feldman is notified that he has been fired as MM's agent.

December 16   *There's No Business Like Show Business* premieres in New York. MM's musical performances receive mixed reviews, including some that accuse her of vulgarity.

ca.
December 21   Deserting Hollywood and Twentieth Century-Fox, MM flies (incognita) to New York and takes up residence in the Connecticut home of Milton Greene, his wife Amy, and their infant son.

1955

January 7   MM and Milton Greene hold a press conference to announce the formation of Marilyn Monroe Productions. Introduced as "The New Marilyn Monroe," she mentions that she would like to play Grushenka in *The Brothers Karamazov.*

January 10   Having flown back to Hollywood (with Greene) the previous day, MM returns to Fox for *Seven Year Itch* retakes and portraits. It is Fox's intention that she remain there to start work on *How to Be Very, Very Popular.*

January 15   Instead of attending a planned meeting with *How to Be Very, Very Popular* writer-director Nunnally Johnson, MM flies back to New York. Fox suspends her again.

February 1   MM meets Broadway producer Cheryl Crawford, who invites her to visit the Actors Studio, which Crawford cofounded.

February 4   MM, with Cheryl Crawford, observes a class at the Actors Studio. She is introduced to the studio's artistic director, Lee Strasberg, famed teacher and proponent of "the Method." He invites her to take classes at the studio, and she soon arranges for him to give her private instruction.

February   MM begins intense study with Strasberg, whom she soon begins to regard as a father figure. She also becomes close to his wife Paula and daughter Susan. Eventually, she feels comfortable taking Actors Studio classes along with other actors. Strasberg also urges her to begin psychoanalysis, and her schedule eventually involves five sessions per week, along with three private lessons with Strasberg and observing two studio classes. In addition to her work with Strasberg, MM also studies with former Shakespearean and film actress Constance Collier.

March 9   MM and Marlon Brando serve as "celebrity ushers" at the premiere of Elia Kazan's *East of Eden*. The event is a benefit to raise money for the Actors Studio.

March 31   Atop a pink elephant, MM appears at Madison Square Garden as part of the gala charity opening of the Ringling Bros. and Barnum & Bailey Circus. Other participants include Milton Berle and, as ringmistress, Marlene Dietrich.

April 8   Edward R. Murrow speaks with MM on live television for the *Person to Person* show. Her usual vivacity in interviews is nowhere in evidence, and it is observed that Amy Greene, appearing on the program along with her husband, Milton, seems far more at ease than MM.

Spring   MM renews her acquaintance with Arthur Miller and begins seeing him secretly.

June 1   On MM's twenty-ninth birthday, *The Seven Year Itch* has its world premiere at Loew's State Theatre in Times Square. The outside of the theater is emblazoned with a far-larger-than-life cutout of her in the skirt-blowing scene. Her escort for the premiere is Joe DiMaggio.

July 22   *How to Be Very, Very Popular*, with Sheree North in the role intended for MM, is released to mixed reviews and moderate business.

July 26   MM signs with a new agency, the Music Corporation of America (MCA), which promptly begins lengthy negotiations with Twentieth Century-Fox on her behalf.

October 1   Fox releases another MM reject, *The Girl in the Red Velvet Swing*. Joan Collins appears in the role that had been offered to MM.

October   MM lobbies hard for the title role in Elia Kazan's new film, *Baby Doll*. Although author Tennessee Williams believes she would be ideal for the role, Kazan decides she is too old to play the nineteen-year-old child bride. Instead, he casts Carroll Baker, who is five years younger than MM. Having lost *Baby Doll*, MM sets her sights on Terence Rattigan's play *The Sleeping Prince*, originally suggested to her by Charles Feldman. She intends to use the bonus from her new Fox contract to buy the property (for $125,000) on behalf of Marilyn Monroe Productions.

December 31 MM signs a new contract with Twentieth Century-Fox. The terms include $100,000 per film for four films over a seven-year period, the right to make films elsewhere, approval on two cinematographers, and director approval, with a list of sixteen names submitted as directors she would work with. (Otto Preminger is not included.)

1956

January MM and Milton Greene reach an accord with Fox about the first film of her new contract: *Bus Stop*, from the play by William Inge, to be directed by Joshua Logan. Logan, directing his third film, is one of the names on her "approved" list.

February 9 MM holds a press conference to announce the first film from Marilyn Monroe Productions: *The Sleeping Prince* (later retitled *The Prince and the Showgirl*). Laurence Olivier, who has agreed to costar, direct, and coproduce, is also present, as is author Terence Rattigan.

February 17 Demonstrating the results of her past year of work and study, MM performs at the Actors Studio. With Maureen Stapleton, she presents the Anna/Marthy scene from Eugene O'Neill's *Anna Christie*. The audience violates Actors Studio protocol and applauds at the end, with the consensus that her performance is a marked success. (She herself feels otherwise.)

February 27 Having flown back to California two days earlier, MM returns to Fox to begin preproduction on *Bus Stop*.

March 1 Studio head Jack L. Warner announces that Warner Bros. will be distributing the Marilyn Monroe Productions film *The Sleeping Prince*.

March 5	Having been informed that her association with MM is at an end, Natasha Lytess unsuccessfully attempts to contact her former charge. Her role as coach will now be assumed by Paula Strasberg.
March 12	The former Norma Jeane (Baker) Mortenson/Dougherty/DiMaggio legally changes her name to Marilyn Monroe.
March 15	MM arrives in Phoenix to begin shooting on *Bus Stop*. The company will later move to Sun Valley, Idaho, for further location work.
April 5	Following her return to Los Angeles, MM is hospitalized for bronchitis and exhaustion. She resumes work on the Fox lot nineteen days later.
May 29	MM finishes work on *Bus Stop*.
June 29	MM marries Arthur Miller in a civil ceremony in White Plains, New York.
July 1	MM completes her conversion to Judaism and (re)marries Arthur Miller in a Jewish ceremony in South Salem, New York.
July 14	The Millers arrive in London for the shooting of *The Sleeping Prince*.
August 7	*The Sleeping Prince* begins filming following a week of rehearsals. It is instantly apparent that the influence of Lee Strasberg (first by phone and later in person) and Paula Strasberg (always live and in person) increases the tension between MM and Laurence Olivier.
August 31	*Bus Stop* opens in New York, earning MM her best reviews to date.
November 16	Shooting concludes (eleven days late) on *The Sleeping Prince*. In addition to the ongoing conflict involving MM and Laurence Olivier and the Strasbergs, there has been steadily escalating tension between Arthur Miller and Milton Greene and general hostility from the British crew toward the perceived-as-aloof Americans.
December	Laurence Olivier arrives in New York to show the first cut of *The Sleeping Prince* to Jack L. Warner. The film is deemed overlong and not especially amusing. To ratchet up its box-office potential, it is decided to include MM's character in its title, which becomes *The Prince and the Showgirl*, and to create a sexy ad campaign.

1957

MM spends the year in the Millers' Connecticut house and New York apartment, attempting to have a baby, setting up housekeeping, working with a new psychoanalyst, and studying privately with Lee Strasberg. She oversees the expulsion of Milton Greene from Marilyn Monroe Productions and supports Arthur Miller in his ongoing dealings with the House Un-American Activities Committee and his subsequent indictment for contempt of Congress. He, meanwhile, begins work on a new screenplay, *The Misfits*.

June 13

MM and Arthur Miller attend the premiere of *The Prince and the Showgirl* at Radio City Music Hall. Though some critics deem it her best performance to date, the reviews overall are mixed, and the box-office receipts are disappointing.

September

Twentieth Century-Fox approaches MM about a possible second film on her contract: a remake of *The Blue Angel*, to costar either Spencer Tracy, Fredric March, or Curt Jurgens, directed by Charles Vidor. Depressed over her recent miscarriage, MM initially feigns interest in the project.

1958

January 13

As the year begins, it appears that MM is agreeing to accept billing under Spencer Tracy in *The Blue Angel*, now to be directed by George Cukor. On this date, however, she informs her agents that the project is off.

March 17

Billy Wilder, learning that MM is considering a return to work, sends her a two-page treatment for a comedy tentatively titled *Not Tonight, Josephine!* Although subsequent reports vary widely over how positively she responds to it, she and Arthur Miller decide that she should do the film.

April 15

Twentieth Century-Fox, pleased over the news that MM will be returning to work—albeit not for Fox—formally releases her from any obligation related to *The Blue Angel*.

April 22

The *New York Times* runs the premature (and inaccurate) announcement that MM will appear with Maurice Chevalier in Fox's film version of Cole Porter's Broadway musical *Can-Can*.

May–June   Richard Avedon shoots MM for *Life* magazine. The elab-
               orate layout has her portraying love goddesses of the
               past—Lillian Russell, Theda Bara, Clara Bow, Marlene
               Dietrich, Jean Harlow—as well as herself. The spread will
               be featured in the *Life* issue of December 22, which will
               turn out to be the magazine's biggest-selling issue up to
               that time.

July 8   MM arrives in Los Angeles with Paula Strasberg and secre-
               tary May Reis to start work on the film now titled *Some Like
               It Hot* (formerly *Not Tonight, Josephine!*).

July 14   Arthur Miller contacts John Huston about the possibility of
               directing the screenplay in progress, *The Misfits*.

July 30   MM begins prerecording her songs for *Some Like It Hot*.
               She nails "Runnin' Wild" on the fourth take.

August 4   *Some Like It Hot* begins shooting at the Samuel Goldwyn
               studio in Hollywood. Location work will be done in
               Coronado, California, where the Hotel del Coronado will
               stand in for the movie's Seminole Ritz.

September   Arthur Miller flies to California to be with MM and soon
               notifies Billy Wilder that she is pregnant.

October 20   Dozens of takes are required to get MM to correctly deliver
               the line "Where's that bourbon?"

November 7   As many as twenty-nine days behind schedule, *Some Like It
               Hot* concludes shooting with the scene in which Tony Curtis
               kisses MM after her rendition of "I'm Through with Love."

December 16   MM, now back in New York, has a miscarriage.

1959

January   Two contrasting sneak previews for *Some Like It Hot* are
               held in the Los Angeles area. The first, in Pacific Palisades, is
               greeted with stony silence and walkouts. The second, a few
               days later six miles away in Westwood, is, in the words of
               Jack Lemmon, "an absolute smash."

February 26   At the French Film Institute in New York, MM receives
               the Crystal Star (Étoile de Cristal) from the Académie du
               Cinéma as Best Foreign Actress of 1958 for her perfor-
               mance in *The Prince and the Showgirl*.

March 4	Twentieth Century-Fox notifies MM that her next film will be Elia Kazan's *Time and Tide* (later retitled *Wild River*), which will start work on April 14. Eventually, Kazan will decide to use Lee Remick instead.
March 17	MM attends the premiere of *Some Like It Hot* in Chicago. Twelve days later comes the New York premiere, at which she is also present. Most critics feel that she has given one of her best performances.
May 13	MM receives another award as "Best Foreign Actress" for *The Prince and the Showgirl*. This time, it is the David di Donatello prize from the Academy of Italian Cinema (Accademia del Cinema Italiano).
August–September	As Arthur Miller continues to revise the screenplay of *The Misfits*, Fox producer Jerry Wald moves ahead with plans for *The Billionaire*, to costar MM and Gregory Peck under the direction of George Cukor.
September 17	Twentieth Century-Fox notifies MM that she will be beginning work on *The Billionaire* on November 2. A day later, the studio agrees to her participation (following *The Billionaire*) in *The Misfits*.
September 19	Escorted by George Cukor, MM attends a luncheon at Fox in honor of Russian premier Nikita Khrushchev. The following day, she meets with Cukor, Jerry Wald, and screenwriter Norman Krasna to discuss *The Billionaire*.
September 22	Back in New York, MM attends the opening night of Yves Montand's one-man Broadway show. As Miller is still working on *The Misfits*, she is escorted by Montgomery Clift.
October	Having set her sights on the role of Holly Golightly in the upcoming Paramount film of Truman Capote's *Breakfast at Tiffany's*, MM performs workshop scenes from the novella at the Actors Studio. Although Capote is delighted with her performance (as is Lee Strasberg), Paramount gives the role to Audrey Hepburn. It is believed that reports of MM's behavior during the *Some Like It Hot* shoot were a factor.
October 14	A planned *Billionaire* rehearsal with Jack Cole at the Dance Players Studio in New York falls apart when MM fails to

	appear. Though she works sporadically with Cole over the next few days, she does not seem to be ready for the impending shoot.
October 24	George Cukor, in New York to scout *Billionaire* locations, meets with MM and learns that she is unhappy with the script. Fox engages Arthur Miller (who has now completed *The Misfits*) to work on rewrites.
November 9	MM, now in California with Miller, begins work on *The Billionaire*, which is being retitled *Let's Make Love*.
November 13	Arthur Miller submits his script revisions. Gregory Peck, dismayed over the now-diminished size of his role, withdraws from the project. Producer Jerry Wald and the Fox casting department hurriedly seek a replacement.
December	The quandary over a leading man is finally resolved with a suggestion from Arthur Miller: Yves Montand, fresh from a successful Broadway appearance. Earlier, Montand had appeared in the (French) film version of Miller's *The Crucible*.
December 15	Having done wardrobe tests the previous month, MM makes a new round of hair, costume, and makeup tests. Two days later, she views them with George Cukor, Jerry Wald, Fox head Buddy Adler, and others studio personnel. No one approves of the results, and a devastated MM fails to report to the studio over the next week.
December 23	Arthur Miller is engaged to write (anonymously) more script revisions. Meanwhile, Clark Gable, who had initially turned down *The Misfits*, agrees to star in it.

1960

January 6	MM arrives on the Fox lot, spends thirty minutes rehearsing, and then leaves.
January 18	On the first day of shooting, George Cukor is compelled to shoot around MM, who has sent word that she will not be coming in. She begins seeing a new psychiatrist, Dr. Ralph Greenson, who recommends a cutback in her medications.
January 25	MM begins shooting the "My Heart Belongs to Daddy" sequence. Viewing the rushes, studio head Adler is once again displeased with how she looks.

January 27	MM shows up for filming but leaves before any shots are made. Later that day, her agents inform Fox that she is scheduled to begin work on *The Misfits* between April 1 and April 14.
January 29	MM shoots her first scene with Yves Montand. Although her lateness and memory lapses continue, their rapport is good. She is now working under the tutelage of Paula Strasberg following an earlier estrangement.
February 25	This day marks the end of a week when, for the first time, MM has shown up for shooting every day. The film is now ten days behind schedule.
March 4	As shooting concludes for the day, the production is shut down due to a strike by the Screen Actors Guild.
March 10	MM receives the Hollywood Foreign Press Golden Globe Award as Best Actress (Comedy or Musical) for *Some Like It Hot*.
April 12	With the strike settled, production resumes on *Let's Make Love*. MM is seldom able to work more than four hours at a time.
June 20	MM shoots her final scene for *Let's Make Love*.
July 1	Back in New York and beginning preparations for *The Misfits*, MM is informed that her next film for Fox will be *Goodbye Charlie*.
July 17	MM flies to California for final dubbing on *Let's Make Love*, after which she will fly to Reno on the July 20 to begin work on *The Misfits*.
July 21	The first scene shot for *The Misfits* corresponds with the opening of the film, with MM, Thelma Ritter, and Eli Wallach at a Reno rooming house. The film will continue to be shot roughly in sequence.
August	*The Misfits* continues shooting in and around Reno. The temperatures are nearly unbearable, and MM frequently calls in sick. She is increasingly reliant on barbiturates and other medications. Moreover, the Miller marriage is now in a parlous state, due in part to MM's feelings about the constantly revised script and Miller's antipathy (shared with others) toward Paula Strasberg.

August 21   The planned premiere of *Let's Make Love*, to be held in Reno with MM in attendance, is canceled near the last minute due to power outages caused by a devastating fire.

August 27   MM is admitted to a Los Angeles hospital to rest and detoxify. During her weeklong stay, John Huston seeks further financing to complete the film. Arthur Miller is angered that MM's illness, not Huston's gambling, is being cited as the cause of the production shutdown.

September 6   MM returns to work in Reno, where filming will continue until October 18.

September 8   *Let's Make Love* is released to mixed reviews and a tepid-at-best box-office response.

October 24   *The Misfits* resumes shooting at the Paramount studio in Hollywood.

November 4   Over schedule and over budget, *The Misfits* concludes filming.

November 6   Clark Gable suffers a heart attack.

November 11   MM, now in New York, announces that her marriage to Arthur Miller is over.

November 16   Clark Gable dies.

December 13   MM informs Fox that she will not do *Goodbye Charlie*.

1961

January   MM begins to formulate plans for an NBC-TV production of the play *Rain*. She will star as Sadie Thompson, and Lee Strasberg will direct.

January 20   In Juárez, Mexico, MM obtains a divorce from Arthur Miller. She has selected this day—on which John F. Kennedy is inaugurated president—in order to attract as little attention as possible.

January 31   MM, with Montgomery Clift and Lee Strasberg, attends a "preview" opening of *The Misfits* in New York. Arthur Miller is also present. The reviews over the next few days are mixed, and the box-office returns are a disappointment.

February 5   MM, in severe distress, checks into the Payne Whitney Psychiatric Clinic in New York. Later, she is transferred to the Columbia-Presbyterian Medical Center, where she remains until March 5.

March–April A reasonably rejuvenated MM continues, through her agents and attorneys, to battle with Fox over *Goodbye Charlie*. George Cukor, initially scheduled to direct, is now working on another project, so Fox enters into discussions with Lee Strasberg. Although he has not directed films, Strasberg demands a high salary, and the project eventually falls apart.

June 27 NBC informs MM's attorney Aaron Frosch that *Rain* is being canceled. The chief sticking point is Lee Strasberg; the network will not consider a director who has no television experience, and MM refuses to work without him.

June 28 MM is hospitalized in New York. She has gallbladder surgery the following day and remains at the Manhattan Polyclinic Hospital until July 11.

September Now back in California, MM discusses a new film with Twentieth Century-Fox: a remake of the 1940 comedy *My Favorite Wife* titled *Something's Got to Give*.

November–December Heeding the advice of her psychiatrist, MM moves toward agreeing to make *Something's Got to Give*, while noting that she does not yet find the script acceptable.

1962

January 2 Fox production head Peter Levathes announces the upcoming production of *Something's Got to Give*.

January 12 MM makes an accepted offer ($57,500) on her first house, a secluded Spanish-style residence in the Brentwood section of West Los Angeles. Near the entrance, set in tile beneath a coat of arms, is the legend *Cursum perficio* ("My journey is ended").

January 24 With Nunnally Johnson as the latest (re)writer assigned to *Something's Got to Give*, MM agrees to do the film, pending her approval of the script.

February MM flies to New York to confer with the Strasbergs about *Something's Got to Give*. Later in the month, she flies to

Mexico to buy furniture and fittings for her new home; she also meets members of the Mexican government and film industry.

March 5   Accepting the "World Film Favorite" award at the Golden Globe ceremony, MM appears notably unsteady. The following day, she goes to Fox to meet with Peter Levathes. "I guess I'm reporting back," she says.

March 30   Following further rewrites of the script by George Cukor and Walter Bernstein, MM approves the new Nunnally Johnson version of *Something's Got to Give*.

April 10   MM arrives at Fox on time and does six hours of wardrobe, hair, and makeup tests. It is announced to the press that she will be appearing at President Kennedy's birthday celebration in New York on May 19.

April 13   MM flies to New York to meet with Lee Strasberg. It is agreed that Paula Strasberg will serve as her coach on *Something's Got to Give* at a salary of $3,000 per week.

April 20   Back in California, MM informs producer Henry Weinstein that she is ill and will miss the starting day (April 23) of *Something's Got to Give*.

April 30   One week late and still feeling unwell, MM begins filming *Something's Got to Give*. The following day, she is sent home due to illness.

May   During the first three weeks of filming *Something's Got to Give*, MM has done one day of work. Director George Cukor has been shooting around her.

May 11   Peter Levathes contacts MM's attorney to inform him that given the delays caused by her illness, Fox is rescinding the permission it granted for her to go to New York for the presidential gala.

May 14   MM, accompanied by Paula Strasberg, performs extremely well on her second day of filming and patiently does take after take when the dog in the scene does not perform correctly.

May 17   Having done two more full days of work, MM works a partial day and then flies to New York. The following day, she is notified that she is in violation of her contract.

May 19	At Madison Square Garden, MM performs a medley of "Happy Birthday" and "Thanks for the Memory." She is the last of the twenty-three performers on the program and is, by all accounts, the hit of the evening.
May 21	Although MM returns to work, she informs Cukor that she is too tired to shoot her close-up. The following day, running a fever, she says she cannot work with Dean Martin, who has a cold.
May 23	Cukor shoots MM's swimming scene. At first, she wears a flesh-colored suit, and then she performs nude. After the seven-hour shoot, she poses for photographers and comments that the photos will knock Elizabeth Taylor off the front covers of all magazines.
May 24–31	MM works five days and calls in sick twice.
June 1	On her thirty-sixth birthday, MM works a full day and is then given a surprise birthday party on the set. That night, she appears at a charity baseball game at Dodger Stadium.
June 4	Having become ill with a sinus infection as a result of her appearance at the baseball game, MM notifies the studio that she will not be coming in. Cukor shoots around her with Dean Martin and Cyd Charisse on what will be the last day of filming.
June 5–6	With MM still sick at home, studio executives decide to move forward with plans to replace her. Cukor leaks this story to columnist Hedda Hopper, also implying that MM's inability to perform well stems from mental illness.
June 8	After talks with her attorney and her psychiatrist break down, Fox fires MM. It has already been decided that Lee Remick will replace her. MM also learns that the studio plans to sue her for $500,000.
June 9	Dean Martin announces his refusal to do the film with anyone other than MM.
June 11	Twentieth Century-Fox formally announces the suspension of production on *Something's Got to Give*.
June 18–19	Fox executives begin to reconsider the shutdown and firing.
June 23	Peter Levathes meets with MM at her home to discuss a possible reinstatement. The studio's demands include

discharging Paula Strasberg. MM listens noncommittally, and they plan another meeting. Later that day, she has the first of three sessions with photographer Bert Stern. The photos include fashion shots for *Vogue* and nude and seminude studies.

June 28   MM and her attorney meet with Levathes at Fox. A main topic of discussion involves making changes to her support staff.

July 4   MM gives an in-depth interview to Richard Meryman of *Life* magazine. The interview—for which she will be commended for her candor—will run in the August 3 issue.

July 12   MM appears to cover some serious territory in a meeting at Fox. A verbal agreement is reached by which she will receive a salary increase for *Something's Got to Give* and $500,000 for a second film, which will probably be *I Love Louisa* (later retitled *What a Way to Go!*). The studio demands that she fire Paula Strasberg, Dr. Ralph Greenson, and publicist Patricia Newcomb; relinquish her director approval; and give up the right to inspect the daily rushes. She demands script approval on *Something's Got to Give* and the replacement of George Cukor with Jean Negulesco. Fox then insists that she issue a public apology.

July 27   MM receives yet another rewritten screenplay for *Something's Got to Give*, this time by Hal Kanter. Negulesco, for his part, feels that the Nunnally Johnson script should be the one used.

August 1   MM speaks by phone with stand-in Evelyn Moriarty and informs her that *Something's Got to Give* appears to be back on track and will resume shooting in October. *I Love Louisa* will follow, and another possibility is a biography of Jean Harlow. Later that day, Gene Kelly phones to discuss *I Love Louisa*, in which he plans to costar.

August 4   MM dies of an overdose of Nembutal and chloral hydrate, possibly between 9:00 and 10:00 p.m., although it will be reported that she does not die until early the following morning.

August 5	MM is pronounced dead at 3:50 a.m. by her physician, Dr. Hyman Engelberg, who has been summoned by Dr. Greenson. Engelberg phones to notify the police at 4:25.
August 8	MM's funeral and interment are held at Westwood Memorial Park.
August 18	The Los Angeles County Coroner terms MM's death as "caused by self-administered drugs [and a] 'probable suicide.'"

1963

April 18	Twentieth Century-Fox releases *Marilyn*, a feature-length compilation of scenes from MM's work at the studio. While no footage from *Let's Make Love* is included, there are clips, mostly hair and makeup tests, from the uncompleted *Something's Got to Give*. Rock Hudson serves as on-camera narrator for the documentary, directed by Harold Medford.
May 13–late July	The reconstituted *Something's Got to Give*, now titled *Move Over, Darling*, is filmed at Fox under the direction of Michael Gordon. Doris Day, James Garner, Polly Bergen, Chuck Connors, and Don Knotts perform in the roles originally given to MM, Dean Martin, Cyd Charisse, Tom Tryon, and Wally Cox.
December 19	*Move Over, Darling* premieres in New York to mixed reviews and excellent returns. Some reviews mention its tumultuous backstory and note that Doris Day does not do a nude swimming scene.

1964

May 13	*What a Way to Go!* (formerly *I Love Louisa*) premieres. Shirley MacLaine stars in the role originally intended for MM, who had already given her OK to director J. Lee Thompson. Although Edith Head's costumes win better reviews than the film itself, Fox once again has a financial success.
November 18	A final MM-connected project is released. *Goodbye Charlie*, directed by Vincente Minnelli, stars Debbie Reynolds in

the role Fox originally intended for MM—who, it appears, was wise to have rejected the project, which is notably unsuccessful. While the first phase of MM's association with Twentieth Century-Fox has now ended, the constant marketing and repackaging of her films will continue.

1

Apprenticeships

For Norma Jeane, it was always about the movies. Homes and circumstances changed incessantly, family members and loved ones came and went, security was fleeting, affection often temporary. The one constant was film, so connected to her that it was part of her life even before she was born. And not only was it simply a matter of being born in the heart of filmmaking, since her mother worked as a cutter in film labs. Moreover, she was baptized by the most show-bizzy pastor ever, superstar evangelist Aimee Semple McPherson.) For the little girl who grew up to be Marilyn Monroe, motion pictures were inherent.

The circumstances of Monroe's early life have been so written about as to constitute an American equivalent of *Oliver Twist*. There was the mother, Gladys, who seemed to fit in all too well with her family's history of mental instability. There was the anonymous father, whose identity is still open to some dispute. There was the succession of foster homes—terrible and unsettled enough on their own, later heightened by the constant self-mythologizing Monroe was prone to in later years, when she referred to her young self as a "waif" and told dark and unverifiable tales of child abuse. There was also the stretch of time, nearly two years, when a nine-year-old girl with a living parent was compelled to live in an orphanage.[1] Then back to more foster homes.

Norma Jeane, whose last name was variously termed Baker (after her mother's first husband) or Mortenson (after the second), needed something different. Fortunately, there were a couple of sunshine rays. She herself was a reasonably bright child with an imagination that could often transcend the dreary uncertainty of present realities. There was also a fairy godmother of sorts in Grace McKee, Gladys Baker's close friend and former coworker.

---

[1] It's been recounted that Monroe's film debut may have occurred while she was living at the orphanage. A scene shot at the Los Angeles Orphan's Home used some of the residents as extras, supposedly with Norma Jeane among them. The movie in question is Warner Bros.' *Little Big Shot*, directed by Michael Curtiz, but the record shows that the scene was filmed approximately two months before Norma Jeane's arrival at the home. Still an intriguing thought, however.

Possibly even more movie-struck than Gladys, Grace was compelled to assume charge of the young Norma Jeane after Gladys was institutionalized. It was through Grace's eyes that the little girl began to see life as a thing with some cinematic potential, and even during her time at the orphanage, Grace would take her out for movies and ice cream sodas. As some Monroe biographers have noted, Grace was somewhat obsessed with Jean Harlow, and even early on, she could see some similarities, at least potentially, between the "Blonde Bombshell" and Gladys's little girl. Small wonder, then, that Harlow—the platinum-hot comedian and glamour queen dead at twenty-six—became a template and inspiration for Monroe, who in later years frequently considered starring in and even producing a Harlow biopic.

There isn't an enormous amount of information about the films young Norma Jeane went to see. Later on, she would cite Marie Dressler as the kind of performer she wanted to be when she got older—a telling aspiration, since Dressler was majestically proficient in both comic and dramatic roles and was, understating the case, the antithesis of sex appeal. Although Dressler's *Dinner at Eight* would have been heady fare for a seven-year-old, it did run at Grauman's Chinese Theatre, that first-run palace of Hollywood art where both her mother (prior to her commitment) and Grace McKee frequently took her.[2] In 1935, the Grauman's bill of fare featured several items that could enrapture the young Norma Jeane: Shirley Temple in *Curly Top*, for example, and Harlow and Gable in *China Seas*. It's also been reported that Norma Jeane was taken to see Claudette Colbert as *Cleopatra* and, in her post-orphanage time, Bette Davis in *Jezebel* and Norma Shearer as *Marie Antoinette*. Most likely, too, she would have seen *Gone with the Wind*, that ultimate chunk of studio professionalism and confident storytelling. In any case, she held on tightly to her movie dreams: Marie Antoinette facing the revolutionary hordes or Scarlett O'Hara escaping the Yankees may have been dangerous, but either of them would offer a whole lot more allure than having to worry about the latest foster family packing up and dumping you with somebody else.

[2] In addition to its stature as a gorgeously prime piece of Hollywood entertainment, *Dinner at Eight* contains so many references to Monroe's later career that it might have been unfair to posterity if she *hadn't* seen it early on. Besides Dressler, it has a killer performance (possibly her best) by Jean Harlow, under the direction of George Cukor. Cukor worked far less happily with Monroe (in *Let's Make Love* and the uncompleted *Something's Got to Give*) than he did with Dressler, Harlow, and the other *Dinner* cast members. Two other MM connections were originally up for roles that went elsewhere: Clark Gable, her final costar, in the role taken by Edmund Lowe, and Joan Crawford, who became one of her most conspicuous detractors, in the role played by Madge Evans.

As she entered her teens, Norma Jeane blossomed, famously, into a pretty young woman with a sensational figure. She was also, for the time, rather tall at five feet, five and a half (or possibly six) inches, which meant that her size-seven shoes seemed discouragingly larger than the tiny star-lady feet memorialized in cement at Grauman's. She was taller than, say, Betty Grable and Ginger Rogers—a particular favorite of Norma Jeane's—at five foot four, though the much-admired Greta Garbo was five foot seven, as was Jennifer Jones, and Rosalind Russell was a towering five foot eight.[3] Norma Jeane, then, was taller than most peers in life and on the screen, if not unreasonably so, and her identification with movie royalty continued unabated. Clark Gable, for her, was in a special category, not least because her mother had shown her a photo of a mustachioed man she said was Norma Jeane's father. That there was a resemblance gave Norma Jeane permission to pretend that her father had really been Gable, instead of some anonymous man she never knew.

By 1942, when the barely sixteen-year-old Norma Jeane married friend of the family James Dougherty, the movies were providing an even steadier anchor for the country than they had during the Great Depression. The world was at war, younger and older men were enlisting or being drafted, and women were undertaking responsibilities they had never been allowed to hold before then. In all of this, the movies promised something more special than the radio shows people could hear at home. While some significant films used the war as a source for drama, it was the fantasy entertainments that seemed the most indicative of what the country needed—musicals with Betty Grable, the comedies of Abbott and Costello, exotic lunacy featuring Maria Montez. The popularity of these films, filling America's need to be entertained, was such that they would run in theaters far longer than they had previously, often three or four weeks instead of one. If the movies had been something of a necessity for decades, the war gave that importance an urgency so vivid that the point would never be missed by, say, glamour-struck teenagers, even married ones, who'd been raised on a diet of film.

Norma Jeane was not quite eighteen when, with her husband off at war, she became a working woman. For anyone believing drone technology to be a thing of the twenty-first century, think again: her first job was at Radioplane,

---

[3] Later in the 1940s, there would be future Monroe costars Adele Jergens and Lauren Bacall, both at five foot nine, virtual giantesses in film annals up to that time. In 1953, some minor movie sorcery in *How to Marry a Millionaire* could sometimes make Monroe and Grable appear to be the same height, with Bacall only a little taller.

a factory that made radio-operated drone planes used for military target practice. It was real Rosie the Riveter work, at least until a crucial moment when army photographers arrived at the plant to shoot a "women at war" piece. Norma Jeane was among those selected to pose working on Radioplane equipment, and photographer David Conover saw very quickly how she lit up in front of a camera. A modeling career soon began to seem like a possibility, and not only because four hours of modeling paid the same as a whole week at Radioplane. Some, not all, of the eventual Marilyn Monroe can be seen in those early photos. Her brownish hair often appears to be an unruly bush, the front teeth are too prominent, and the face seems fuller and softer in a way that indicates baby fat. Yet there is something there, as Conover saw, a definite glow that is so noticeable that it's not simply a hindsight "Marilyn-to-be" aura. There were, as people sometimes say about houses, good bones, even at the beginning. It would then be up to her to do the work to stand out from the crowd, from all those other young women trying to angle for modeling jobs around the time the war ended.

"Wow factor" charisma may be innate, and it also requires a good deal of hard work to burnish it. Norma Jeane rose to that particular challenge with a vengeance, taking courses, listening to advice, practicing and studying and polishing and honing. She paid attention to posture and deportment, she learned to pose to maximum advantage, and she listened to those who told her something needed to be done about her smile and her hair. Directing the upper lip downward and emphasizing the lower teeth was a good remedy for the smile issue, which is why there are some shots in her films where Monroe can be seen maneuvering her lips into place. As for the hair, she was initially resistant about getting it lightened and straightened, in large part because of the resulting expense and upkeep. Finally, in connection with a shampoo advertisement she was doing, she became a true blonde, as opposed to her natural "California blond" shade, which is really a brown hue that photographs lighter in the summer. All this was done with thought as well as dedication. Her modeling agent in those days, Emmeline Snively of the Blue Book Modeling Agency, spoke to a Monroe biographer about her work ethic:

> She was the hardest worker I ever handled. She never missed a class [and] did something I've never seen any other model do. She would study every print a photographer did of her. I mean she'd take them home and study them for hours. Then she'd go back and ask the photographer, "What did

I do wrong in this one?" or "Why didn't this come out better?" They would tell her. And she never repeated a mistake.

A lot of models ask me how they can be like Marilyn Monroe and I say to them, honey, I say to them, if you can show half the gumption, just half, that little girl showed, you'll be a success, too.

The work extended apart from modeling classes to a good deal of independent study. Later on, there would be sneering mockery of the books Monroe read and allegations that she would be seen carrying them around with their titles facing outward without ever opening them. No, she did read, and her drive for self-improvement extended to both her mind and her body. In the latter category was a modern edition of Andreas Vesalius's classic treatise on human anatomy, *De humani corporis*, which she would pore over intently earlier and later in her career. Dreams bred ambition, intent fostered determination, study led to results.

By mid-1945, Norma Jeane had left Radioplane and was actively seeking modeling jobs. Eventually, she signed with Blue Book, took the prescribed training courses, and began to go out on calls. In her initial application, she did not mention acting as an ambition, although she did cite some singing and dancing ability. Nor, it soon became clear, was her modeling career destined for the fashion end of things, not with that figure. Snively soon began to direct her toward the less chic, if lucrative, direction of pinups, and the Norma Jeane Dougherty modeling portfolio soon began to include the covers of magazines with titles like *Swank*, *Sir!*, *Laff*, and *Salute*, along with the slightly more sedate *Personal Romances*, *U.S. Camera*, and *Pageant*, as well as the incontestably respectable *Family Circle*. In addition to her willingness to work hard, she became recognized for her good-natured professionalism, which she deployed to mask a marked lack of self-confidence. By the spring of 1946, she was on her way, and some early movies of Blue Book models show a sweetly assured Norma Jeane with more manageable hair and a smile so large and genuine as to seem all-encompassing.

Two major changes came early in 1946: the decision to end her marriage to Jim Dougherty and the move toward an acting career. The divorce was, all things considered, a foregone conclusion, as with many wartime marriages; the acting career was less so. It would later be reported that the only time Norma Jeane had shown any interest in acting came during her stint at Van Nuys High School, when she auditioned unsuccessfully for a role in the comedy *Art and Mrs. Bottle*. That, as it happened, came less out of thespian longing than from the desire to be near one of the boys in the cast. While nothing more was heard of her dramatic ambition after that, a young girl raised on movies and living in the center of the film universe would hardly be immune to the attraction. With the war over, the movie studios were still buoyed by immense wartime profits and turning out product like there was no tomorrow. There was not yet a major threat from television or the notion that business would fall off alarmingly when the movie companies were divested of their theater chains. They were still busy and hiring, and it may have been the last time it was this easy for a young person with good looks and no experience to sign on with a studio. It was hardly an immense leap of faith that caused the Helen Ainsworth Agency to sign Norma Jeane for representation. Enough people had seen the cheery and shapely young woman on those magazine covers.

The first stab at a movie career was an interview at Paramount that amounted to nothing. Little is known about that event other than that it happened; Paramount at that moment would not have been as propitious a fit for Norma Jeane as a couple of the other studios. Twentieth Century-Fox was a bit more suitable, at least on the surface. As with the other major studios—MGM, Universal, Paramount, RKO, Warner Bros.—it functioned as a self-contained factory, producing dozens of features and scores of short subjects each year. The profits ensured that there was a large personnel roster of technicians, laborers, creative artists, and executives—also talent, both the stars and, way down the list, the group known as "stock" people. These were the young men and (possibly more numerous) women who showed up for work, posed for photos, took classes in acting and singing and dancing, and occasionally were assigned small roles in movies. If they were really lucky, such an appearance—or, alternatively, the personal or professional interest of a studio executive—might lead to larger roles. Or not. Film history is liberally scattered with the names of people who started in humble contracts and then rose—from Joan Crawford, probably the ace example, in the 1920s, to Lucille Ball in the '30s, Ava Gardner in the '40s, and all the way to Harrison Ford in the '60s. Gable and Harlow, too, had early experience doing extra work. If the work wasn't necessarily demeaning, it involved a good deal of waiting for an opportunity that quite possibly wouldn't happen. Stock contracts such as that given to Norma Jeane in 1946 were usually based on six-month increments, at which point they could be renewed or terminated. Meanwhile, you could be called upon to be an extra in a crowd scene, appear at the opening of a supermarket, pose for endorsements of products you never used, or show up at studio functions to look attractive and, in some cases, available. As far as actual "acting" was concerned, it might be an insignificant role in a feature, reading lines to someone else in a screen test, or getting doused with water in a comedy short.

Norma Jeane's advent at Fox has been subject to as much myth-making, and elevation, as every other part of her life. (Save, possibly, her relationship with the Kennedys—that one has gone way over what should have been the prescribed limit.) It's unclear exactly how the ball got rolling, and this is where some of the legend kicks in. It's been written that some of Norma Jeane's modeling work was spotted by Howard Hughes—not the best judge of talent, if certainly a connoisseur of the female figure.[4] This, apparently, was a fabricated news item dreamed up by Snively—and so convincing that it made Hedda Hopper's syndicated column. Snively then prompted talent agent Helen Ainsworth to follow up, which was done with a call to Fox casting director Ben Lyon. The incontestable fact is that one day in July 1946, Norma Jeane Dougherty, just back from a Nevada residency needed to obtain a divorce, met with Lyon at Fox. He was no faceless studio suit; in the 1920s and '30s, he had been a popular leading man, serving as love interest for the likes of Gloria Swanson and Pola Negri and, significantly, Jean Harlow. While never in the highest star ranks, Lyon was consistently likable and engaging. Later in the 1930s, he moved to England and continued working, sometimes alongside his wife, silent (and early movie musical) star Bebe Daniels. After the war, he and Daniels came back to California, and he moved to a position behind the camera. He had worked with enough actors to be considered a good judge of talent, and it was in that capacity that he served a brief tenure at Fox. Shortly afterward, Lyon and Daniels returned to England and had flourishing careers as an "Ozzie and Harriet"–type couple on radio and television.

What, exactly, did Lyon see in that twenty-year-old woman when she walked into his office on that summer day? Not surprisingly, the name "Jean Harlow" has been frequently invoked to describe Lyon's reaction. This sounds suspiciously hindsight-propitious, since Harlow had been a favorite of the young Norma Jeane and Lyon had worked with her on the film that brought her overnight fame, *Hell's Angels*. If the sunny sexuality of the

---

[4] Hughes was always signing young women to personal contracts and then not giving them any work. Jane Russell was the exception, but then his management of her subsequent career was nothing to brag about. If MM's initial tenure at Fox was well short of sensational, she was still better off there than at the beck and call of a breast-obsessed mogul whose aberrations were politely termed eccentricities.

young Norma Jean (she had dropped the "e" professionally) recalled Harlow, it was less in her early, blatant *Hell's Angels* persona than in the later post–Production Code Harlow, with darker hair, who can be seen in a film such as *Wife vs. Secretary*. There was also something of the modified simmer of the young Lana Turner in Norma Jean and possibly a little of the warmth of Fox's former musical mainstay, Alice Faye. Plus, and not surprisingly, there was an air that recalled Fox's current leading breadwinner, Betty Grable. With her cheery, everything-on-the-surface, "this is me" persona, Grable turned out one successful Technicolor musical after another in the 1940s, seldom with much differentiation. Whenever Fox tried to alter the Grable matrix, especially after World War II, the public turned away. While studio head Darryl Zanuck stayed in steady pursuit of such Grables redux as June Haver and Vivian Blaine, finding a new Grable was not necessarily on Lyon's agenda.

There is still some mystery and contradiction surrounding those first days at Fox. Evidently, during their meeting, Lyon had Norma Jean read lines originally written for Judy Holliday to speak in George Cukor's 1944 film *Winged Victory*. This, apparently, was enough to show that for all her lack of dramatic experience, she wasn't hopeless. On July 25 (and this date is definite, as verified by a surviving Fox memo), Lyon notified the Fox legal department that Norma Jean would be given a screen test and, if that was judged a success, would be put under contract. It's always been recounted that she made her screen test only two days after meeting with Lyon and that it was shot silently, in Technicolor, on the set of *Mother Wore Tights* (starring Betty Grable, naturally), then in production. Though the test itself has not resurfaced—as with much studio ephemera, it wound up in a landfill long ago—there are a few photos of a smiling Norma Jean, hopeful and with a hint of nervousness, standing on a somewhat anonymous-looking set of a park bench and some shrubbery. The setting is generic, and the gown is downright peculiar—a fussy concoction with a tight-fitting off-the-shoulder bodice that erupts midway into a procession of ruffles decked with some kind of dotted trim. (Except for an excessive number of bows that seem arbitrarily attached, she comes close to looking like a giant chess piece.) The tradition continues to note that the test was directed by Walter Lang, then directing *Mother Wore Tights*, and shot by Fox's ace color man Leon Shamroy. Perhaps it happened that way, but then the record shows that *Mother Wore Tights* did not commence shooting until mid-October and that on August 14, Norma Jean shot a non-silent screen test with a Fox stock-contract actor named Robert Cornell. Most probably, she did two tests, one of them silent and in color.

Perhaps, too, she did a (later) test connected with *Mother Wore Tights*. At any rate, she made an impact judged sufficiently favorable for her to be offered a six-month contract at $125 per week, renewable at that same rate for another six months.[5]

There was, soon enough, the issue of what she should be called. "Norma" had gone out of fashion since the 1920s, when superstar Norma Talmadge had probably been the inspiration for Gladys Baker's choice of her daughter's name. "Dougherty" was a nonstarter, "Mortenson," from that elusive non-father, was no better, and "Baker" seemed prosaic and flat. Only the "Jean," without that second "e," was a possibility, with its recollection of the great Harlow. Indeed, modeling agent Snively, when cooking up some early promotion for the starlet-to-be, had come up with the moniker "Jean Norman," which was as close to that platinum template as one could get. Ben Lyon, though, was thinking farther afield. There was something about this young woman that reminded him of a performer he'd worked with fifteen years earlier in a Warner Bros. film titled *Her Majesty, Love*. Although she had success in films, Marilyn Miller was a creature of Broadway, a dancing enchantress who'd captivated vast audiences in the Ziegfeld Follies and as the centerpiece of the hugely successful shows *Sally* and *Sunny*. Miller was one of those people like Gertrude Lawrence (and, some would allege, Marilyn Monroe), whose personal magnetism was so intense that her deficiencies as a performer could not deter audiences from loving her. Lyon may have loved her as well, since some sources mention that he had a relationship with Miller prior to his marriage to Daniels. What is more verifiable is that Lyon, possibly with some input from his wife, came up with the name "Marilyn" and that Norma Jean suggested her mother's maiden name of "Monroe." The alliteration was almost musical, which was why there had already been a Marilyn Miller (born Mary Ellen Reynolds) and a Marilyn Maxwell (born Marvel Marilyn Maxwell).[6] Norma Jean herself was less than happy with "Marilyn" and later said that she wished she'd held out for "Jean Monroe" as a stage name. "Marilyn Monroe" it was, however, and a decade later, it became

---

[5] Again, the history opposes the legend. Numerous accounts of Norma Jean's first contract with Fox put her salary at $75 a week—low even for 1946. Enter, then, an authentic Fox contract, signed by Norma Jean, which has the correct, higher number. It sold at auction some years back and even bears a notary seal.

[6] Something else was shared by these three Marilyns, and it's a sad parallel: none of them lived very long. Maxwell was dead of a heart attack at fifty, and Miller was only thirty-seven when she died, with shocking suddenness, after surgery. And talk about shocking: Monroe, of course, was gone at thirty-six.

her legal name as well. Although accounts have always suggested that Lyon came up with the name just as she was starting her Fox contract, there is, once again, documentation to show that legends can take a while to form: it was not until early December 1946 that a Fox attorney notified the publicity department and Lyon that the professional name of Norma Jean Dougherty "has been designated" Marilyn Monroe.

For Norma Jean, now Marilyn, the possibilities seemed dazzling. She had a contract with one of the largest and most successful movie companies, she'd passed her screen test, and she was being groomed, trained, and photographed. There was little, however, of much substance. Fox, still flush with the profits that came during and just after the war, could afford to keep young and untried players under shorter contracts as a wait-and-see possibility, without much effort being extended toward developing viable performers. In doing so, Fox was somewhat different from the other studios. For all its busy production schedule and roster of big names, the studio was propelled less by performers than by scripts. At MGM, the star personality came first, and many young players were given sink-or-swim feature-film tryouts. Paramount was a little more staid in that regard, with a mostly conservative outlook that tended to pigeonhole players while taking few chances. Warners, RKO, Columbia, and Universal were all bang-for-the-buck kinds of places, with endless B-movies and short subjects providing ready exposure for the contract actors to, again, sink or swim. Fox, under the guidance of Darryl Zanuck, had its marquee names in Betty Grable and Tyrone Power and a few others, though for the most part, the Fox actors were interchangeable. If Alice Faye got pregnant, Grable could step in, or later June Haver; Anne Baxter, with her low-profile versatility, could always take over for Gene Tierney or Jeanne Crain, and on and on. Zanuck saw to it that the scripts were constructed so as to be virtually actor-proof. (Director-proof, too.) If Clifton Webb was inimitable, he was an exception. As for the stock people like Marilyn Monroe and Robert Cornell, they were window dressing, if that. This fact became clear to Monroe when, during the early months of her Fox contract, she waited for a casting call that seemed to never come.

Would that history was completely clear about Monroe's first film job at Fox. Most people are aware of *Scudda Hoo! Scudda Hay!* as her first documented role, and she herself later recounted the untruth that she'd been cut out of it. Before then, at least one possibility has been set forth in some annals of early Monroe. The film in question is *The Shocking Miss Pilgrim*, one of Fox's first attempts to widen the set-in-granite Betty Grable configuration of romance overlying a brassy show-biz setting. "Shocking" may have been the operative word, in that *Miss Pilgrim* did not have the usual Grable backstage trappings—and, crucially, it gave her next to no opportunity to show her legs. Even her hair was darkened. Instead of the usual formula, it was a proto-feminist tract about a young typist who goes to work in a man's world. Bold departure, indeed, and also rather dowdy and lacking in a detectable spark, which may be why Fox kept it on the shelf for the better part of a year before releasing it. Monroe is nowhere in evidence in the movie, and indeed, she did not arrive at Fox until six months after shooting had ended. Perhaps she was in an unused retake or coming-attractions trailer; the accounts that state that MM played a telephone operator, or just the voice of an operator, don't take into consideration that the film is set in a pre-telephone era. She did, however, have an incontestable *Pilgrim* connection: the first truly high-profile result of her Fox contract came on February 24, 1947, when she appeared briefly on one of radio's most popular programs, the *Lux Radio Theatre*. In a scripted interview with host William Keighley, a slightly nervous MM stumbles over a few words to plug both *The Shocking Miss Pilgrim* and Lux Soap. Keighley offers some backstory about her "discovery," purportedly while posing in morale-boosting wartime photos, and MM states that her screen test was made—ahh!—with film "left over" from *Miss Pilgrim*. Nothing is said regarding her participation in it or any other Fox film.

In both its title and its meek self, *Scudda Hoo! Scudda Hay!* has to mark one of the most unpropitious starts ever to a brilliant career. And as far as can be determined, it is square one for Monroe. It is also a fairly good demonstration of the mindset then at work at Twentieth Century-Fox. Far from being a low-budget programmer, it was one of the studio's "A" pictures for 1947, with a budget of around $1.7 million. But . . . it's a movie about training a pair of mules. That's where its mind is and where its ethos lies and what its title indicates. (It's what is said to the mules to get them to stop loafing and start moving.) As such, it is well in line with one of the Fox tendencies of the 1940s, which involved bucolic stories in which animals, mostly horses, were as significant as people. *Home in Indiana, My Friend Flicka,* the inevitable *Thunderhead, Son of Flicka,* and more, usually shot in Technicolor with nice location vistas and some romance between young and appealing(ish) contract actors.

June Haver, the above-the-title star of *Scudda Hoo! Scudda Hay!,* had started out at Fox in an insignificant bit in *The Gang's All Here.* So had Jeanne Crain. Then both of them were given leads in *Home in Indiana* in 1944 and went on from there. Haver was almost exactly the same age as Monroe—nine days younger, in fact—and had been performing since childhood. Almost immediately, she was put into the Technicolor musicals that defined Fox even more than its horse stories. She was pleasant without being very distinctive, which seems to have been enough for her to be promoted informally as a younger successor/threat to Grable. It was at that point that Fox cast her (alongside her *Home in Indiana* costar, Lon McCallister), in *Scudda Hoo!* Given the arc of Haver's career up to 1947, it's clear that someone like Monroe, with a contract, some hope, and a fair amount of ambition, could see the ascension of Haver as a model and precedent. Perhaps she could even see herself as a Haver-like figure to challenge Grable or even Haver herself. Having had the six-month option of her contract renewed, plus that much-heard radio appearance, Monroe could muster at least a modicum of self-assurance that she was on her way.

If many of the Fox films of the 1940s, the ones below the caliber of *Laura* or *The Snake Pit*, blur together indistinctly, *Scudda Hoo! Scudda Hay!* does, at the very least, stand out. Not, it must be said, as a star vehicle for Haver or as an endearing love story between a boy and his mules or as early proof that a very little Natalie Wood was a natural on camera. It's all due to its odd status, legendarily, as both Monroe's first film and the one she's not in. She herself, in a *Person to Person* TV interview in 1955, stated that she'd been cut out of it. For years, books stated that she could only be seen in a couple of indistinct long shots, paddling a canoe with another Fox contract hopeful, Colleen Townsend. There was even proof of the deletion in stills of a scene, no longer in the film, of Monroe and Townsend sitting in the canoe speaking with actor Robert Karnes. Yet, as keen-eyed Monroe scholars finally observed, she did make it into the film, with a spoken line. Fifty-one minutes and forty-one seconds in, Haver and Wood are standing on the steps of a church. We can see parishioners leaving the sanctuary, and suddenly, while Wood is speaking, a blue pinafore and white blouse enter from screen right, arm in arm with a darker woman's suit. You wonder if you'll ever see the face, and then, after about three seconds, you do. It's a smiling, medium-blond Marilyn Monroe with somewhat prominent front teeth. As she begins to speak, she exits the frame, but it's clearly MM saying "Hi, Rad!" to Haver. "Hi, Betty," Haver replies, so we have a name to go with the face and the pinafore. A minute later, there's a dissolve to a lake, and while Haver, McCallister, Wood, and friends talk in the foreground, there are blond Monroe and brown-haired Townsend off in the distance, paddling away from the camera in three shots.

Monroe is on-screen for less than a minute, and her face is visible for something like two seconds. Betty, friend of Rad, is otherwise a blank—one of those minor characters who can end up on the cutting-room floor without anyone, save the actor herself, being upset. Too tiny a start to be able to prove anything to anyone, it might serve as a warning to aspiring young players that this, too, might happen to you.

After the non-role of Betty, Monroe's days at Fox were numbered, even as she continued to collect her paycheck for several more months. She could possibly have done background work in one of the "Fox Loves Horses" pictures, *Green Grass of Wyoming*; there's a square-dance scene with a lot of young people dancing while Burl Ives sings, and MM might be in the background somewhere. Something like this would, in any case, be one way to get some work out of a young contract performer on the way out. So, as it happened, was *Dangerous Years*, which would serve as Monroe's first released film, preceding *Scudda Hoo!* by a couple of months. A product of the B-movie factory of longtime Fox producer Sol Wurtzel, *Dangerous Years* was one of Hollywood's earlier looks at juvenile delinquency. Aside from its place in the MM canon, it's notable for casting a number of former child actors in adolescent-to-adult roles—"Dead End Kid" Billy (now William) Halop, Ann Todd, Scotty Beckett, Darryl Hickman, and Dickie Moore. *Rebel without a Cause* it's not, even for a bargain-price hour-long film shot in two weeks. The delinquency comes early, ending with an accidental death followed by way too many scenes of testimony and atonement, and a great deal of the bad influence comes out of a den-of-teen-iniquity roadhouse called The Gopher Hole. Yes, it has a sign with a cartoon gopher on it, and the featured waitress there, Evie, is Marilyn Monroe, with ten lines to speak, a close-up, and a total screen time of about a minute. As she banters a bit with Moore, it's clear that although she appears to have some self-assurance, she's still a newbie, and some of her line readings give the impression that she's reciting a script she doesn't quite comprehend. And though she's certainly pretty, it's a softly rounded teenage attractiveness that's a lot closer to, say, Haver than it is to the more mature Monroe. Naturally, the only reason to spend any time at all discussing this performance is because it's her. Who else would, at this early point, rate the effort?

Even before *Dangerous Years* wrapped, probably a few days after she shot her scenes, Monroe received notification that Fox was not renewing her contract. Effective August 25, 1947, she was out of a job. Her agent, Harry

Lipton, later remembered that her initial reaction to the termination was one of devastation—and then she quickly moved to a philosophical "that's life" kind of attitude, with a resolve to keep on keeping on. She was already taking acting classes at the respected Actors' Lab in Hollywood and would also soon study briefly in a class led by Charles Laughton. Retreat was not an option, even as employment was a challenge. She obtained a few modeling jobs, did a couple of "starlet caddie" gigs at celebrity golf tournaments, and may have returned to Fox to do background work on the musical *You Were Meant for Me*. Perhaps more consequential than these was her first try at live theater: a second lead in the comedy *Glamour Preferred* at a small showcase theater in Beverly Hills. Although she had worked hard during rehearsal, she was initially paralyzed by stage fright during the actual performances—a harbinger of the professional insecurity that would become an essential part of her work ethic.

Although Monroe frequently gave off an air of helplessness, she knew how to connect with people. She met and soon became attached to actor John Carroll (a leading man at small Republic Pictures) and his wife, MGM talent director Lucille Ryman. Ryman later recalled that the young MM was both appealing and, with her neediness, draining. For all the "poor me" vibes she sent out, she could be quite resourceful in her networking, most successfully with the formidable Joe Schenck. He was a film pioneer and Fox executive, and the bond they formed—whatever it may have been—raised many eyebrows. Before many months had passed, Monroe had another film contract, most likely due to Schenck's speaking on her behalf to another studio chief.

Harry Cohn was *the* Hollywood mogul, a man made up of a wildly jumbled mixture of personal crudity and professional acumen. People loathed him liberally and admired him grudgingly, which was why he was an industry legend long before his death. Under his despotic reign, Columbia Pictures was a tight ship—a smallish yet prominent player in the studio system, run efficiently and economically and without even the cursory sentimentality of some movie studios. Like the other companies, Columbia had its roster of low-rung stock players, any of whom could be called on to appear in small roles in the studio's many grade-B films or comedy shorts. For Monroe, Columbia may have seemed a comedown after the glossier upmarket Fox, even as her time there yielded some big consequences. One was a major role in an admittedly insignificant film; the other came with two associations that spanned both the professional and personal fronts.

Natasha Lytess was a central part of Monroe's life for seven years, an imperious figure so hated by most MM associates that she could hardly even be termed controversial. Teacher, actress, student of Max Reinhardt, and self-appointed oracle, Lytess had little focus, save her own personal needs, beyond drama. She was immersed in acting, although her own film performances are not particularly distinctive, and in her position as a drama coach at Columbia, she did her utmost to impose her principles on the studio's more malleable young players. Her recollections of meeting Monroe for the first time are etched in bile, which was surely a natural extension of the way their partnership ended. Having just signed with Columbia, Monroe showed up for her appointment dressed, in Lytess's words, like a "trollop." Neither was her voice a thing of promise, although Lytess's memory of her voice sounding "squeaky" is belied by that *Lux Radio Theatre* recording. Nevertheless, there was something that drew them together: MM's need for a teacher, Lytess's need to impose her precepts on a willing pupil, and some weird sort of personal interdependence that, in truth, has flummoxed a whole host of Monroe biographers. Lytess expounded grandly, MM listened and absorbed, and so it would go for the entire first half of Monroe's movie career. When an inherently curious person has an education that is inadequate or curtailed, a great and fillable gap opens. Monroe was like a sponge with Lytess, drawing in all the directives, commands, and endless recountings of theatrical lore. When it came to the actual work of being an actor, it involved gesture, character delineation, line-by-line study, and, past and above everything else, diction.

Her training in live theater led Lytess to place clarity of pronunciation at the very top of the actor's toolkit. While the intangibles of characterization were vital and necessary, it was enunciation, for Lytess, that would remain the hallmark of her work with Monroe. It was a tactile manifestation of their collaboration, of studying the text and conveying an author's work to the listener. Given the slurry rush of some of Monroe's words in *Dangerous Years* and her stumbling over a few words in her scripted talk with Keighley, it's easily understandable why Lytess would drill her in the importance of speaking distinctly. It was the question of proportion that posed the problem, which is why so many of Monroe's performances, early and later, have been rightly criticized for the way she can overpronounce her lines. Intelligibility was a major mark of older-school acting, which is why the Method actors of the 1950s drew heavy fire for what was perceived as "mumbling." Lytess's training and relentless absorption in all things theatrical could often blind her to some of the needs of film, especially if a microphone would be nearby to pick up every syllable. Monroe's natural tendency was to speak in a rush that could often seem breathless, which was not great for film in most instances. To remedy this, Lytess imposed a style of speaking involving overly stressed consonants. As will be seen and heard, this could frequently be stiff, unspontaneous, and altogether self-defeating.

Columbia, as Monroe saw immediately, did not operate as Fox did. Physically, it was a far smaller plant, which played quite smoothly into Cohn's wish to know everything that was going on, and it had neither the economics nor the predisposition to keep performers under contract without putting them to work. Given her inexperience, Monroe could easily have been put into any insignificant role; she might even have gotten called upon to play, say, someone's haughty girlfriend in a Three Stooges short. Instead, someone at Columbia, possibly producer Harry Romm, thought of her in connection with a major role in an upcoming feature. Specifically, it was a musical titled *Ladies of the Chorus* and would require singing and dancing as well as acting. To prepare for her audition before Cohn, Monroe worked with—and soon became personally involved with—arranger and coach Fred Karger of the studio's music department. Karger quickly observed that there was indeed a singing voice there, pleasant in tone if slight in volume, and after some work, he went with Monroe to her audition with the great Cohn. As the terrified woman launched into "Love Me or Leave Me," Cohn barked, "I can't hear her." Karger retorted that a microphone would make it all acceptable, and Cohn eventually agreed.[7]

A film born of expedience and penny-pinching, *Ladies of the Chorus* is one of the few 1940s B-musical films that is at all well known today. That, it goes without saying, has nothing to do with its stature in the movie-musical canon and everything to do with it giving us the first long look at the fledgling Monroe. It also demonstrates some of the particular traits of its hopeful, overtaxed genre. After the largest historical epics, musicals were the most expensive films being produced in the 1940s, due to the enormous preparation they entailed as well as the multitude of production requirements. This

---

[7] During the audition, Cohn observed that MM was carrying a Christian Science publication, and, recalling how his first wife had been a practicing Christian Scientist, he apparently had one of his rare sympathetic impulses. Although Cohn had issued the edict that the cast members of *Ladies of the Chorus* would need to do their own singing, this did not apply to the film's top-billed player, Adele Jergens. She was dubbed by Virginia Rees, who did the honors again a year later when Jergens appeared in Columbia's *The Traveling Saleswoman*—singing Monroe's song from *Ladies of the Chorus*, "Every Baby Needs a Da-Da-Daddy." For Jergens, being cast as MM's mom in *Ladies* was something of a comedown from previous glamour roles; unless you're Bette Davis, playing mother to someone nine years your junior was hardly a sign of good things to come.

did not mean that studios were not also capable of doing them on the cheap as well. Columbia, like Universal and the insignificant Monogram, had a special knack for turning out short black-and-white pieces featuring lesser names, musical specialty acts, and flimsy scripts, all in the name of supplying product and, often enough, occupying the bottom slot of a double feature. While westerns and mysteries shot for piddling sums could make virtues of necessities, the corner-cutting with musical quickies could be quite a bit more conspicuous. Somehow, as part of a large-scale moviegoing diet, this was seen as sufficient. Columbia, after all, had already turned out such un-remembered things as *Sing While You Dance*, *Talk about a Lady*, and *Two Blondes and a Redhead* and would later land in the rock-and-roll era with the likes of *Don't Knock the Rock* and the memorably titled *Cha-Cha-Cha Boom!* Even alongside these, *Ladies of the Chorus* was a poverty-level enter-prise, shot on a no-time-to-waste schedule totaling ten days. Economy of time, money, and artistic inspiration—all those account for why someone as untested as Monroe could be given a big role and a chance to prove herself.

For a film of low ambitions and meager means, *Ladies of the Chorus* does have a heart and a message: love can overcome snobbery and class distinctions. Indeed, the cause for the snobbery comes with the untruth of the title, for these women are not from the chorus-girl wing of musical comedy. They are, instead, burlesque strippers, the kind to establish dread and loathing in upright American families who were familiar with, and fearful of, the likes of Gypsy Rose Lee and Lili St. Cyr. The problem was that this film was shot in 1948 by a major studio and thus subject to the dictates of the Motion Picture Production Code. So no undressing, no bumps or grinds or teasing or G-strings or any of it. These ladies truly rated the term—showing little more than their legs, they prance about with as much decorum as good-will. The word "burlesque" is spoken but never "stripper," and the number that makes MM's Peggy a star, "Anyone Can See I Love You," has her twirling and posing in a long gown that makes her look like a Disney princess.[8] It's certainly not burlesque, as Monroe seems buoyed on a cloud of dreamy, self-willed romanticism. Her second number follows only a minute later, and this is the one where the Karger coaching really paid off. "Every Baby Needs a Da-Da-Daddy" is a minor-key rhythm number, and Monroe handles it like

---

[8] "Anyone Can See," sung and later reprised by Monroe as a warm sigh, is a nice enough song and also an emblem of the movie's poverty: it has the *exact same tune* as the title song, sung by Monroe and chorus before and after the opening credits. It's more languid in the solo version, but this is cost-cutting on quite an obvious scale.

a pro. While close microphone placement was doubtless a help, this is so significantly different a voice from the later breathiness that it gives lie to the notion that her singing was only a matter of baby whispers set to music. "EV-ry baby," she belts, in loud and full tones far more authoritative than her acting.[9] Along with the song, there is also dance, sort of, and the truth is that she was never much of a dancer. She could, however, be set off admirably by her dance mentor, Jack Cole, more as a matter of gesture and placement than anything approaching Rita Hayworth or Cyd Charisse. In "Anyone," she waves her arms and spins to the music, and in the va-voom "Every Baby," she does some lunges and kicks and at one point starts to imply that she might bump and grind. As would happen in a couple of later films, director Phil Karlson sustains the illusion of a coherent dance performance by cutting away from Monroe to various reaction shots backstage or in the audience. That's as far as she could go.

Monroe's singing is good enough that the film could have used more of it. Instead, there's a plot and dialogue, and as in *Dangerous Years*, she's still groping to bridge that gap between saying the lines and understanding them. The blissfully opaque quality she gave off in, say, *The Seven Year Itch* has its roots here, only it's born less of choice than of inexperience. Clearly, she was still not used to the camera, and her scenes with Jergens and leading man Rand Brooks show the difference between a fledgling film performer and one who's logged some screen time. Brooks could see what he was dealing with: "She hadn't had much film training, so I'd move her back and tell her where the light was." Some of the lines she speaks don't land, and not all her movements are properly coordinated, as in a catfight scene that has her turning away from the camera apologetically. Brooks, Jergens, and Nana Bryant (as Brooks's non-snobbish dowager mom) are all clearly more seasoned—which, in these desultory circumstances, plays into the notion that Peggy is a nice, unworldly girl, however much she's been gaining fame as a striptease artist. It's as if she was still too young—though, of course, she wasn't—to be considered a sexpot, and the sweetness of the performance is, besides her singing, the main takeaway here. These come in blessed contrast to two "specialties" that come late in the movie. One involves a comedian and a little boy with matching speech impediments, and the other is the Bobby

---

[9] In addition to her *Ladies* songs, MM also made a test record of a piece Karger co-wrote called "How Wrong Can I Be." On the long-unheard disc, which resurfaced in 1992, Monroe comes off as a capable, confident vocalist. An excerpt of the recording turned up on the soundtrack of the 2017 Oscar winner *The Shape of Water*. Yes, the one about the big fish.

True Trio performing "Ubangi Love Song." Even for an hour-long B-minus musical, these are hideous.

The acting style is not the only unformed part of Monroe's performance, since it was still early on in the physical transformation from starlet to Marilyn. While her hairline has been expanded via electrolysis and the color is further along the road from dark blond to platinum, the 1940s Rita Hayworth style, with lots of waves, is hardly a vintage MM look. Nor is the heavily applied dark lipstick and definitely not the rather unfortunate hat she wears in a flower-shop scene. Her face hasn't quite begun its rapturous love affair with the camera, either, as when her lower lip seems to pout petulantly. The magic of plastic surgery, the following year, would make some small but telling changes, adding a little more to the chin while slightly shortening the nose. The teeth, too, aren't quite there, although it was under Karger's direction during her time at Columbia that Monroe began to wear an orthodontic retainer that would eventually pay some iconic dividends.

Ladies of the Chorus was not released until early in 1949, and the few critics who took the time to write about it were kind to Monroe. Compliments such as "Nifty warbling," from *Daily Variety*, should have provided her with a professional boost, but by then, she was long departed from Columbia Pictures. She herself later declared that this came from her unwillingness to yield to Cohn's lord-of-the-manor advances. Other accounts suggest that Cohn simply didn't like her acting and refused to renew her contract. Perhaps it was both or something else entirely. What is verifiable is that she was out of Columbia after six months and just the one film—plus a decidedly odd appearance in a Gene Autry western bearing the uncatchy title *Riders of the Whistling Pines*. It can't be called a performance, since it's only a still photo of Monroe that's supposed to be the dead wife of one of the characters. Shown several times during the film, the MM glamour shot even inspires Autry to sing an uptempo ditty titled "Hair of Gold." *Riders* was shot a few weeks after *Ladies of the Chorus*, and MM might not even have known that she was sort of in it.

What would have happened to Monroe if Columbia had not dropped her? She might have found herself in an actual role (if that's the word) in an Autry film or in a comedy short. According to not-always-reliable Hollywood chronicler Garson Kanin, she shot a screen test for *Born Yesterday* that made quite a good stab at what will always be known as the Judy Holliday role. Little if nothing else happened, and years later, Cohn would be plagued by jokers sending him cards or flowers with messages like "Thank you for my career, Harry—Love, Marilyn." At least, in 1952, he managed to get a little more mileage out of the instantly forgotten *Ladies of the Chorus*: MM's "Da-Da-Daddy" number was excerpted in the Columbia feature *Okinawa* as a movie-within-the-movie being watched by a group of sailors, and a reissue of *Ladies* sported a new opening credit that gave MM over-the-title billing. She herself would later recall the film with disdain, doubtless partly fueled by the fact that her performance should have opened some career doors and didn't.

By mid-September 1948, Monroe was looking for work once again. Her relationship with Karger was on a one-sided road to oblivion, and his seeming rejection of her on top of her treatment by Fox and Columbia could only have felt devastating in both personal and professional ways. There were modeling jobs, this time for girlie-type pinups, and little else besides some encouragement from Lytess and others who thought, as *Ladies of the Chorus* reviews would say, that she had promise. When, or how, this promise might be fulfilled was another story entirely.

2

Breakthroughs

Because of the way Marilyn Monroe lived and died, there are events that will always remain shadowy and indeterminate. Some are controversial and others simply mysterious, much of this due in part to the ever-changing ways in which she would speak of herself. Six biographies can recount six different ways something seems to have occurred, professionally as well as personally, and who's to know what's correct? So it is with a central occurrence in both her public and private arenas, her first meeting with Johnny Hyde. Hyde, the high-powered and well-connected William Morris agent, was the strongest single external force in Monroe's early career, with an interest in her fueled by a love that frequently skirted the obsessive. Monroe, who lived with him for a time, never said yes to his repeated marriage proposals. She did, however, allow him to take the reins of a career that, after the Columbia termination, was in desperate need of guidance.

A small man with an assertive personality and a heart condition, Hyde most probably met Monroe on December 31, 1948, at a New Year's Eve party hosted by producer Sam Spiegel. He was a guest, and she was, essentially, set decoration, in a way similar to how she had served at her friend Joe Schenck's poker nights. Hyde's interest and his attraction were immediate and fast became so all-encompassing that before long, he was plotting how to leave his wife and children. There were practical aspects to his sponsorship as well: he spirited Monroe away from her former agents and had her sign with William Morris, he began taking her out on high-visibility dates to draw industry attention, and he mapped out some further cosmetic alteration. The hair was further lightened and eventually shortened, while a slight nose bobbing and a chin implant finally gave her face its now-accustomed symmetry. He also began to scope out jobs for her, the first one to pan out being small in size and huge in implication.

Love Happy is a good example of a film that finished in a far different place from where it started. In some ways, it's a Marx Brothers film that isn't, since Groucho isn't in it all that much; moreover, it's worth noting that after it was done, all three brothers hated it. This is the sort of comedy caper mystery that ranges far and gets no place, some drivel about stolen diamonds and a theater troupe. And since Vera-Ellen is in it, there are dance numbers. Conceived as a vehicle for (and partly by) Harpo Marx, it was underfinanced, underorganized, and in most particulars a plain mess. Much of the blame can be laid at the feet of Lester Cowan, an independent producer better able to talk the talk than to walk the walk. The script had already passed through multiple hands before shooting began in July 1948, after which Cowan and company continued to tinker with it incessantly. A great deal of the touch-up is obvious in the completed film and mainly involves Groucho's on- and off-screen narration as Sam Grunion, a detective on the case. There's also some especially garish product placement that comes near the end because Cowan needed some quick sponsor cash to finish the shoot. This, in short, is not a film where the seams show; instead, they dominate.

Monroe, of course, is the film's most celebrated feature, and her bit was one of Cowan's add-ons, shot many months after most of the rest. She's on the screen a total of thirty-one seconds and speaks thirteen words—far less, all told, than in *Dangerous Years*, let alone *Ladies of the Chorus*. So why does *Love Happy* qualify as a milestone? The reasons span both the performance and its aftermath. Most important, it's the first time Monroe's sexuality reads on film. When she sang and danced in *Ladies of the Chorus*, both her inexperience and the Production Code ensured that she was exuberant and cheery rather than smoldering. Here, jammed into a more-than-tight strapless gown, she undulates in a fashion that's both carnal and comical.[1] She slithers into Groucho's office in an exaggerated fashion that stops just short of drag queen caricature, and blessedly, she finally comprehends the full meaning of her lines. She is, in fact, quite in on the joke. "Mr. Grunion," she begins plaintively, and then the Lytess-mandated diction kicks in, far more conspicuously than in *Ladies*: "I wanT you To helP me." Groucho responds accordingly, and as she turns to leave, she adds, "Some men are following me," with a slight smile coming in near the end that almost looks as if she's about to break up. It's odd. Is Monroe, the actor, laughing at Groucho? Or is she, as Grunion's client, taking accustomed delight in the effect she has on all men? Maybe it's

---

[1] Take a close look at that gown. It gives the impression that it should be showing off her cleavage but doesn't. Once again, the Production Code has cast its shadow and ensured that the bodice be constructed to cover up what we would normally expect it to expose. This kind of coverage—often done with brooches or cloth flowers—was one of the features of the Code years, and some years after *Love Happy*, it prompted one of MM's wittier quotes. Speaking of the Code vigilantes, she offered this analysis: "The Johnston Office spends a lot of time worrying about whether a girl has cleavage or not. It seems to me they ought to worry if she doesn't have any."

both. What's certain is that she's there to be laughed with, not at, and this attitude would form the basis for a fair amount of Monroe's career. The entire scene is self-contained, unconnected with any other part of the film, which in this case sets it and her off in optimal fashion.

Between the one day she spent shooting *Love Happy* and the time she would be on the road promoting it, Monroe garnered no more film work. Instead, she would revert to her former persona for the most important photo session of her life. The stories go that either she was behind in her car payment or she owed rent. In any case, she needed fifty dollars quickly, and Hyde was out of town. She called up photographer Tom Kelley and was soon posing naked on red velvet for the most famous calendar pinup of all time. This wasn't acting, exactly, but did require the physical coordination and concentration she had steadily been acquiring since she left her factory job four years earlier. Nude modeling was not, in 1949, judged to be a respectable form of employment, and the models were almost never credited. (MM herself signed Kelley's release form as "Mona Monroe.") The more popular of the two Kelley poses that made it onto calendars, the one known as "Golden Dreams," was a huge hit for a while without anyone knowing who it was. When it was finally revealed that Monroe—now an emerging movie star—had been the model, something like all hell broke loose. (So did *Playboy* magazine, which featured it in its first issue.) The wonder is how, in that buttoned-up time, she was able to turn it into something of a triumph, in a sense one of her most successful performances.

Shortly after the red velvet, she spent nearly six weeks on the road doing intensive publicity work for the as-yet-unreleased *Love Happy*. If Cowan was incompetent as a producer, he did understand MM's impact and came up with a way to use her to give his product a desperately needed boost. Since she was not otherwise engaged, Monroe went on a tour to promote *Love Happy*, in which she got special "and Introducing" billing on-screen.[2] As with everything else connected with this film, the junket ended up being a trifle off-kilter, what with this bit-part actress (billed as both the "Mmmmmm Girl"

[2] Here, as in other films, that "Introducing" credit can seldom be taken at face value. Monroe had, of course, already begun in films, and so had the other two actors supposedly being introduced, Paul Valentine and Bruce Gordon. Many long years after *Love Happy*, Valentine chuckled as he recalled the haphazard experience of shooting *Love Happy*, which included Cowan stiffing him for at least part of his salary. Cowan, for his part, got more bang for his buck when, in 1952, he rereleased *Love Happy* under the slogan "The Film That Discovered Marilyn Monroe." With this and *Ladies of the Chorus* being recycled, it's something of a wonder that Twentieth Century-Fox didn't try the same thing with *Dangerous Years* or possibly even *Scudda Hoo! Scudda Hay!*

and the "Woo-Woo Girl") sent out to give interviews for a film that had not yet opened—and would not play in most theaters for a long eight months. Yet for Monroe, it was an exercise in self-presentation as helpful as her sessions with Natasha Lytess or her intermittent studies at the Actors' Lab. It was, again, not performance in the conventional sense, yet it involved a kind of acting: MM plugging this supposedly dynamite movie (and pretending it wasn't a jerry-built dog) while playing to the press with various fabricated versions of her own biography. She attended parties, gave interviews, and made special appearances at sports events. And always posing for pictures. In its way, it was a minor victory, especially in Rockford, Illinois, where a kind of "advance premiere" was set up and MM did gag work with Harpo's stand-in and gave out endless autographs. It was during this leg of the trip that her private past and public present crossed paths in a rather touching fashion. When the former resident of the Los Angeles Orphan's Home visited the Rockford Children's Home, which was both an orphanage and a children's hospital, she threw the promotional schedule out of whack by insisting on spending time with every child there.

Monroe went back to California and, as it happened, back to Twentieth Century-Fox, where Hyde had come up with another film. *A Ticket to Tomahawk* was a healthily budgeted Technicolor western with an amiable tone and, in Dan Dailey and Anne Baxter, engaging stars. As with *Scudda Hoo! Scudda Hay!* Monroe spent weeks on location, this time in Durango and Silverton, Colorado. Playing one of a quartet of Old West "entertainers" making the maiden journey on the Tomahawk and Western Railroad, she was given a character name (Clara) but no billing or distinguishable lines.[3] The troupe appears intermittently in the film and most visibly in a musical number, "Oh, What a Forward Young Man." Monroe is given some modest choreography, a dubbed voice, and a quick, nice one-on-one moment with Dailey. She stands out in her scenes both because she's Monroe and because of the Technicolor. She's the only blonde, and, additionally, she's dressed in yellow, thus drawing the eye. The ringlet hairdos she wears don't conceal the fact that her face is well on its way to assuming its now-familiar contours.

---

[3] Even so, she does get mentioned by name. In the epilogue that closes the movie, it's revealed that Dailey's and Baxter's characters are now married and have five daughters. Leaving his family by train, Dailey calls out to the quintet by their names, which happen to be those of the actresses playing the four performers and their "manager," Madame Adelaide: Connie (Gilchrist), Barbara (Brown), Marion (Marshall), Marilyn (Monroe), and Joyce (MacKenzie). Little Marilyn is a blonde, and Marshall and MacKenzie were Fox-contracted "stock girls" of the same sort as MM in her early stint at the studio.

Having a real role, naturally, would have been helpful, and that would be taken care of very shortly.

In whatever light one might care to assess her ability to make connections, her next role—the really important one—came as a result of whom she knew as well as what she could do. As would be expected, Johnny Hyde had a good deal to do with getting Monroe cast in *The Asphalt Jungle*, and she also had a major sponsor in-house at MGM, the studio producing *Jungle*. MGM casting director Lucille Ryman and her actor-husband John Carroll had been early Monroe advocates, and Ryman would maintain an ongoing belief in her potential. The part in question was the young mistress—a word not spoken in film at the time—of a Midwestern attorney who is both married and involved way too deeply with a big-time jewel robbery. The robbery would be the central incident of *The Asphalt Jungle*, and the cast would be drawn not from name stars but from actors able to embody the thieves, enablers, hangers-on, and law-enforcement officers associated with the case. The director, John Huston, had long since established his film credentials, and his clout and talent were sufficient for MGM to consent to produce a stark and rough film instead of the usual softer-edged gloss that was its trademark. For Angela, the mistress, Huston wanted Lola Albright, who had recently made a good impression supporting Kirk Douglas in *Champion*. Albright's asking price of $1,500 per week was too rich for Huston's budget, and Ryman quickly suggested Monroe, whom Hyde was also promoting.[4] Huston agreed to an audition, and Monroe spent days working on the scene with Lytess. Suffering from a major case of nerves, MM did it, unconventionally, sitting on the floor with her shoes off. Huston approved.

The Asphalt Jungle is, even more than a take on a heist gone wrong, a rough and unflinching story about losers. Some are blunderers, most are damaged, a few are slime, and the one acknowledged "genius" (Sam Jaffe, who is superb) is brought down because of his own terminal flaw: a preoccupation with nubile young women. Not even the police chief comes off as a worthy role model. This is riveting stuff and nearly revolutionary in its time, given its status as a product of the MGM Dream Factory. For the many who admire Huston's work, it's a key part of that powerful march from *The Maltese Falcon*

---

[4] Ryman had an additional ace in the hole where Huston was concerned: he owed her quite a bit of money. Ryman and Carroll owned the ranch where Huston stabled his horses, and, inveterate heavy gambler that he was, Huston was far behind in his rent. Ryman, then, was able to call in a marker to get him to consent to a Monroe audition. Such private exigencies can often be a part of moviemaking, and Huston's gambling would also be a factor when he directed MM for the second time, in *The Misfits*.

and *The Treasure of the Sierra Madre* to, eventually, *Fat City* and *Prizzi's Honor*. So, is it fitting or just strange that its merit is sometimes swept aside in favor of its status as the Movie That Made Monroe? Her role was not judged large enough for her to be billed in the opening credits, though she does appear in the cast list at the end. As with the other women in the cast (Jean Hagen, Dorothy Tree, Helene Stanley, Teresa Celli), she is less intrinsic to the story than a noteworthy appendage, and still she can be seen as both essential and indelible.

The *New York Herald Tribune*, in its review of *The Asphalt Jungle*, paid Monroe an interesting and possibly debatable compliment, saying that she imparted "a documentary effect to a lurid exposition." Using the word "documentary" to describe any of MM's performances can seem plain lunatic, and yet that is precisely how Huston places her in the film's context. Her character is, in fact, one of the main motivators, albeit not deliberately so, for both the robbery and the double-cross. Huston doesn't simply show Monroe-as-Angela; he grants her a glowing presentation. The sleek new haircut is eye-catching and even somewhat timeless, while the makeup and lighting are a vast improvement over anything seen previously, perfectly setting off Angela as an irresistible and pricey object of attention for lecherous older men—a sex object, obviously, but in a yielding, assuring, insinuating way. Fittingly, she is first seen from a higher angle looking down as she's curled up languidly on a sofa. Sweetly self-absorbed, she does appear to dote on her "Uncle Lon" Emmerich, and Louis Calhern is pretty brilliant as the smooth operator whose infatuation with her leaves him terminally overextended. In a couple of telling moments, Huston shows the essence of the relationship: Emmerich leans down to give Angela a deep kiss, and she quietly pulls away. (The subtle look of almost revulsion that crosses Monroe's face shows a born actor at work.) After Angela goes to bed, Emmerich fondles the shoe she's left behind, a rather pathetic pseudo-upscale thing studded with jewels. He contemplates it as he plots to come out on the winning end of the heist—which, conceivably, could enable him to give Angela shoes decorated with *real* jewels. After this, there are several scenes in which Angela is discussed and not seen, in effect making her a sort of spectral tempter, a prompting force for some ill-laid plans.

Monroe received a few excellent reviews for *The Asphalt Jungle*, which certainly justified the belief Hyde and others had in her. As if it weren't already important enough to her career, it also marked something of a formal beginning to her collaboration with Lytess. At Monroe's (and possibly Ryman's and Hyde's) request, Lytess stayed on the set while MM filmed her scenes, giving her assurance, correction, and even overt direction. The routine developed quickly in subsequent films: after the director called "Cut," or sometimes even during the scene, Monroe would look over to Lytess, who was usually positioned near the camera. If Lytess felt the scene could be better, she would shake her head, and Monroe would ask to do the scene over. This was quite audacious of her, especially as a newcomer, and the polar opposite of being a "team player" on a movie set. Monroe, by implication, was setting herself up, alongside her coach, as her own auteur, rather than that role going to the director, however competent or accomplished he might be. (All of Monroe's directors were male, which surely makes for some proto-feminist hypothesizing.) What began here with Lytess soon grew into a prerequisite both feared and loathed, as most of Monroe's directors would resent the way Lytess's opinions—or Monroe's whims—were given precedence over their own. Huston, for his part, was amenable to having MM's coach on the set, and perhaps he didn't notice the moment in *Asphalt Jungle* when Monroe, still on camera, looks over to Lytess for assurance. It comes in her first scene, as she's leaving Calhern, and it's quite noticeable.

Also noticeable is that ongoing plague in Monroe's early performances, the stilted diction Lytess taught her. Her very first line comes out as "What's the big idea standing there staring aT me, Uncle Lon?" Later, there's "WaiT, you wait right here" and, defiantly to a cop, an oddly cadenced reading of "Haven'TYou bothereD me enough, you Big Banana HeaD?" Perhaps, to take the most accepting view of it, someone like Angela would strive to rise above unsavory circumstances by paying overly careful attention to the way she speaks. Yet it's something that keeps turning up, one way or another, in most of the films on which Lytess worked with Monroe. "You will have to work on diction," Lytess told Monroe during their first meeting. "Diction, diction, diction." She may have thought she was dealing with another dim starlet, but that was not who Monroe was. She worked hard and, in her insecurity and need to learn, followed every directive and pronouncement Lytess gave her. This included the miscalculation over the enunciation of consonants. As a number of MM observers have noted, this can work fine in comedy, where an overcalculated reading might be used for humorous effect. With drama, it can give her work an oddly Amateur Night tinge and detract from her unique physicality (also the result of work and study) and the devastating glow that occurs when Monroe is properly lit and photographed. Lytess gave Monroe confidence, validation, solace, some good training, and even purpose. She also gave her a couple of bad technical habits, as well as the cocooning over-protection that could stray into self-defeating realms.

The traditional lag time from a film's shooting until its premiere meant that there was about a six-month span between making *The Asphalt Jungle* and reaping the benefits of some good notices. During that time, as guided by Hyde, Monroe stayed busy. If the work was steady, it also formed the most nondescript part of her legacy. First was an independently produced drama starring Mickey Rooney, *The Fireball*. It was a sort of exposé about the fast rise and the faster fall of a brash (it's Rooney, after all) roller-derby star who is brought low and then redeemed after he contracts polio. Monroe, as a skating groupie named Polly, has a few scenes and four lines. Mostly, she is shown watching Rooney or the other skaters, and all in all, the circumstances are so humble that it appears as if *The Asphalt Jungle* hadn't happened. Her hair (which always required touching up) has gone back to a slightly darker shade, and Angela's sleek pageboy has reverted to a longer, less interesting look. In some shots, Monroe takes the camera particularly well, and one striking moment has her at a party, sitting on a sofa with her legs folded under her and sporting a different upswept hairdo. As she watches Rooney going on at full blowhard tilt, she purrs an acid-tinged "Oh, brother!" It's just enough to make one believe that there's some Monroe going on there.

Her role in MGM's prizefight drama *Right Cross* came right afterward and gave her even less screen time as well as no screen credit at all. She does, how-ever, have a name, and it's a honey: Dusky Ledue, a model being pursued by sports reporter Dick Powell. While the initial scripts gave Dusky something of a substantial role, the final screenplay and the finished film give MM-as-Dusky one short scene and all of eleven words to speak. (Twelve if we count a "Hello" that is seen but not heard.) We're almost back to *Scudda-Hoo!* ter-ritory here, with a couple of differences. Sitting in a restaurant booth with Powell, holding a cigarette, she seems reasonably sophisticated and assured, looking rather like a post-Emmerich Angela who'd kept going successfully. The MGM lighting and photography are once more a boon, and the diction comes into play again when Dusky tells her would-be seducer that his propo-sition is "RighT from left field."

Not, in sum, the sort of role to make an ambitious actor leap with joy. Neither was the television commercial, Monroe's one known venture into that territory, that she shot around the same time. Not for cosmetics or shampoo, which might have been predictable, or for toothpaste, which would have been a sweet harbinger of her "Dazzle Dent" spokesperson in

The Seven Year Itch. Instead, it was for motor oil, specifically a famously purple-hued concoction called Royal Triton, manufactured by the Union Oil Company of California. A phalanx of male admirers push MM's convertible, "Cynthia," to a filling station, where she commands, "PuT Royal Triton in Cynthia's little tummy . . . Cynthia will just love thaT Royal Triton." Not even these petroleum-driven circumstances can deter the Lytess partiality to the letter T.

Aside from her rendezvous with Cynthia, 1950 would be a crucial year for Monroe on both public and private fronts: two major breakthrough roles, a studio contract, and, finally, the death of Hyde. Far less significant, and most likely done in that same interim time as *The Fireball, Right Cross*, and Royal Triton, was possibly the most extraneous film of her career. If her role was not the smallest in her canon, the movie itself was a bafflement and her performance one of her more stilted. *Home Town Story* is one of those strange old films that fall outside normal commercial moviemaking, financed by General Motors, shot independently, and only later picked up for distribution by MGM. Instead of being an overt commercial for GM cars, it was a sneakily wrought plea for free enterprise, arguing in a heartfelt fashion that big corporations are the backbone of America and that anyone who disputes this notion is wrong and possibly subversive. Jeffrey Lynn, who starred as a crusading newspaper editor who finally sees the light, later said that he was unaware, during the filming, of the didactic purposes underlying this project. Though the writer and director, Arthur Pierson, had already worked with Monroe on *Dangerous Years*, this was hardly the occasion for a sentimental reunion. As Iris Martin, a secretary in the newspaper office, Monroe exudes a fair competence while overemphasizing her consonants and being on the receiving end of what is now known as sexual harassment. (The unwelcome attention comes from a reporter played by Alan Hale Jr., far more aggressive here than he would be on *Gilligan's Island*.) Even more than *Love Happy, Home Town Story* was intent on spotlighting Monroe as a sex object. Wearing a succession of tight sweaters and a sturdy brassiere, she walks from her desk to Lynn's office several times for the sole purpose of demonstrating that she is, in that loaded 1950s word, stacked. If her previous films had shown her attractiveness, here it is the shape that matters the most—possibly even more than whatever argument GM was trying to make about big bosses making the nicest guys and liberals needing to change their notions.

Lynn remembered one day of filming *Home Town Story* when Monroe bounded onto the set exclaiming, "I've got it, I've got it, I've got it!" This well may have been the moment when she learned that she was being cast in a film that was to *Home Town Story* what the Sistine Chapel ceiling is to a two-year-old's crayon scribble. At the time, MM's performance in *All about Eve* rated less critical attention than the one in *The Asphalt Jungle*. Yet, given the film's subsequent place in the pantheon and given Monroe's own preeminence as icon deluxe, her role as Claudia Caswell, graduate of "the Copacabana School of Dramatic Art," offers a great deal—far more, in fact, than may have met many eyes in 1950, when most observers were so dazzled by so much in the film that MM's presence was not judged a necessary standout.[5] As with certain other Monroe roles, there is a fair amount of autobiography going on in *All about Eve*, in this case stemming less from who Monroe was than from who people, even back then, thought she was. Miss Caswell is a luscious and dim opportunist, willing to do whatever it takes—short of learning to act—to become a star. She is obviously the mistress, or at least trophy friend, of the grandly snide columnist Addison DeWitt, who "sponsors" her until turning his eye to someone (Eve Harrington) who has all the talent and cutthroat smarts that Claudia lacks. This tallies exactly with the view taken of Monroe, then and later, by industry people. Instead of DeWitt, it was Hyde, constantly singing her praises to whoever might wish to hire her. And Miss Caswell's own artless dim-bulb personality was echoed by the way many saw Monroe: ambitious in a vacuous way, manifestly untalented, willing to use her body and anything else in order to get ahead. That the real Monroe was far more than this, and far different from this, did not particularly matter to those willing to give her jobs, not respect. She was, to them, a joke, and such a diminution continues even to this day, when some prefer to see her in terms of her life, real or mythical, instead of her achievements.

Joseph L. Mankiewicz, the writer-director-auteur absolute of *All about Eve*, was not prominent among those who credited Monroe with genuine talent, citing her "glued-on innocence" as having been a positive factor in her casting. Later on, he would pay tribute to her association with Johnny Hyde as being the only time in her life she was truly respected: "More than anyone in her life, I think, [Hyde] provided her with an honest *ego* of her own." It was Hyde's intense lobbying, Mankiewicz noted, that persuaded him to hire her for *Eve*. More important still, that lobbying was crucial in persuading

---

[5] Not that the critical reaction in 1950 was complete silence. The *Hollywood Reporter* critic had a particularly well-directed comment: "Marilyn Monroe's chorine is right out of *Esquire* and grand."

Twentieth Century-Fox to sign her to a subsequent one-year contract, despite what Mankiewicz recalled as Darryl Zanuck's vehement opposition.[6]

It might have been sufficient that *All about Eve* provided Monroe with her second role in a worthy film. There was much more, however, for the role presented her with the first real opportunity to play comedy. It would quickly prove to be her primary gift, although she herself would have found this to be a demeaning assessment. Her coaches and teachers were always hanging dramatic moons in front of her—Cordelia, Anna Christie, Blanche DuBois, Sadie Thompson, Lady Macbeth, Grushenka. Alongside them, Monroe's totemic roles—Lorelei Lee, the Girl Upstairs, Sugar Kane—might seem unworthy, reductive, trifling. Part of this comes with the high-handedness that traditionally opposes itself to most comedic acting, as if it genuinely poses that much less of a challenge. In this elevated mindset, the "Great Roles" are traditionally given over exclusively to utter seriousness. Monroe, with her drive toward validation and self-improvement, would never have ascribed to the maxim "Dying is easy, comedy is hard." Thus, she was never completely able to judge the magnitude of her own achievements, to comprehend the things she could do better than anyone else. Yes, her material could be of lesser quality and even condescending intent, but she herself, through both hard work and instinct, had the gift for going far beyond its limitations. She became her own author, which is why one of her best directors, Billy Wilder, so approved of the comedic persona—or is it person?—she was able to create.

With the role of Miss Caswell, MM was given an award every bit as worthy as that Sarah Siddons prize that provides the frame for *All about Eve*. She was even allowed to hit it out of the park the moment she opened her mouth. She enters the frame on the arm of George Sanders, managing to have a coexistent veneer of elegance (the restrained hairdo) and crassness (the projectile bodice). When Bette Davis's Margo declares that she does not recall seeing her before, she offers, "We've never met. Maybe that's why." The line, of course, is both absurd and funny, and Monroe speaks it with a forthright dimness that makes it land perfectly. She has not yet acquired the girlish whisper of Lorelei Lee, which would not have suited this role in any case, nor has she yet cultivated that open-mouthed look so famous from *Niagara*

---

[6] That Monroe and Zanuck were never a good match can be seen in a number of the opportunities she was, and was not, given during their joint time at Fox, as well as some insulting things he was reported to have said about her. Mankiewicz, who worked somewhat more harmoniously with Zanuck, had his own reservations as well. In *All about Eve*, Margo Channing famously derides her director boyfriend's association with the famously heterosexual Fox studio head: "Zanuck, Zanuck, Zanuck! What are you two—lovers?"

onward. The overenunciation does appear ("meT"), and this time, it finds the right home. Miss Caswell *would* have those manicured consonants, which she (like Lytess) would mistake for mature, if perhaps "glued-on," assurance. She is, after all, angling to be a stage actress, as opposed to, say, playing a burlesque queen in a cheap movie. Celeste Holm, who shared a scene with her, would observe, "She had a strange delivery, which was something she'd learned from a bad coach." Exactly how bad a coach Lytess was could be debated; it's quite likely, in any case, that she did not have one of the great senses of humor and might not have been able to comprehend completely how the techniques she was imparting could be used to produce laughter. "I don'T want to make trouble," Monroe-as-Caswell announces. But if it's not trouble, it's something that is, fortunately, both congruent and disruptive. And coupled with the peculiar delivery is a heightened skill at reacting to others, as when her eyes momentarily acknowledge, then move past, the insults DeWitt tosses her way.

Monroe's final scene in *Eve* is very short, although it did account for her being part of the location shoot at a San Francisco theater. Her voice is in a lower register than before, befitting someone who's just thrown up after bungling an audition. As with her bit in *Love Happy*, an odd smile crosses her face, and here it's a matter of . . . what? Self-absorbed hopefulness, maybe? Miss Caswell is not long for DeWitt's company, and she may be headed, as one character notes, "back to the Copacabana." Her inept machinations have thus been offered in counterpoint to Eve Harrington's cutting-edge skill at self-advancement, and the contrast between these two approaches is fascinating to observe. And, as with *The Asphalt Jungle*, the fascination does not come simply because she's becoming Marilyn Monroe. The evidence is more than clear that as a performer, she is on her way.

3

A Fox Blonde

All about Eve was only midway through filming when, on May 11, 1950, Marilyn Monroe signed a one-year contract with Twentieth Century-Fox. This time, her salary would be $500 per week, to be raised to $750 if the contract was renewed at the end of that year. Several factors were at work with all of this. One, assuredly, was the aggressive push from Johnny Hyde. Like many successful agents, he was not averse to bullying, badgering, and probably blackmailing to get his clients well situated. Another consideration was Monroe's ongoing friendship—however it was manifested or seen by others—with company cofounder Joseph Schenck. There was also the simple and incontestable fact that she had figured conspicuously in two of the year's major films, neither of which had yet opened. *The Asphalt Jungle* had already been augarnering enthusiasm—including for her work—in advance screenings, and *All about Eve* was an all-but-preordained success both critically and commercially. These are credentials on which a solid career can start to be constructed.

One factor not weighing upon this Fox contract in any kind of positive way was the esteem of Fox's head of production, Darryl F. Zanuck. Zanuck, before he was studio chief, had been a screenwriter, and he was frequently an astute judge regarding script construction. This was in large part why Fox, at its best, could be viewed as a place where intelligent and thoughtful films might be made. Yes, there was always the commercial stuff, the vehicles for Shirley Temple and Betty Grable and all those other staples of midrange moviegoing in the 1930s and '40s, up to and including *Scudda Hoo! Scudda Hay!* Balanced against these were films that took chances of one kind or another: *The Grapes of Wrath, How Green Was My Valley, The Ox-Bow Incident, Laura, Gentleman's Agreement, The Snake Pit,* and others. If not always completely successful or worthy, they all shared a reasonably sincere effort to raise their sights well past the lowest common denominator. So it was that, in one way or another, Zanuck could be judged as well intentioned as it was possible for a golden age studio head to be. Of course, for every *A Letter to Three*

Wives, there would be several pieces on the order of, say, *Oh, You Beautiful Doll*.[1] That's what studios were. That's what they did.

Zanuck, then, was at best a sage assessor of how intelligent filmmaking could operate. His judgment with actors could also be adequate, though not consistently so, which is why so many Fox casting sheets played out like a game of musical chairs. Betty Grable declined Zanuck's invitation to go dramatic in *The Razor's Edge*, so Anne Baxter came in (and won an Academy Award). Peggy Cummins proved way overparted to star in *Forever Amber*, so enter, with a dye job, longtime contractee Linda Darnell. Nor were Zanuck's thoughts for *All about Eve* particularly sound; could anyone see Marlene Dietrich instead of Bette Davis? Later, there would be a rather dismaying procession of Zanuck "protégées" who were displayed in the cinematic equivalent of boxing above one's weight: Bella Darvi, Irina Demick, Genevieve Gilles. These Zanuck handpicked to appear in major roles. Monroe would not enjoy such favor. Let Joseph Mankiewicz comment on Zanuck's earlier and later aversion to her: "The only person importantly associated with *All about Eve* with no supportable claim whatsoever to having brought her [MM] back to Twentieth Century-Fox . . . was Darryl F. Zanuck. Upon my proposal of her name his opposition was instantaneous [and] vehement." In discussing Monroe, Mankiewicz also alluded to Zanuck's personal distaste over her supposedly louche reputation, during her early Fox stint, as the plaything of certain studio executives. That belief may or may not be accurate. The fact of the matter is that Zanuck's own personal conduct was generally observed to be on a similar level, only with the additional and massive overlays of power and gender, coupled with an especially seamy quid pro quo.

Monroe's new Fox contract, then, came despite Zanuck—and also in spite of some major changes in the studio since her first arrival there in the summer of 1946. That had been a time when the studios were still riding the wave of their huge wartime success. Then came the dawn—in fact, several dawns. The divestiture of the studios from their theater chains wreaked havoc with the former guarantee that most films would make something of a profit. This was followed, with great dispatch, by the rise of television, which decimated audience interest. At Fox, economic concerns also came to the

---

[1] Zanuck's judgment would not have uplifted a desultory piece of Technicolor like *Beautiful Doll*, but he was very involved with shaping *A Letter to Three Wives*. The original story had five wives, writer-director Joseph Mankiewicz pared it down to four, and Zanuck could sense that something wasn't quite clicking. He ordered the expulsion of one more wife, so out went the storyline with Anne Baxter as a too-doting mom. The final trio emerged triumphant, and so did Mankiewicz. And so did Zanuck.

fore with several projects that had gone so far over their original budgets that they could not be anything other than bloodletting money losers: *Captain from Castile, Carnival in Costa Rica,* and the ruinously expensive *Forever Amber.* The reaction to all these setbacks would be, at Fox as elsewhere, a more fiscally conservative approach to the film program with a far tighter management of budgets and costs. For a time, circa 1951, an edict was in place that dictated that no film could cost more than $2 million—a rather low figure considering the more than $6 million price tag on *Forever Amber.* This might mean, at least on the surface, that the studio's roster of contract talent could be more actively employed, as opposed to sitting on a back bench, as Monroe had done in 1946. Someone like Hyde would have observed that she could benefit from this leaner style and be put to work in a somewhat more substantial way than she had been the first time.

The films Monroe did at Fox at the start of her contract have been held up as an example of corporate myopia. "They have Marilyn Monroe, for chrissakes," this mindset runs, "and all they can give her are these nothing little roles in the unimportant movies?" Then, of course, the whole "dumb blonde" charge comes into play, as if Fox were all too intent on following the dim lead of Miss Caswell. Ultimately, the record and the circumstances provide something of a corrective. The first three films MM did as part of her Fox contract—*As Young as You Feel, Love Nest,* and *Let's Make It Legal*—were all lower-budget projects of the kind that, in the pre-divestiture days, could be called "programmers." Workmanlike, unimportant time passers, they were made to supply product, not score artistic points, and they were being done by all the studios at this time. Monroe was not being put into them simply because Zanuck didn't like her; in fact, most or all of her "love goddess" predecessors were compelled to test their mettle in pieces like these. Jean Harlow had big billing but unimportant roles following her initial splash, Betty Grable endured a long decade in mostly minor pieces, and over at plush MGM, Lana Turner and Ava Gardner were compelled to prove themselves before being handed major challenges. In the studio days, this was the way unseasoned performers (of both genders) were tested.

With Monroe, there was also the question—and it might be held still valid even now—about the exact nature of her ability. Yes, as *The Asphalt Jungle* and *All about Eve* showed, she photographed not only well but glowingly, with a physicality, an ease with her own body, that put her far beyond the "flashy starlet" category. Just watch that moment in *Eve* when she slips out of her wrap and goes on the attack for a big producer. (She's not only presenting, she's deploying.) There was also an interestingly quirky way with dialogue, or at least there was when all those Lytess consonants didn't get in the way. Some of this was instinctive, since Monroe was an intuitive performer. She could project a natural effervescence with the best of them, and despite all the ballyhoo, she was never simply about the whole sex angle. However they costumed her, however much she flaunted those curves, there was still the innocence and girlishness under all the sheen. (Even in *Niagara*, where she's playing a major-league film-noir femme fatale, there's a moment when she bursts into the infectious giggle of a giddy adolescent.) An equal amount of it came through all the hard work she did: going through her roles line by line, creating motivations and backstories for even sketchy characters, working to find meaning in every word and gesture. This can be questioned and argued with, but she may have been her own kind of Method actor long before her much-vaunted sojourn in New York under the aegis of Lee Strasberg and the Actors Studio. That could be, in fact, one reason she and Strasberg connected so well so quickly. Bear in mind, too, that while working on a Eugene O'Neill script can certainly provide enormous challenges, so can being handed a role in slag like *Love Nest* and attempting to turn it into something that can be even fleetingly honest and legitimate.

What she did not have was versatility, at least in the conventional sense. She could find infinite variations in her created persona—the differences, say, between Lorelei Lee (*Gentlemen Prefer Blondes*) and the Girl Upstairs (*The Seven Year Itch*) are so numerous as to shut down any criticism. In other contexts, especially those involving more "traditional" roles, she could flounder. Take, for instance, her work in *River of No Return*, a performance for which she was soundly and correctly criticized. Granted, she was doing a studio-mandated film that she did not want to be doing (except for the songs). Granted, too, she was working with a director, Otto Preminger, who was— putting it gently—not considered an actor's best friend. And Preminger's conflicts with Monroe and with Natasha Lytess made for a fraught on-set ambience that may have been standard on a Preminger movie but was hellish for Monroe. There was also a crass and clumsy script with virtually no motivations for its characters. All this, and yet there's that performance—stiff aurally and visually, filled with misreadings and misreactions, an amateur's effort that should never have been filmed. It's fair to ask, "Why is she so bad?" and then move on to "Wouldn't *anyone* else have been better?" Gardner and Turner definitely would have. Grable, too, and possibly, heaven help us, June

Haver. Regardless of the harsh and unsympathetic director and the crass screenplay, Monroe has to take her share of the responsibility.

In failure as well as success, she always depended on outside guidance, and seldom in the big-studio era would any actor be as overtly reliant on a coach. Along with the intense (and perhaps stifling) Lytess, there was the much-respected Michael Chekhov, nephew of the playwright Anton Chekhov and student of Konstantin Stanislavski. Of all the Monroe teachers, he may have been the most sincere and selfless in his belief in her capabilities, as can be seen by his casting her as Cordelia to his Lear in a workshop scene. Still, one wonders if he may have been overly dazzled by her magnetism and drawn in by those same protective feelings that so many others had toward her. In any case, he was never on one of her film sets, and his death in 1955 prevented her from working further with him. Then there were the Strasbergs, Lee and Paula, and who can possibly break down all the dynamics of their relationship with Monroe? They believed in her and encouraged and taught and praised her and in return demanded both fealty and large sums of money. Sometimes, in considering their impact on her career and life, one can go back to that snarky Celeste Holm remark about MM having gotten bad coaching. While her work with the Strasbergs wasn't bad, to be sure, there are whiffs in their relationship of dependency and possible exploitation. Not to mention the mandated psychoanalysis, which may in some particulars have had the reverse of the intended result.

Monroe's 1950 contract with Fox was something of a tryout. The standard amount of contract time for "serious" talent could be as long as seven years, and there was palpable caution attendant on hiring her. While it would be months before she was given an actual role, there was a sort of false start. Alongside Fox leading man Richard Conte, she shot a screen test for a never-made crime drama called *Cold Shoulder*. The test survives and gives a fair idea of what she could and could not do at that time. Her hair is styled in the *Asphalt Jungle/Home Town Story* pageboy, and the outfit she wears—obviously part of her own wardrobe—has been seen in previous films, including *All about Eve*. She plays the girlfriend of gangland hood Conte, warning him that a couple of guys are after him. Conte spits out, "You dumb broad! You stupid little . . ." and threatens to hit her. She replies, "Go ahead! It won't be the first time I've been worked over today! I'm getting used to it."

As was her standard procedure, Monroe worked hard with Lytess in preparing the scene, and Conte would later recall her focus and concentration when they made the test. That, unfortunately, doesn't mean that she delivers a good performance. While Conte could do these snarling roles without breaking a sweat, Monroe is, in contrast, pushing very hard, working the emotions and facial expressions as strenuously as she is delivering those artificially overenunciated T's. Her exertions recall the screen test a teenage Lana Turner made for Scarlett O'Hara: when there's not enough experience or training to be effective, go large. Noir melodramas such as *Cold Shoulder* were standard fare in 1950, and many other contract players—Jean Peters, say, or Linda Darnell—could take on a role such as the one Monroe is trying to do here. It simply was not in Monroe's skill set. There would be, at the time and later, countless accusations about her lack of acting ability, and that's hardly the truth of it. Obviously, as *Cold Shoulder* makes plain—and as *River of No Return* would do later on—Monroe could not convince in certain mainstream types of roles. Even without some of the mistraining she got from Lytess, neither her private nor public projections of herself could lend themselves to these particular conventions. The closest she would come would be in *The Asphalt Jungle* and, the next year, in *Clash by Night*, and even there she's doing things in a way another actor could not or would not do. The character she ultimately inhabited, the "Blonde" seen in her most successful comedies, was forged from equal parts of her own self, her intensive study and work, and sheer, pure instinct. It could never transfer into standard-issue roles, any more than copyists like Jayne Mansfield or Joi Lansing could duplicate it. Had *Cold Shoulder* been made—it was slated to star Victor Mature along with Conte and Monroe—it would likely have been efficient, watchable, and at moments gripping. Monroe would have stuck out like a sore thumb, and her work would have been judged harshly. Conceivably, it could have sabotaged her career early in its ascent.

With the death of *Cold Shoulder*, Monroe was essentially back to her "stock girl" role of 1946—posing for photos, on the lookout for opportunities, attending public events, and doing product endorsements. Johnny Hyde was still plugging away on her behalf, and there were also the standard chores of a contract actor. As one of her company's most photogenic employees, she was naturally called to the photo studio again and again. She still seems a little unformed in many of these photos, and the hairstyles aren't yet optimal, but her modeling experience certainly puts her in good stead. Since studios were always issuing "holiday art" of attractive young actors, Monroe was called on in 1950 to be Twentieth Century-Fox's Thanksgiving sweetheart. Most studios played up the cheesecake for Halloween and then went restrained the following month, posing a star-in-training at a sumptuously arranged table, knife in hand to carve the bird. Not at Fox. Did Pilgrims, female or otherwise, ever wear fishnets? MM did, in an abbreviated Pilgrim outfit complete with buckled peaked hat, armed with a musket and stalking a live turkey. Normally at complete ease before the camera, she seems somewhat unnerved in these photos, and small wonder.

By the fall of 1950, Fox was finally coming up with an on-screen slot for Monroe by expanding a minor role in a screenplay being readied for filming. It's worth noting again that there's long been criticism that the studio wasted her talent by giving her small, unimportant parts in small, unimportant films. Her most singular "biographer," Norman Mailer, called them "an abominable waste . . . films which are non-films." Really, though, what else, given the circumstances, could they do with an idiosyncratic talent, not yet a big name, who so blatantly defied normal notions of casting? There was no mold, nor were there many opportunities for the clever showcasing she had had in *The Asphalt Jungle* and *All about Eve*. It was not simply a lack of respect, though doubtless that was there as well, especially given the general notion regarding her "connections." The truth was that she needed the experience and seasoning this work could provide. Her first three Fox films, sitcoms for a slightly pre-television age, would be the conduit. Obviously, they were far less urgent and accomplished than *Asphalt* and *Eve* yet were not completely negligent in showcasing her. On the surface, they recall her intermittently spaced bits in *The Fireball* and *Home Town Story*, with Monroe dropped in every so often to supply a bit of sex and flash. The auspices, however, were sometimes notably better, and in performance as well as in presence, she more than took advantage of the possibilities they offered.

The first of the trio was also, by fair measure, the best. *As Young as You Feel* has at least one claim to history besides MM: it marked the first time a work by Paddy Chayefsky made it to the screen, in this case a short story called "The Great American Hoax." The relevance of the story's slant put it in line with Fox's socially conscious uplift, although, as extended and softened for the screen, it plays out as one part Frank Capra and another part conventionally "warmhearted" family comedy. A sixty-five-year-old factory worker is fired as part of his company's mandatory "retirement" (sans pension) policy and decides to do something about it. Posing as the president of the factory's parent company, he impresses everyone—including the real president—with his wisdom and insight, and instead of being arrested, he gets his job back. That's the central Chayefsky arc, to which were added a couple of love plots, some screwy relatives, and one gorgeous secretary. Seventy-six minutes of screen time is hardly enough to encompass all this in a fully realized form, and thus some very talented actors are treated insufficiently. The most egregious waste is of the divine Thelma Ritter, in possibly the least endearing role of her career, as the complaining daughter-in-law who clings to the memory of her long-ago career in vaudeville as a chanteuse named (really) Della Robbia. Jean Peters and David Wayne, as the young lovers, are given more than Ritter but not enough, and a young Russ (then Rusty) Tamblyn gets barely enough time to make an impression. The most fully thought-out characters are the senior (Monty Woolley) and the factory executive and his neglected wife (Albert Dekker and Constance Bennett). Woolley gives one of his standard likably stentorian portrayals, Dekker makes a convincing feet-of-clay blowhard, and Bennett is quite touching as the elegant helpmate who has settled for too little for too long.[2]

There is also Harriet, the exec's secretary. Wearing crisp examples of Hollywood-stylish sexy office wear, Monroe is completely convincing as both a competent worker and the object of Dekker's roving eye. He calls her "dear" and goes ballistic when he sees her out with another man, but both censorship and the truncated screenplay have seen to it that the film won't convey just how far the infatuation has gone. Significantly, and despite her low-cut necklines and flashy jewelry, Harriet is not simply the secretarial equivalent of a Copacabana graduate; that particular denigration would come in a slightly later Monroe film, *Monkey Business*. Monroe speaks her lines more rapidly than usual, which makes those consonants less onerous and gives the character a certain calculated precision. Harriet only loses her cool once, when her boss is being completely impossible and, when he turns his back, she sticks out her tongue—an easy and well-timed laugh getter. One striking aspect of the performance comes with the confident way Monroe holds the screen. The camera has liked her before, but here, with a vintage "early prime MM" hairstyle and greater assurance, she's really starting to radiate. There's also a moment of genuine warmth that looks ahead to *The Seven Year Itch*, when Harriet compliments the incognito senior on the speech he's just given. "I want you to know I think your speech was grand. I felt real honored just

---

[2] Hollywood's highest-paid actress two decades before this, Bennett was given fifth billing to Monroe's sixth. Oddly, all the credited cast members are billed above the title onscreen, which makes *As Young as You Feel* not only the first time that MM is billed above the title but also the only film to give such august treatment to the supporting likes of Clinton Sundberg and Minor Watson. Bennett's dance with Woolley in the country club sequence is a special treat, and as a wittily hardened observer of the Hollywood scene, she had a pithy comment concerning Monroe when she saw her on the set: "There's a broad with a future behind her!"

to hear it." Even with the overenunciation, she's completely open and sincere, giving intimations of the vulnerability lurking on the other side of that assured exterior; it's too bad that the script drops her completely in the final quarter. Only a few minutes of performance were enough to rate high praise from a tough observer at the *New York Times*. Bosley Crowther, all too frequently billed as the "dean of American film critics," loved *As Young as You Feel* and called MM's performance "superb." Later on, in assessing her work, he would habitually be far less generous.

As Young as You Feel was an important film for Monroe in all sorts of ways. While it did not mark the very first time her chronic lateness was an issue, it set the pattern for everything to follow, with cast and crew members of both low and high stature being forced to wait, and wait some more, for her to arrive on the set. Wayne, the only actor to make four films with her, later recalled both the waiting and his subsequent realization that "something was going on which I didn't know about: this girl had a little power going for her." This "power" was mostly her rumored affair with Schenck, as well as her sponsorship by Hyde. Unfortunately, Hyde, age fifty-three, died on December 18, 1950, three days after shooting commenced on *As Young as You Feel*. A grief- (and possibly guilt-) stricken Monroe would sometimes be seen crying off camera, and because life cycles are such peculiar things, it was at this precise point that her path crossed that of two powerful men. Harmon Jones, the first-time director of *As Young as You Feel*, had edited four films directed by Elia Kazan, and Kazan came to visit the set accompanied by Arthur Miller. Evidently, and despite MM's vulnerable condition, a number of sparks flew; she promptly embarked on a short affair with Kazan and filed Miller away (as it were) for future reference.[3]

Clearly, Monroe proved herself with *As Young as You Feel*. However, despite Fox's active production roster, there did not seem to be anything in the way of a follow-up for a while. *Life* magazine was terming her one of the "Apprentice Goddesses" of film, as well as a "Busty Bernhardt," yet there were some long weeks with just the steady procession of pinup poses and the prospect of being an Oscar presenter.[4] Then it was Monroe herself, not one of her

[3] Kazan, who had already directed Miller's *All My Sons* and *Death of a Salesman* on Broadway, was working with the playwright on a screenplay that ultimately went unfilmed, *The Hook*. Kazan had already met MM the previous summer prior to shooting *A Streetcar Named Desire*, and it's generally thought that he visited the *As Young* set less to see his colleague Jones than to renew his acquaintance with Monroe. Upon such machinations are marriages and movies sometimes founded.

[4] Monroe's only trip to an Academy Awards show—she was one of six of *Life*'s "Apprentice Goddesses" handing out an award—came in pre-television times but was filmed in color. Wearing a (predictably) low-cut black gown with a billowing full skirt, Monroe presents the sound recording

powerful friends, who used a combination of enterprise and exhibitionism to correct the situation. Assigned her umpteenth photo session, she opted for maximum exposure. At the studio's wardrobe department, she changed into a few scraps of black lace that approximated a negligee. Then she began the long walk across the Fox lot to the photo studio. The sight of a barefoot Monroe, hair slightly tousled, slowly undulating over a six-block expanse was enough to stop traffic and draw crowds. If people at the studio already knew who she was, they could now see that her audacity and determination went far beyond being labeled a busty anything. Shortly after this, she drew all eyes when she arrived late at a studio dinner in honor of Fox exhibitors. Forgetting Tyrone Power, Susan Hayward, and others in attendance, the theater owners stampeded over to MM. Who was she? What was her next film? Preternaturally poised in strapless black velvet, Monroe replied, "You'll have to ask Mr. Zanuck or Mr. Skouras" (Spyros Skouras was Fox president).

A new film followed quickly, and again, it was a small role slightly expanded. This time, the focus was less on comic timing than on sheer physicality. If *Home Town Story* made hay with Monroe in tight sweaters, *Love Nest* goes a good deal farther. This is conspicuously less ambitious than *As Young as You Feel*, simply a little slice-of-unreal-life comedy about a veteran and his wife owning and operating a small Manhattan apartment building. The main complications, such as they are, come with a Lothario con man who woos one of the tenants, and with Bobbie (aka Roberta), the most luscious ex-WAC in the history of the military. As with *As Young as You Feel*, it's the seniors and MM who make the greatest impression. The aging "love pirate" is Frank Fay, famous in the 1920s as a comedian and emcee, then later as the star of the hit play *Harvey*. (Fay's renown behind the scenes was equal, if less sterling; nearly everyone in show business considered him one of the most bigoted and unpleasant people ever created. Even when he was sober.) The latest object of the con's affections is played by silent-screen star Leatrice Joy, and the two of them make a pretty good match—he's almost charming in an off-kilter way, and she's sweetly appealing. Their romance makes for a lot more interest than the bland competence supplied by June Haver and William Lundigan and is notably more palatable than the smarmy presence

---

award to *All about Eve*. Though she looks up from the podium only fleetingly, she manages to present a reasonably professional front. It may, in fact, be one of her bravest performances, as a major case of nerves nearly reached crisis proportions following a wardrobe malfunction shortly before she was due onstage. Fortunately, a quick sewing repair was able to rescue both the dress and MM's composure.

of future TV star Jack Paar, who would later write about Monroe with note-worthy condescension.

A half hour of film has drifted by, unexcitingly, before Monroe enters, wearing a tight suit and a hat, along with a slightly less becoming hairstyle than in the previous film. She's beginning to raise the pitch of her voice just a shade, and again, the diction works far better in a light context. At one point, she breaks out into the infectious giggle/laugh that will resurface intermittently over the next decade, perhaps most prominently in *The Prince and the Showgirl*. As her third sequence in the film makes clear, the concern is far less about how she sounds than about how she looks. The bikini had already made a steamy impact on European beaches; in America, it was more notoriety than actuality, and there was no way an actor in a 1951 studio film could wear a costume exposing her navel. Consequently, there is a scene in which, for no real reason, Monroe is shown sunbathing in a two-piece polka-dot swimsuit that gives off bikini vibes without actually going the full distance. Even so, director Joseph Newman keeps the camera at a somewhat cautious distance, which belies the furor when she first walked onto the soundstage. June Haver later recalled the terror MM could undergo even while creating a sensation:

> When Marilyn walked on the set in her bathing suit and walked to the beach chair, the whole crew gasped, gaped, and seemed to turn to stone. They just stopped working and stared [and] just gasped and gaped at Marilyn as though they were stunned.
>
> Anyway, Marilyn was aware of it and she just loved it. . . . The crew's reaction gave her confidence because she was always nervous, always had trouble getting into a dialogue scene. Just on the first word or two, she had trouble getting them out. . . .
>
> But the warmth of the crew's reaction to her relaxed her. She suddenly seemed to be another person. She lost her shyness. I think it's the only time she felt confident—when she was in that bathing suit.

Countless writers, perceptive and otherwise, have written of the bifurcation of Marilyn Monroe, of the fantastic and sex-propelled creation MM and of the lowly, terrified Norma Jeane lurking behind it. She herself mentioned the duality frequently, in interviews and in the "memoir" cobbled together after her death. *Love Nest*, even more than her most flamboyant previous moments, is where that newly created bombshell persona really starts to take hold. It does so most strikingly in a sequence that can variously be termed amusing, titillating, or exploitative. Jim (Lundigan) and Connie (Haver) quarrel, and since Bobbie's away for the weekend, he takes refuge in her apartment. She returns home shortly after sunup and immediately begins undressing—both before she knows a man is dozing on her sofa and afterward. The camera lingers on Monroe as she removes her suit and stockings and walks around in a black slip. When she takes a shower, the soundtrack presents her satisfied sighs. Finally, she emerges wrapped in a rather abbreviated towel. If each shot of her is brief, the overall impact is decided. This, then, would set the tone for the professional route she would be traveling. She hasn't been given laugh lines in the film, but she's great to look at and, as is implied, fantasize about. In comparison with the pert, shorter Haver, with her ponytail and drab blouses, Monroe is real danger.

Monroe was rushed straight from *Love Nest* into another time-passing comedy which was, in reality, something of a digression. On the surface, *Let's Make It Legal* would appear to be on a par with its two predecessors and with some notable Monroe-connected historical resonance. It was cowritten by F. Hugh Herbert, who had directed and written *Scudda Hoo! Scudda Hay!*; his cohort, I. A. L. Diamond, had written *Love Nest* and, years later, would join with Billy Wilder to write *Some Like It Hot*. Vestiges of *All about Eve* are also present, since the star is Claudette Colbert, the original Margo Channing who was replaced at the last minute by Bette Davis; playing her daughter here is Barbara Bates, the Eve-like interloper in the last scene. Unfortunately, no amount of history can make *Let's Make It Legal* anything other than a chore to get through. Comedies, even putative ones, are supposed to have some humor; here there's virtually none, with a parents-divorcing-and-finally-reuniting premise played out tediously in static scenes of people standing around talking. "It's 10% Improper! It's 40% Illegal! It's 100% Hilarious!" was the way the ads termed it, hopefully and inaccurately. Colbert, at her greatest, was the most sparkling of comediennes in the '30s and '40s; here she can be little more than grimly professional. As her character's former and future (more or less) husbands, Macdonald Carey and Zachary Scott go through the motions with one eye to being a pro and the other toward the Fox paycheck. While a very young Robert Wagner tries for some verve as the son-in-law, poor Bates is trapped in a role intended to be so unlikable as to be thoroughly alienating.

There is also, in the midst of these sour circumstances, Monroe—not much of her, since the rush to put her into the movie gave her only four short sequences and, in a movie overstuffed with dialogue, some twenty lines. As with *Love Nest*, it's more about how she looks, specifically the sparks she can give off in a succession of tight outfits, including a bathing suit clearly not intended to be gotten wet. Her character, Joyce, is a Miss Caswell with a little more brain power and far fewer scruples, an opportunistic gold digger whose sole claim to respectability is having been crowned Miss Cucamonga. As if this weren't sufficiently déclassé, Herbert and Diamond went so far as to delve into some of MM's own personal history. It was well known in the Hollywood community that Monroe, like Joyce a cheesecake model, had been a fixture early in her career at Schenck's poker nights.[5] Accordingly, Joyce is shown serving as decor and server at a poker party. It's not very much compensation that she seems completely assured on-screen, doesn't overdo the diction—although the *Los Angeles Times* called it "execrable" (ouch)—and pulls off one of the movie's closest approximations of a laugh line. When her advance toward the wealthy Scott is rebuffed, Carey asks her, "What happened to that vibrating motor of yours?" "He turned off the ignition" is the comeback, delivered ruefully with the right kind of pouty inflection. There's also a moment in *Let's Make It Legal* that is so spot-on that it almost seems patched in from another movie, illuminating volumes in a brief two seconds or so. During the first exchange between Monroe and Carey, they discuss the impending arrival of tycoon Scott, who she's read is the country's most eligible bachelor. "And you'd like to talk him out of it," Carey offers, referring to both singlehood and fortune. MM replies simply, "Unhunh." It's hardly a simple yes: it comes from all the way down in her lowest vocal register, with teeth flashing and jaw jutted forward in a fashion that reveals decades, perhaps centuries, of knowing sexual opportunism. In contrast, just a few seconds earlier, she had called Carey "Daddy" in her soon-to-be-patented Lorelei Lee voice. Thus, amid the least propitious circumstances this side of *Ladies of the Chorus*, she makes a genuine, wholly idiosyncratic impact. In something as arid as this, it's best to be grateful for even the tiniest valid moments.

A couple of months earlier, Monroe had taken matters into her own hands when her studio was lagging in giving her opportunities. Unfortunately, *Let's Make It Legal* presented her with an opportunity that seems virtually

---

[5] Carey, who shared all four of her scenes with her, was the latest colleague to note the special treatment she was thought to be getting. "She was riding the coat-tails of Joe Schenck at that time," he recalled. "When it was time to go to the set they sent a big limo for her . . . and a Jeep for me!"

meaningless. A role like this should have come after *Love Happy*, not after *The Asphalt Jungle* or even *As Young as You Feel*. This is doubtless why, on the set, she indulged in her first recorded instances of temperamental behavior. A penchant for lateness had already been observed during *All about Eve* and *As Young as You Feel*. This time, when reprimanded for tardiness by director Richard Sale, she bolted from the set in a display of anger usually reserved for actors with more than, say, four lines in one scene. This time, at least, she returned a few minutes later and apologized. Throwing a fit on the set would not be considered a way to move ahead in one's career; neither, for that matter, was being handed an all-but-nothing role in a routine movie. However unprofessional her behavior, Monroe's reaction had some honesty about it. Having had her Fox contract renewed—this time for seven years— and having begun to prove herself as a performer, she was confronting a future where small and potentially demeaning roles were subordinate to endless cheesecake publicity. Hyde was no longer around to help map out a career progression, and her hard work in Chekhov's acting classes obviously did not guarantee much respect from her employer. There needed to be more.

4

Seriously

One of the distinctive aspects of Marilyn Monroe's charisma came with the fact that there were always those who wanted to help her or, in some fashion, rescue her. While the hangers-on and opportunists would come in due time, earlier in her career, there were some without a seamy agenda who simply wanted to offer assistance or even kindness. Drawn by her on- or off-screen magnetism, they were a refreshing respite from all the ones demanding payback of one kind or another. Complicated person that she was, Monroe was well aware of this phenomenon, and her air of helplessness was both very real and quite deliberately deployed. In no way did it hurt her cause that she was always willing to burnish her mythology by adding an extra layer of pathos. Even as the reality was bad enough, there were always ways to make situations that much more pitiable. She knew, for example, that it was rather more appealing to tell people she was an orphan instead of letting it be known that she was illegitimate and had a mother who was constantly in and out of mental institutions. The tweaks and reshaping usually served very well, and she was rarely ungrateful to those who helped her as a result. But, as with many other ambitious persons, she would frequently move forward to the next sponsor or mentor without much in the way of a backward glance. Her own real-life cast of characters, many of them, were sort of like her roles in movies such as *Love Nest*—enter with a splash, serve a function for a time, then exit.

Sidney Skolsky was one of the more clear-eyed, and long-lasting, of MM's "sponsor figures." A longtime columnist for *Photoplay* and other publications, he was smart, opinionated, well connected, and—given the business he was in—a person of integrity. Like many Hollywood hopefuls, Monroe had cultivated Skolsky's friendship early on, and he remained the only journalist with whom she would maintain a consistent personal association. Their relationship bore particular fruit in the summer of 1951, shortly after she completed work on *Let's Make It Legal*. At that point, only one film in her "blonde trilogy," *As Young as You Feel*, had been released, so her renown was mainly a matter of photos, publicity, and accumulated goodwill resulting from *The*

Asphalt Jungle and *All about Eve*. Fully aware that her potential extended beyond roles involving a few lines and a tight bodice, Skolsky did some major politicking on her behalf with executive producer Jerry Wald. Wald had been in charge of some sizable hits at Warner Bros.—*Mildred Pierce, Johnny Belinda, Key Largo*—and, with fellow writer-producer Norman Krasna, had formed a production company to make and release films through RKO.[1] Having already worked on a series of emotion-propelled melodramas at Warners, Wald was now preparing a similar story for RKO. It had a role for a healthy and sensual young woman.

Clash by Night had not been one of Clifford Odets's more commercially successful works, which had a good deal to do with the fact that it was a stark drama that opened on Broadway shortly after the United States declared war on Japan. That it was off the boards after only six weeks was a relief to its star, Tallulah Bankhead, who had had her own clash with producer Billy Rose and had been unnerved by the Method approaches of costar Lee J. Cobb and director Lee Strasberg. For Wald, the plot of the play was well in line with those he'd done at Warners with Joan Crawford: a Staten Island housewife and mother, restlessly trapped in a dull marriage, finds excitement and, eventually, tragedy with another man. Although Wald originally intended to cast Crawford in the role of Mae, the final and probably more sensible choice was Barbara Stanwyck. The central triangle was completed by Paul Douglas and Robert Ryan, who'd had another role (Joe) in the original play. The setting changed coasts, from Staten Island to Monterey, and the shock of Odets's ending (husband kills lover) was softened to merely attempted murder, along with a sort of reconciliation between Mae and her husband. Given the presence of three stars well into their forties, Wald was on the lookout for a younger, sexier, and commercially viable pair to play the secondary couple of Mae's brother and his fiancée, a cannery worker. This was Skolsky's point of entry with Wald, after which Monroe closed the deal by showing up for a meeting dressed in tight pants and a clinging blouse. (This was per both Skolsky's advice and MM's own dress-for-success ethos.) The agreement between Fox and RKO stipulated that Monroe would be given over-the-title billing along with the trio of leads, an arrangement that proved beneficial

[1] RKO, one of the smallest of the major studios, had long had fiscal and management issues. None of them, however, compared with the erratic (a gracious term) leadership of the studio by Howard Hughes, who had acquired RKO in 1948 and eventually ran it into the ground. At first, Wald and Krasna worked harmoniously with Hughes; then, as was not uncommon, things grew sour. After he left RKO, Wald moved to Columbia and later to Twentieth Century-Fox, where he and Krasna would collaborate on one of the least propitious of all Monroe films, *Let's Make Love*.

to all parties. She was, after all, being given a big-time opportunity to prove herself in a film made without Fox having to finance it. If it and she turned out well, her success would benefit future endeavors at Fox; if it didn't pan out—and studio people like Zanuck suspected it might not—her career at Fox could be wound down. She was, after all, widely considered to be a garish and empty flash in the pan. Let a "respectable" role in a worthy film offer any evidence, yea or nay.

Monroe approached this new project with excitement and a fair amount of terror. RKO was a smaller, more tightly managed company than Fox, there would be an extensive amount of location shooting in Monterey, and she was being called on to stretch herself more than at any time since *The Asphalt Jungle*. Her role was larger than any since the long-ago *Ladies of the Chorus*, and she would be interacting with proven professionals. Even her hunky counterpart, Keith Andes, had had extensive stage experience. Perhaps most intimidating of all, the film was going to be directed by Fritz Lang, whose stern reputation was a byword in the industry. Aware of MM's work with, and reliance on, Natasha Lytess, Lang struck a deal: Lytess would be allowed on the set as long as she and Monroe did not work together on the role beforehand. Lang's rationale for this was sensible as well as autocratic: he wanted the performance to emerge from an actor's evolving relationship with both the director and the other cast members, without preconception. In that way, there would be at least the possibility for something less calculated and more spontaneous. Well and good, it would seem.

The trouble started early, with Douglas's loud resentment of the press coverage given to Monroe, whose publicity was beginning to snowball. (Stanwyck's sad and clued-in reply to Douglas: "It's this way, Paul: she's younger and more beautiful than any of us.") Along with the buildup and pinup photos and general ballyhoo, there was the *Collier's* magazine story that ran a few weeks before shooting began. Long and laudatory, the piece was part interview and part biography, with touches of mythology tossed in by Monroe, who knocked two years off her age, and the Fox publicists, who quoted Darryl Zanuck, unconvincingly, as saying that MM was "the most exciting new personality in Hollywood in a long time." The situation with Lang heated up quickly as he realized that Lytess, more than he, was directing her performance. Monroe, observing his hostility, as well as that of other crew and cast members, became still more terrified, to the extent that she would vomit before coming onto the set and frequently break out in an unphotogenic rash. Finally, Lang told Wald that he wanted Lytess kept off the set. Not for the last time, Monroe dug in, staying away from the set until the conflict was resolved and Lytess was permitted to return. Later on, when *Clash by Night* was given a sneak preview in Pasadena, Wald realized that it had all been worth the trouble when he saw a stack of response cards that raved about Monroe. He was even more gratified when *Clash by Night* was released right after the sensational story broke about MM having posed for a rather celebrated nude calendar. Far from turning off audiences, this revelation helped the film's grosses no end.[2]

Clash by Night is an atypical, if not odd, entry in the filmographies of both Lang and Monroe. It has some of the same elements of film noir as other Lang films, as well as the physical and emotional violence also seen in, say, *The Big Heat* or *Human Desire*, yet it's an oddly uneven work that lurches about too much for its own good. While the realistic Monterey setting is well observed, Lang insists on overlaying it with some heavy-handed symbolism involving crashing waves and dark clouds that demonstrates how much better his use of visual metaphors had worked in *Metropolis*. Ultimately, at its core, it's as much a women's melodrama as *Mildred Pierce* or other Wald titles, with dramatics that get far closer to Crawford than to Odets. Fortunately, Stanwyck's direct and unsentimental approach helps keep it grounded, especially in her love/hate scenes with Ryan, as always one of the most resourceful of film actors. They and Douglas, more than Lang, are able to negotiate most of the hairpin emotional turns set forth by the script. So is Monroe, who gives one of her most fully realized performances.

Peggy, the cannery worker who becomes engaged to Mae's brother Joe, is less a part of the central drama than an involved bystander, not unlike MM's participation in *The Asphalt Jungle*. As in the three comedies she had just completed at Fox, Monroe drops in and out of the narrative in generally short scenes, if with a profound difference. This is probably the most "normal," or perhaps "real," role of Monroe's career: a positive and assertive young woman with a mind of her own, willing to work on a relationship yet consistently able to hold on to her own beliefs. There's an element of pre-liberation feminism that underlies both the character's independence and the way she defends the errant Mae; she sees herself on even—if sometimes slightly violent—footing with her man, and, like Mae she is drawn, if briefly, to the irresistible heel Earl (Ryan). Monroe looks the part as well as acting it, and

---

[2] As it happened, nude calendars had already figured in the *Clash by Night* script. In one scene, Jerry (Douglas) angrily orders his uncle (J. Carrol Naish) to "Take down them dirty pictures you got hangin' up!" Sometimes art can imitate life even when it doesn't intend to.

instead of garish starlet wear, she is clothed in blue jeans and housedresses, albeit as snug-fitting as the usual MM on-screen wardrobe. (Quite partial to jeans in real life, Monroe supplied her own for the film. She favored men's cuts, which hugged the hips somewhat tighter.) She is shown sorting fish on an assembly line and, later, working on a boat, managing to seem plausible in both situations. Peggy banters with Joe and even smacks him, flirts with Earl, and gets amusingly bombed at Mae's wedding reception. Monroe is utterly at ease in all of this, never betraying the turmoil and nervousness that attended the creation of her performance. She falters a tiny bit only in her final scenes, when Mae is preparing to leave her husband. There, as she negotiates heavier dramatics, Monroe's diction becomes a little more stilted and calculated, if not destructively so. Overall, she plays with a naturalness and youthful vigor that were seldom seen in later films, managing to stand out at the same time as she remains part of the ensemble. She had worked hard, and the reward would be a sizable number of fine reviews. Apart from the general sensation and the subsequent calendar brouhaha, she had shown herself to be a resourceful actor.

Monroe's work on *Clash by Night*, if not her conduct on the set, was a pretty sure guarantor that there would, or could, be more substantial work to come. When she returned to Fox, she was greeted with an onrush of films—four, in fact, in less than six months. These were a sort of Marilyn and the Three Bears—one role tiny, two medium-sized, one large. And in spite of the resistance from Zanuck and other decision makers, she was allowed two further potential opportunities to prove herself in dramatic roles. Specifically, she made screen tests for two upcoming Fox dramas, *Wait 'til the Sun Shines, Nellie* and *Night without Sleep*. The *Nellie* role, that of a straying wife in turn-of-the-century Illinois, was a close miss that eventually went to Jean Peters. The film's director, Henry King, was not so much opposed to Monroe as resistant to her affected vocal delivery. He told Peters: "It wasn't that I didn't want her. It was just that I told [Zanuck], 'If you make me use her, you'll really have to give me another ten days of shooting time to get her to stop talking that way!'" For the *Night without Sleep* test, Monroe worked intensively with Lytess to prepare the scene, the result was an unqualified success, and she promptly started work on the film, which was eventually retitled *Don't Bother to Knock*.

Don't Bother to Knock was based on a short novel by Charlotte Armstrong, *Mischief*, which had run in 1950 in *Good Housekeeping* magazine and soon afterward was published as a stand-alone book. Armstrong specialized in suspense thrillers, and this one had an unsettling premise: a family of three travels to New York, and while the parents are in the hotel ballroom for an award ceremony, their little girl is left upstairs in the care of a young woman who soon proves to be—here's an understatement—monumentally unsuited to the job. The tenor of the story recalled a previous Fox drama dealing with a woman's mental instability, *Leave Her to Heaven* (1945), including the use of child endangerment as a troubling plot point. There were even, given the setting, echoes of a slice-of-life *Grand Hotel* story, with various fringe characters becoming involved with the central narrative. The role of Nell, the disturbed babysitter, was far removed from conventional heroine roles, and of course, Monroe had been proving herself to be anything other than a standard-issue leading lady. For Fox, it was an astute way to move her career a step forward: without spending much money, there was the potential to make an impact punch and also to see what she could do in a larger—and quite difficult—role. The budget, in fact, would be so low ($550,000) that Fox was all but guaranteed to make a profit even if it turned out disastrously. With the Monroe Sensation well under way, people would go to see it even if, ultimately, they didn't think she was up to the job. Then surely, her detractors believed, she could go back to flashy drop-in roles in which she looked good and didn't count for much. As it turned out, *Don't Bother to Knock* was a major success for a grade-B project, earning back something like four times its initial cost. Besides serving as a testing ground for Monroe, it was also a kind of tryout for another leading woman. Anne Bancroft, a twenty-year-old New York actress with television credits and Actors Studio training, would be making her film debut in the second female lead of Lyn, the lounge singer. Bancroft's roles at Fox over the next few years were uniformly undistinguished. The glory would come later.

The low budget of *Don't Bother to Knock* made for a tight shooting schedule and the stated intention to capture as many shots on the first take as possible. That, at least ostensibly, precluded the usual Monroe-related delays and excessive reliance on the presence of Lytess, and for a good part of the shoot, she did conduct herself with the get-it-done professionalism of someone seeking to do well with a big and taxing assignment. Director Roy Baker, a Hollywood newcomer, opted to shoot in sequence, which at the very least could help an actor in building and shading a characterization. Zanuck, for his part, seemed to believe that MM's success with her screen test might give her the confidence to get through the shoot on her own, without having Lytess on the set. Push, in fact, came to shove, in the form of a somewhat testy and patronizing memo Zanuck wrote to Monroe: "You have built up a Svengali, and if you are going to progress with your career and become as important talent-wise as you have publicity-wise then you must destroy this Svengali before it destroys you." Temporarily chastened, MM started the film without on-set coaching. Soon enough, she adopted the distressing habit of, after Baker called "Cut," running to a phone to call Lytess for reassurance or direction. Baker's displeasure about this was magnified when, a little later, she finally demanded Lytess's presence on the set. With this, a shoot that had been proceeding with relative smoothness began to fall behind schedule. Monroe became increasingly uncertain about her lines and was, it was clear to all, prioritizing her coach's opinions over those of the director. Finally, on the last day of filming, the trouble worsened to the extent that Baker ordered Lytess off the set, stating that he was capable of giving MM all the direction she required. Monroe quickly retorted, in front of the cast and crew, that he was incapable of doing this, and so Lytess remained. The difficult final scene was captured quickly afterward.

It would be nearly seven months until the public and the critics would be able to assess Monroe's work as the alarmingly disconnected Nell. The initial reviews were quite mixed, and though there have been some laudatory reassessments in later years, her work in *Don't Bother to Knock* remains, most likely, the most controversial and even divisive performance in the MM canon. (Another contender for this prize is *The Misfits*.) The film, too, has been both praised and damned, even apart from its questionable psychology and somewhat bumpy pacing. It does get off to a confident start, for after the Twentieth Century-Fox trademark, there immediately begins a fine urban clatter courtesy of composer Alfred Newman. This is to clue the audience that the film is set in Manhattan; it also sends a message to knowing viewers that this is a budget enterprise, since Newman's music had been used less than two years earlier in Elia Kazan's *Panic in the Streets*. (That film, like this one, starred Richard Widmark.) The economy of the production is, in fact, somewhat of its raison d'être. In addition to its "public screen testing" of Monroe and Bancroft, it facilitated a no-frills narrative that benefits the story. This is not one of the city's plusher hotels, nor are there the extraneous digressions that would have come in a more lavish kind of film. Even the music, what there is of it, becomes a part of the narrative, since it consists of a series of pop songs piped into the rooms from the hotel lounge.[3] There's

---

[3] If it doesn't really sound like Bancroft singing "How About You?" and "Manhattan" and other numbers, it shouldn't, since the voice belongs to singer Eve Marley. In someone's misshapen notion of downscale sophistication, the lounge is called the Round-Up, and Bancroft is called upon to wear an unfortunate "rodeo chic" costume. Mrs. Robinson's fur coat suited her far, far better.

also the simple fact that no film studio in its right mind would have given a big budget to such unpleasant material. Or, for that matter, would it cast a breakout new star in such an off-kilter role. Even Widmark, who receives top billing, made his sensational film debut in *Kiss of Death* as a psychotic thug . . . in a supporting role. Here Nell holds center screen and, film noir auspices notwithstanding, there's something troubling about it.

Armstrong had structured *Mischief* to read as a movie scenario, with constant cutting between the central trio (man, woman, and little girl) and the parents and the hotel bystanders. The film—with its new title aiming to lure in the avid MM fans—maintains this layout, with a major assist from a group of players quite familiar to devotees of '40s and '50s film and television: Lurene Tuttle and Jim Backus as the parents, Elisha Cook Jr. as Nell's uncle, and such familiar faces as Jeanne Cagney, Verna Felton, Olan Soulé, and a true film-cultist figure, "Queen of the Extras" Bess Flowers. While he generally followed the contours of Armstrong's narrative, it was decided that screenwriter Daniel Taradash should provide a major change of backstory to make Nell both more comprehensible and more piteous. In the novel, she's a standard-issue psychopath who murdered her parents by setting fire to their house. Since it couldn't be proven that she'd started the fire (but we know better), she's come to New York to live with her aunt and uncle, passively yielding to their attempt to give her a fresh start. At first phlegmatic, she quickly turns lethal, all of her malevolence directed outward. She isn't a killer because of anything other than her own inherent lack of humanity and empathy; she's also a bigot who spits out a foul racial epithet at one point. The film's Nell has traveled a significantly different route. Her own psychosis was directed not at her parents but at herself: she had slashed her wrists after learning that her pilot boyfriend was killed in action. There are, again, the uncle and (unseen) aunt to try to give her a life, but now Nell's derangement is resurrected because she conflates her hotel pickup, Widmark's Jed, with the memory of her dead lover; the fact that they're both pilots helps the confusion. The haywire that results from Nell's misdirected passion is directed mainly toward little Bunny (Donna Corcoran), and after the smoke clears, Nell is given a pathetic coda. In the book, she's led off unceremoniously, as blankly malevolent as ever; the film, in contrast, shows a girl who couldn't help it, who meant well while at the same time lacking the resources to handle the stress and the memories. As several graphic close-ups of her wrists have already demonstrated, she's intending to harm herself more than she would harm others.

Unsurprisingly, Monroe did rigorous preparation for Nell, working hard with Lytess and on her own to build up a construction of inner and outer traits that would animate this rather slippery character. We might pause here to stand back in wonder that someone taken and treated so unseriously would be working this hard to create validity and truth in a role that many actors would not go near. Monroe was seen, at the time and later, as the latest and ultimate incarnation of the "Fox blonde"—a sunny, photogenic character whose dramatic ability rarely strayed past love scenes and perhaps an on-screen tantrum. Still, even at that point, she was felt to be a little outside the mold, due largely to a forthright presentation of overt sexuality well removed from the less complicated "here I am" presentation of a Betty Grable. (Try to imagine Grable in *Don't Bother to Knock*. Or June Haver.) For Nell's exterior, Monroe darkened her hair to something approaching its original shade; she also toned down the makeup, especially the lipstick. When first seen, Nell has fleeting vestiges of the photogenic Monroe glamour, yet she's so withdrawn as to evoke Lytess's later, harsh assessment of the anonymous starlet she met at Columbia back in 1948: "Unable to take refuge in her own insignificance." There's also been a good deal of hindsight speculation over how much of her own family history Monroe called on to create Nell. The struggles of Monroe's mother, Gladys Baker, have been frequently recounted, with the emphasis on a perception that "reality" was a concept too frequently beyond the woman's grasp. Nell's psychology also overlaps notably with both Monroe's insecurity and her history of what are now called abandonment issues. There's even a hint of the "Nell attacking Bunny" thread in the fact that MM often claimed that at the age of one, she had to fight off her grandmother's attempts to smother her with a pillow. (Della Hogan Monroe Grainger was institutionalized in August 1927 and died that same month.) Perhaps, then, Monroe summoned forth her awareness of this legacy of trauma to create Nell's dreamlike self-containment. This aspect of the performance drew some criticism so harsh as to verge on the insulting:

> She is supposed to be a "sick girl" and she plays the part like a sick girl. This may have the sound of praise; but when you see her you will be uneasily aware that her portrayal is reinforced by virtually no acting resources whatsoever. (*Los Angeles Times*)

The story is that Marilyn Monroe is being groomed by Twentieth Century-Fox for razzle-dazzle stardom . . . but if they also expect her to act, they're going to have to give her a lot of lessons under an able and patient coach. . . . To be sure, the role is one that Bette Davis or even Olivia de Havilland might have a little trouble getting over without a running start. . . . It requires a good deal to play a person who is strangely jangled in the head. And, unfortunately, all the equipment that Miss Monroe has to handle the job are a childishly blank expression and provokingly feeble, hollow voice. With these she makes a game endeavor to pull something out of the role, but it looks as though she and her director, Roy Baker, were not quite certain what. . . . All in all, Miss Monroe needs much more practice than she shows in "Don't Bother to Knock." This is [something] we think you and she should be told. (*New York Times*)

Some other reviews were less discouraging, including a praising-with-faint-damnation assessment from maverick critic Manny Farber. In naming *Don't Bother to Knock* one of the most effective films of 1952, Farber cited as a leading asset "Monroe's amateurish manner and childishly blank expression [which are] used without the usual glamour treatment in the character of a paranoiac refugee from a small town." As for the less critical reviewers in the trade press, most of them cited what was felt to be a creditable job and— like that long-ago assessment of her in *Ladies of the Chorus*—noted that she showed promise.

None of the critics, in 1952 and over the ensuing seven decades, was completely wrong about Monroe in *Don't Bother to Knock*, setting aside the snide tone that would increasingly mark many of her reviews. It's a complicated and startlingly uneven performance, with moments of acute psychological truth pushed in alongside overreaching effects and even rank inadequacy. It is, above all, a serious and painstaking piece of work, even at its least successful, and perhaps the fairest way to look at it, and her, is to note how little of it is beholden to traditional, presentational forms of movie acting. Monroe's Nell enters the hotel with a hopefulness that seems both tentative and autobiographical, expressed with both the look of trembling optimism on her face and her anxiously holding her hands together. When she speaks to her uncle in the elevator, the excessive emphasis on diction seems, this time, the obvious affectation of a scared little somebody trying to act adult and normal. When Nell is introduced to the Jones family, MM is a shade less blank than the Nell in the novel, though still spacey enough to remind us of the fundamental flaw of logic at the root of this story: it may be a worthy act to give this damaged girl an opportunity, but who ever thought it was a good idea to have that opportunity be child care?[4]

Monroe's careful shadings are especially telling when Nell appropriates Mrs. Jones's finery. Instead of transforming herself into a Marilyn-type glamour blitz, she is able to convey that the new frills can't hide that fact that this is someone who is lost and emotionally at sea. There's enough of an enticing veneer to draw in the willing Jed, while under the confident disguise she remains uncertain and, presently, unstable. The critics who mistook Monroe's dreamlike speech and manner for amateurishness were clearly— and condescendingly—off the mark. It is Nell's "childishly blank expression" she's presenting, not her own purported incompetence as a performer. It's creepy, to be sure, and not least for the way it doesn't remind a viewer of any other performer. It's Monroe, neat.

The amateurish aspects of the performance come in only when she shifts gears and moves from her self-engineered acting realm to more overt, conventionally actorish representations of passion, anger, and derangement. As would be shown again and again over the years, Monroe's performing style was never in sync with the more conventional tenets of film acting. This becomes especially clear with her overenunciation to Widmark: "Ev-ry time you lookeD aT mee, I wanTed To Kisss you." As the habitually myopic Bosley Crowther noted in his *Times* review, a Davis or de Havilland might, with effort, have made something of Nell's more overt displays of madness. It is not to Monroe's discredit that the tools to do this sort of work were not a part of her acting arsenal. Instead, it would be necessary for an insightful director, when she had one (and one she was willing to listen to) to guide her in a fashion that would negotiate a character's path using her own techniques, both learned and instinctive. There is no remaining record of the acclaimed scenes she did in her acting classes, her Cordelia to the Lear of Michael Chekhov, her Blanche DuBois and Holly Golightly, her Anna Christie opposite the Marthy of Maureen Stapleton. Yet there is no denying the praise that these pieces drew from those who saw them. She *did* have the equipment, at least when granted the opportunity and guidance to deploy it according to her own lights. The impatience of many movie directors, whether Roy Baker

---

[4] The main culprit in this is, of course, Uncle Eddie, who is an honored member of that long line of squirrels and weasels Elisha Cook played in his fifty-plus-year career. Perhaps the Joneses were foolish to trust Eddie's judgment, but the ultimate responsibility is his, which makes it somewhat satisfying—in that era of Production Code retribution—that Nell beans him with that heavy standing ashtray. After all, she wouldn't have been there without him.

or Otto Preminger or even Laurence Olivier, would never form a fitting conduit for these idiosyncratic abilities to find illumination.

At the time and later, Monroe remained proud of the job she did on Nell's final scene, as captured on film by a somewhat hostile Baker on the last shooting day. From leaving the hotel room, through the downward elevator trip and the dreamlike terror of her walk through the lobby, to finally being cornered while grasping a razor blade—she finds a realm of stunned pain and madness that could seem uncontrolled only to an ill-tempered critic who refuses to acknowledge that an actor is at work here. Bancroft—who seems far more mature than Monroe—and Widmark both give firm and feeling support, and both would later praise her work. "It was one of those very rare times," Bancroft remembered, "when I felt that give-and- take that can only happen when you are working with good actors." As Nell is led off by the police, she looks at Lyn and Jed and murmurs a wistful "People who love each other . . ." That's all she says, and for both character and actor, it's plenty.

Whether or not the Fox powers believed that Monroe had truly been up to the *Don't Bother to Knock* challenge, they were naturally willing to cash in on a fame that was, even before the calendar revelation, rapidly accruing. In early 1952, as soon as she was finished with Nell, Monroe was rushed into a somewhat odd pair of movies that may be picturesquely termed "portmanteau." Both were modestly conceived in black-and-white—the Fox economy wave was still well in effect—and both used a good deal of contract talent on the fly. *We're Not Married!* was a series of short vignettes with a one-joke premise, while *O. Henry's Full House* found cohesion only in the fact that all five of its sections were adaptations of stories by William Sydney Porter, known to the world as O. Henry. Monroe's participation in both of these was more about appearance than substance, as she received star billing for a minimum of on-screen time. We're nearly back to *Love Happy* with all this, especially with the fleeting opportunity given her in *Full House*. In fairness, Monroe was not being singled out, among the roster of Fox contract actors, to mark time in make-do work. The casts of both films were composed of actors under contract to the studio (Richard Widmark, Anne Baxter, Jeanne Crain, David Wayne) plus a few more specialized add-ons such as Charles Laughton and, from the sublime to the ridiculous, Zsa Zsa Gabor. Naturally, it was not simply contract-mandated fairness that gave Monroe star billing in both films, for by the time they were both released later in 1952, hers would be the biggest-drawing name in either cast. She had taken off that far that fast.

We're Not Married!, for which the exclamation point appeared in the opening credits but not always in the advertising, was centered around what would later be a treasured sitcom trope. An addled justice of the peace (the sublimely dithery Victor Moore) conducts marriage ceremonies before his license goes into effect; two and a half years later, the supposedly married couples learn the truth. The result, as presented by director Edmund Goulding (*Grand Hotel, Dark Victory, The Razor's Edge*), is five mostly comic variations on one theme.[5] Monroe's segment, in which she is paired with Wayne, marks the only time, save for the uncompleted *Something's Got to Give*, she played a mother on-screen. Her maternal instincts take a decided backseat to cheese-cake, since she's playing a beauty contestant—first Mrs. Mississippi and then, after the letter from the governor comes, Miss Mississippi. (You couldn't tell the state from the audio, since none of the actors tries for a regional accent.) Essentially, the episode was put together to allow bookended displays of MM in fancy bathing suits worthy of Miss Cucamonga in *Let's Make It Legal*. As if further proof was needed that she was there mainly to be looked at, it's Wayne and James Gleason, as the pageant promoter, who have the lion's share of both the screen time and the dialogue; even Zsa Zsa, in her segment with Louis Calhern, is given more to do. Nevertheless, Monroe's character, Annabel, has some moxie, as well as the engaging can-do spirit that not only wins pageants but overcomes a husband's regressive notions about marriage. A biographer has also reported that Goulding worked with her to produce what would soon be a Monroe trademark: the whispery voice that sounded something like a baby allowed to grow up way too fast. Take short breaths, Goulding is said to have advised her, before you say each line. The extra air would lift up the naturally low tone in a distinctive, and often delightfully comedic, way. If only, in the amusingly insubstantial *We're Not Married!*, the lines she delivered in that fashion had been at all funny.

From Mississippi, Monroe was quickly shunted to turn-of-the-century Manhattan for *O. Henry's Full House*, a so-so collection of short-story adaptations with, naturally, the scribe's trademark twist endings. Unlike *We're Not Married!* and Fox's earlier *Tales of Manhattan*, it had a director roster as varied as its cast, and as the title implies, there is a quintet of stories.

---

[5] Six episodes were filmed, and the backwoods pairing of Walter Brennan and Hope Emerson was dropped. (The footage survives.) This change necessitated some postproduction tinkering, since in a couple of scenes, it was mentioned that there were six couples. Look closely at the lip movements of Moore, Tom Powers (as the attorney general), and Jane Darwell (as Mrs. Justice of the Peace): they're speaking "six," but what we hear on the redubbed soundtrack is "five."

Nevertheless, in 1952, it played in most theaters as a four-hander, with Howard Hawks's labored and unfunny take on "The Ransom of Red Chief" dropped early on and reinstated only when *Full House* went to television. It might appear that Monroe fared little better than Fred Allen and Oscar Levant in "Red Chief," since she was given marquee-bait star billing for the briefest role she'd had since the time Dusky Ledue fended off Dick Powell's advances.

"The Cop and the Anthem" was the lead-off story in the O. Henry quintet, directed by Henry Koster and starring the formidable Laughton as Soapy, a courtly Manhattan bum seeking to get himself arrested in order to have a warm prison home, with meals, for the winter. The story consists entirely of a series of failed attempts at illegality—stealing another man's umbrella, walking out on a dinner check, breaking a shop window, propositioning a young woman. The sharp turn of an ending is fairly predictable: hearing a hymn as he stands outside a church, Soapy finds redemption and vows to abandon his old ways for a clean new life . . . and then gets picked up for vagrancy. The story, which spans only a few pages, was expanded to include a sidekick and sounding board for Soapy, played by frequent MM cohort Wayne. Soapy himself, who seems vague and indistinct on the printed page, was recast as a glorious windbag, crammed to the brim with lengthy perorations laden with Laughtonian excess. If Laughton's film roles at this time were sometimes low-rent (Captain Kidd meeting Abbott and Costello, a campy King Herod in *Salome*), here was one considerably more worthy of one of the century's finest actors (and great hams). "Three months, I say, are of assured bed, board, and congenial company at the city's expense," Soapy declaims, in the same authoritative tones as that which ordered sailors so despicably on the HMS *Bounty*.

Monroe, predictably enough, played the streetwalker mistaken for an innocent girl, a small but pointed vignette in the story and, again, lightly extended on the screen. Costumed in the tightest fin-de-siècle skirt—no bustle required—she enters from screen right looking smoothly self-possessed as she strolls to a store window. Laughton makes his move with an ineffably seedy invitation to "Come and play in my back yard." "Sure I will, if you buy me a drink," she answers, in a voice deeper and rougher than any yet heard in her films. Then, feeling a policeman's eyes on the two of them, her voice rises and expands to a theatrical "How's dear Cousin Fanny?" punctuated with a heartily fake laugh. As Soapy realizes he's dealing with a professional, Laughton's facial reaction is priceless. He confesses that he's made an error, and again, those harsh, tough tones tumble out. "Mistake? What kind of mistake?" she demands, adding, "You tryin' to kid me?" Soapy makes humble amends in a sublime Laughton aria and by way of apology offers his umbrella to this "charming and delightful young lady." He tips his derby and wanders off as Monroe watches him in transfixed amazement. "He called me a lady," she tells the cop, and as Koster fades to black, we hear one sob. This is done in yet another voice, soft and reflective, not dissimilar to the tone Monroe used for Nell's "People who love each other." In about a minute of screen time, she has etched a sweet and layered portrait of a bruised innocent with a hard, cracked shell. Koster later said that he loved working with her, and though she was terrified of doing a scene opposite the formidable Laughton, she far more than held her own. Quite likely, it was her interaction with him, plus her work with Chekhov and her own sound instincts, that give this cameo such power—without, let it be said, resorting to excessive consonants. Brevity, in this case, has offered up a great deal—fleeting as it is, Monroe's performance in "The Cop and the Anthem" is one of her best.

In less than six months, Monroe had shot four films, attracted major attention in *Love Nest* and *Let's Make It Legal* and, one way or another—including that calendar—was becoming one of the most talked-about people in the country. Even before the release of her final "apprentice" work, it was clear that something major would be happening before long. Small roles, however piquant, would soon be a thing of the past.

5

Detonating

March 1952 began with a deceptive kind of calm that tended to mask the fact that an explosion was imminent. Monroe was now working on her fifth film in six months, a fairly remarkable statistic considering that the public had not yet seen her in anything made after *Let's Make It Legal*. She was, as *Life* magazine put it the following month, "The Talk of Hollywood," ascending rapidly in spite of the unbelievers. Her seemingly effortless knack for causing excitement, oddly disproportionate to the limited opportunities and screen time given to her so far, was a tribute mainly to her own ambition and hard work. As she was exceptionally aware, she was under contract to a studio that still seemed resistant to giving her roles of substance and, by extension, respect. Perhaps the uneven quality of her work in *Don't Bother to Knock* justified some ongoing caution regarding her ability to carry a film, yet it was becoming increasingly clear that her name on a marquee had become a box-office magnet. Even so, they still didn't know, or perhaps didn't wish to know, exactly what to do with her.

That fifth film, *Monkey Business*, marked the end of Monroe's career as a supporting player. As such, it was less a gateway to new glories than simply the final time her bosses juiced up a nothing role to give her big billing along with minimal screen time. The most generous assessment of her participation would be that it gave her the opportunity to work on a significant project alongside big-name actors under a major director—sort of a comedic equivalent of *Clash by Night*, only this time there were no dimensions whatsoever to the character. The overall premise of the film is suitable for a rowdy farce: an anti-aging formula has a haywire effect, turning sober adults into raucous oversized children. (MM's character is already childlike and thus exempted from the transformation.) With Howard Hawks as director and Cary Grant as star, it carried deliberate echoes of *Bringing Up Baby*, with Grant as a fourteen-years-older version of his absentminded professor character. Unlike *Bringing Up Baby*, with its masterfully controlled chaos, there's now a strained quality that undermines the skillful comedy playing of Grant and Ginger Rogers and sometimes pushes things into an abrading frenzy.

Censorship had already toned down some of the more ribald implications of the script, and Hawks was content to use Monroe mainly as an object for leers and whistles. Her main function, it would appear, was to have her derrière pelted with rubber bands (by Rogers) and spritzed with seltzer (by Charles Coburn). Small wonder that her performance drew critical comments along the patronizing lines of "She disproves more than adequately the efficacy of the old stage rule about not turning one's back to the audience."

Lois Laurel, the character MM plays in *Monkey Business*, is a secretary whose mental capacity is such that her boss hands her a document and orders her to get someone else to type it. Having been reprimanded for her punctuation, she announces that she's now reporting for work early. While Monroe had played dumb before, in *All about Eve*, seldom had she been called upon to delineate so enormous a variance between a character's physical and emotional development. This plays out, as might be expected, in both her appearance and the limited amount of dialogue she is given. The nature of her appeal is underscored, and in sledgehammer fashion, when she lifts her skirt to show Grant how well her new synthetic stockings are managing and notes that they won't run or get torn "no matter how hard you try." When Coburn happens upon this questionable tableau, Grant explains to him that "Miss Laurel was just showing me her acetates." The stocking reveal and a subsequent scene with Grant on roller skates—she manages them quite well—necessitated a dress that Monroe despised: a jersey design with a pleated full skirt instead of the usual tight fit that she always favored.[1]

For audiences in 1952, *Monkey Business* was a fun, forgettable romp. For the large number of film critics and cultists who place Hawks at the very top of the directorial pantheon, it's been far more: a subversive meditation on sexuality, arrested development, and the ongoing war between men and women. It's a viewer's choice, really, but again, those comparisons with *Bringing Up Baby* tend to put things in an invidious perspective. The humor seems forced, somewhat in the fashion of that Hawks "Ransom of Red Chief," which was farcical without being funny. Nor was her director

---

[1] Always wanting her on-screen clothes to hug her figure, Monroe would permit Fox's designer, Travilla, to create just one more costume with a full skirt. That one, as the whole world knows, was the classic white "subway dress" in *The Seven Year Itch*. Not that her jersey number in *Monkey Business* was any prudish cover-up; the bodice was constructed to accentuate her breasts more than any on-screen wardrobe had done since *Home Town Story*. MM's second dress in *Monkey Business* was tailored to her tight-fit specifications yet was also somewhat preposterous, with irrelevant flounces and a weird explosion of ball-fringe trim that evokes science fiction more than either screwball comedy or sane couture.

especially taken with Monroe, despite some later protestations he made to the contrary. She was alien to Hawks's well-documented concept of what constituted feminine appeal, though he admitted, after seeing rushes of *Monkey Business*, that she "read" on film far more impressively than she did in person. In spite of this, he could not or would not deal with her in anything other than a perfunctory fashion, and Grant shared his belief that neither her appeal nor her comedic skill was impressive. Given these circumstances, it would have been difficult to make any more of an impression than she had in something like *Love Nest*. Her role was extraneous to the main thrust of the script, and her dialogue was forgettable, except for the amusing "punctuation" line and the allusion to the wear and tear on her stockings. Even in a cartoon comedy like this, there needed to be more, and Monroe only had the opportunity to deliver it in a few shots of her riding with Grant in the new sports car he buys while under the "rejuvenating" influence. Even though the shots were made on a soundstage, with a wind machine and rear-screen projection, Monroe suddenly becomes gloriously alive, with that infectious laugh and, for once, a more maturely sensual appeal. Yet the whole point of her appearance in this film is made plain in a scene following the joyride at a public swimming pool. Grant ventures out on a high-diving board to show off and calls out, "Everybody looking at me?" All eyes, naturally, are on Monroe, and seldom would a rented swimsuit be cut this low. This is what she's meant to be about here, with no interior life to speak of; if she appears to have a sort of crush on Grant, none of it goes anywhere. Where Grant and Rogers are given ample opportunities and can intermittently steer the proceedings away from tedium, Monroe is relegated to being a cartoon getting leered at. Essentially, she's there to serve only as vaguely ridiculous eye candy.

The insignificance of her role contrasted rather starkly with what was going on off the screen. During filming, she began dating Joe DiMaggio, whose fame still eclipsed hers by a good measure. It was a blow to neither the film nor her career when DiMaggio consented to visit her on the set and pose for photos with her and Grant. There was also that calendar, or rather the breaking news that she had posed for it. If that particular sensation now seems exceedingly quaint, it's helpful to remember that there had been nothing like it in the first fifty years of cinema. Public exhibitionism usually took a far more genteel form, and nude models were usually felt to be both immoral and anonymous. The only comparison to be made was Hedy Lamarr's nude swim in *Ecstasy*, and she and the film were foreign. The advice, or directive, given to Monroe by her studio was "Deny it." Instead, she embraced it, and rather than ostracism, the result was another level of fame.

Another issue for Monroe during the shoot concerned her health. Feeling unwell, she was told by doctors that she had appendicitis and that surgery would be necessary. In the great tradition of golden age studio dictates, however, she would have to make *Monkey Business* first, and it was duly observed that her well-known lateness to the set became even more conspicuous.[2] That delayed appendectomy, when it finally occurred, triggered both personal and professional concerns that she dealt with in a unique fashion. Just prior to the surgery, she taped notes to her abdomen cautioning the doctor to cut as little as possible and to allow her to keep her ovaries. Evidently, her directives were heeded, the surgery was successful, and we are left to wonder if there were many other times when an appendectomy ended up making this many headlines. Fortunately, *Monkey Business* marked the end of Monroe's nova-in-waiting period. Even as another publicity crisis erupted—the revelation that she was not an orphan, as she'd claimed—her studio was in the process of moving her up several notches. She would now be considered a full-fledged all-caps star in every way, save the insultingly low salary still mandated by her contract. The promotion would be commemorated with Technicolor, top billing, and a film and role unlike any she had done before or would do again.

Niagara is far too lurid to be considered any kind of great film, so garish and elemental that some might not even call it good. Technically, it's a suspense thriller, and in a larger sense, it can be considered one of the later examples of the genre now commonly known as film noir. In this case, it is that nearly anomalous thing, a film noir shot in color, albeit with plenty of shadows still in evidence. Like *Clash by Night*, it was a product of the postwar enthusiasm for shooting a film on location instead of in Hollywood—or, in Fox's case, on Pico Boulevard in Los Angeles. Instead of simply shooting establishing vistas and process-screen views of Niagara Falls, Fox shipped Monroe and a sizable cast and crew to both the American and Canadian sides of the falls. The results, on the screen, were outstanding—and, truthfully, if anyone other than Monroe had been in the top slot of the movie, the falls would have

---

[2] This marked the first time Monroe's health became an issue during a film shoot. Later there would be countless shooting days lost due to bronchitis and other ailments, plus her painful menstrual cycles. These were compounded, in her final films, by the unfortunate effects of her reliance on prescription medication. It goes without saying that there were psychological aspects to her illnesses as well—and, really, how should one react when a necessary surgery is postponed because they insist on you being available to do a few scenes in a silly comedy?

ended up carrying off the lion's share of attention.[3] Instead, the focus would stay on that brand-new "Talk of Hollywood," and after recovering from her surgery, MM was back at Fox to test a wide assortment of outfits specifically crafted to make her Rose Loomis look as dangerous, and as trashy, as possible. The trip to Niagara Falls followed at the beginning of June, just after Monroe learned (on her twenty-sixth birthday) that after *Niagara*, her career would be moving in a new direction. Fox was casting her, and not Betty Grable, in the role of Lorelei Lee in *Gentlemen Prefer Blondes*. Invigorated by this professional validation, Monroe took the *Niagara* plunge with a degree of relish that can only be termed outrageous.

While Fox's ads for the not-yet-released *Don't Bother to Knock* called Monroe "A Wicked Sensation," poor Nell wasn't wicked. Rose *was*, or at least could be viewed as such, even as Monroe gave the character turns and detours the likes of which hard-boiled cinema had seldom witnessed before. Formerly a waitress in a beer joint, Rose latches onto a fairly well-to-do sheep rancher, George Loomis, in hopes of both security and excitement. When George's finances and mental health take a downturn, Rose decides to move on with someone hotter and younger. Figuring that George is an iffy candidate for divorce, she determines that Niagara Falls will be the ideal spot to get him killed. Counterpointed to the hellish Loomis union is another, more "normal" couple, Ray and Polly, coming to Niagara Falls for a delayed honeymoon. Before the end title comes up, George and Rose and her boyfriend are all dead, and Polly is nearly so.

In spite of the scenery and Technicolor, this is a plot well in line with previous high-tension tales of sex and betrayal. Charles Brackett, who cowrote *Niagara* and served as its producer, had earlier had some contact with the quintessential Evil Woman in all of film noir: *Double Indemnity*'s Phyllis Dietrichson. As played, indelibly and irreplaceably, by Barbara Stanwyck, Phyllis is a conniver par excellence, coldly and efficiently using sex to blind her prey to the fact that the only person she could possibly love is herself. (And then maybe not even . . .) Although Brackett worked with Billy Wilder on a treatment for *Double Indemnity*, he withdrew from the project because he found the subject matter distasteful. By the time of *Niagara*, more than

---

[3] The initial casting idea prior to MM was Anne Baxter. When Fox put Monroe in the role of Rose, Baxter was moved into the other female *Niagara* lead, Polly. Knowing how much attention would be diverted to MM, Baxter said no, and she soon afterward ended her long association with Fox. There was very little that Baxter couldn't play convincingly, and her Rose would likely have been an intriguing cross between Eve Harrington in *All about Eve* and (talk about lurid) Princess Nefretiri in *The Ten Commandments*.

eight years later, he had obviously toughened his stance. For *Niagara*, Brackett and company devised a fascinating variation on the *Indemnity* theme. Rose is cold, no question about it, but she's also hot. A narcissist supreme, she's capable of directing some of her self-love outward if it can get her either money (which Phyllis also had wanted) or sex (which Phyllis hadn't wanted). Nor does her total self-absorption preclude her being smart, since she's put together that intricate plot by which George will supposedly be lured to his death. Then, adding to it all, her Fatal Woman craftiness is overlaid with a Day-Glo display of sexuality unprecedented in Monroe's career and, really, in all of American film. In spite of her appeal and publicity and all those pinup photos, Monroe had not yet (arguably), except in moments of *Clash by Night*, exhibited much genuine sensuality on the screen. Magnetism and sex, sure, and things like her little pre- and post-shower display in *Love Nest*, but for *Niagara*, it's as if all the brouhaha about that calendar gave her permission to push the hardest she ever had on the sex angle. "They think of me this way?" she seems to be saying to herself while she's playing Rose. "So that's what they'll get, only more so." She paints Rose in such vivid hues that even the Technicolor can barely contain her.

Monroe's unbridled display was abetted by one of her most accommodating directors. Henry Hathaway was one of Fox's most reliable craftsmen—efficient and competent and sometimes creative, with a long record of successful westerns and action films. He was known, sometimes notoriously so, to be tough on actors, yelling and haranguing and, as with Debbie Reynolds on *How the West Was Won*, not averse to exposing them to possible physical harm. (Not, to be sure, by laying a hand on them but by pushing them to do difficult stunts.) He was none of that with Monroe, so obliging—and, after her death, recalling her with such affection—that it's been speculated that he had some kind of unrequited crush on her. What a change. After all those drop-in roles and minor films, MM was here being given something like star treatment, with Hathaway and Brackett going so far as to hold frequent meetings with her before the shoot to go over issues of the script, her characterization, and even the casting.[4] Natasha Lytess would be allowed on the set, and Monroe was permitted as many retakes as she wanted. However

[4] Something odd happened when she was called on to assist in a test for the role of Rose's lover, Ted. After doing the test with a handsome (unnamed) young actor, she called producer Brackett to stammer that this guy wouldn't be right for the part. When Brackett asked her why, she replied, "I don't think he'll do the love scenes right." Pressed for more information, she blurted out, "Well, he's a pansy." Normally, MM was extremely accepting of all her gay friends, coworkers, and fans, so perhaps this was an early nod toward her own self-constructed brand of Method acting.

monumental her personal insecurities, she was here being given something like respect.

Directly after shooting *Niagara*, Monroe would veer off into a completely different direction. With *Gentlemen Prefer Blondes*, she presented the Marilyn Monroe persona that would quickly become her trademark, with all its whispery warmth. *Niagara*, then, would be the final statement of another sort of actor, which makes it quite intriguing as both an achievement and an implication. It's not that her work in it is all that easy to analyze, since she and Hathaway and the cinematographer and costume designer have all conspired to give Rose that preposterously gaudy surface. Indeed, there's so much wildness going on with this character that she and others likely undervalued her achievement. Even with that, she is not striving to let the appearance do all the work, in the way some actors hide behind fake noses and other disguises. Reversing the equation she would later encounter in her work at the Actors Studio, she appears to be working from the outside in, using both her craft and her instincts to sort out the mechanics of a woman who's been engineering her appearance to get what she wants. As the sensible Polly comments, when Rose undulates past in skintight satin, "For a dress like that, you've gotta start laying plans when you're about thirteen."

Surely the work of a good actor is to not let the mechanics show through, and Rose's surface is so flagrant that Monroe is able to do her work somewhat under the radar. For Pete's sake, the audience's very first view of Rose involves a nude-under-the-sheets Monroe testily smoking in bed. In the realm of star entrances, this one is delirious. Then, when she gets up, she puts on a slip that shows possibly the greatest amount of cleavage allowed an actor since the enforcement of the Production Code. As if that weren't enough, she extends a leg to roll up a stocking, then dons a bathrobe that all but defines the word "tawdry"—a flimsy thing trimmed in frizz. It becomes a little less lurid when she starts reciting dialogue, since some of those overstressed consonants are intruding upon her first lines. Rose may be calculating and inherently artificial, but not with *those*. In later scenes, the diction relaxes for the most part, particularly in the scene of Rose telling off her husband. Monroe's voice rings out with a force not heard in any other film, and her sneering "Ehhh" as she walks away from George is the aural embodiment of withering contempt. Here, and in other scenes, Hathaway and Brackett permit her to give a clear picture of what she can do as an actor and of who Rose is.

While Rose is not remotely like the sad and deluded Nell, a comparison can be made in that the dynamics of both performances are utterly unlike conventional screen acting of the time. Similarly, if Monroe's Rose and Stanwyck's Phyllis can be viewed as wicked stepsisters, they reside on different planets. Monroe's rhythms, when she was working on all cylinders, were simply not those of other actors, which is one reason all the Jayne Mansfields could sort of imitate her while not really doing it at all. Rose's actions are those of an ice-cold conniver, endlessly lying and exhaustively manipulative, yet because of Monroe's newly minted acting style, she's also appealing and, under all the manufactured blare, even a little delicate. Monroe can do big and unsubtle through her appearance and movement—this is, of course, the great "Marilyn walking" movie—while in her interactions, even when Rose lashes out, the currents are more involved. Critic and novelist Gavin Lambert, writing about *Niagara*, made some intriguing observations about Monroe, some spot-on and some quite arguable. She was, he said:

> [A] rather mysterious girl [who] does not fit in any of the cinema's established categories for blondes. Her acting can at best be described as reluctant [and] she is too passive to be a vamp. . . . For all the wolf calls that she gets and deserves, there is something mournful about Miss Monroe. She doesn't look happy. She lacks the pinup's cheerful grin. She seems to have lost something or to be waking up from a bad dream.

Lambert seemed almost to be reviewing the person rather than the actor. His use of the word "reluctant" made the rather condescending implication that Monroe was being governed by her material, instead of the other way around. He was correct in assessing that she was dissimilar to her predecessors, even as he failed to grasp the fact that this difference was because she had learned and pieced together a style of acting wholly her own. The scene of Rose singing along with the record of her theme song, "Kiss," is a good example: enveloped in Day-Glo colors—hair, makeup, dress—Monroe moans along with the song in an all-but-berserk display of self-directed eroticism.[5] As in *Don't Bother to Knock*, she falters only when she tries to do more conventional "movie acting." This comes in the scene where Rose phones

---

[5] The script had originally specified that Rose's song was to be Cole Porter's "Night and Day," but by the time of shooting, it was changed to the newly composed "Kiss." While Monroe recorded a studio version of "Kiss," backed by a male chorus, Fox pulled the plug on the record's release; apparently, it was felt that the record went a bit too far. As it was, *Niagara* did rate protests from a few "moral-minded" groups after its release. The "Kiss" recording finally came out a long time after MM's death, and the reasons for the studio's caution become fairly plain around the time she begins moaning "take me, take me."

her lover to plot her husband's murder. George has just made a psycho spectacle of himself in public, so she goes over the setup with Ted. "It's maaade to orrrrder," she croons, in a Stanwyck-like baritone that, on Monroe, seems simply forced and odd. In only one remaining film, *River of No Return*, would she again fall back on similar devices, and there it was even less effective. She was simply too original and imaginative to convincingly borrow from others.

For many, *Niagara* begins and ends with the walk. There are two of them, actually, one near the beginning and then the big one when a triumphant Rose thinks her scheme has worked. Way back in *As Young as You Feel*, co-star Constance Bennett had remarked on the prominent and even surpassing quality of Monroe's rear end. From then on, most of her screen wardrobe was tailored for maximum accentuation, which is why she was so unhappy with the full skirt in *Monkey Business*. Even so, that film was the first that truly exploited the way she moved her hips when walking away from the camera. It goes a good deal farther in *Niagara*, since she and Hathaway determined that Rose's lateral propulsion would be one of her defining traits. If the eyes are the window to the soul, Rose's soul is so deficient that, instead, her walk says who she is and how she goes after what she wants. By focusing on it so intently, Hathaway was moving beyond simple leering—although there was still that—to something like transcendence. Rose's walk is so blatant that other women (such as Polly) can feel threatened, and even the musical score comments on it with insinuating variations on the oft-repeated "Kiss."

The long walk, the famous one, comes when Rose leaves Table Rock House with Polly and Ray after reporting her missing husband. At first, there's only ambient street noise; then, suddenly, the Rainbow Tower carillon begins playing "Kiss." Rose, who takes this as the signal that she's now a widow, begs off a ride with Polly and Ray in favor of walking back to the motel. As MM sets off, she opens her mouth wide and shows pretty much all her teeth—but this isn't any normal smile. It's something akin to a lion stalking prey or perhaps a vampire coming in for the kill, and it's so voracious that a viewer may gasp. Then comes that sideways/forward walk, for which Hathaway parks his camera to capture about sixteen seconds of Monroe, in a red jacket and a black skirt, moving briskly away from the camera, across the plaza outside Table Rock House. What's traditionally been reported as the longest walk ever captured on film isn't really, since it's easy to find longer walks taken in all kinds of movies. What it is, though, is indelible, hypnotic, and funny, and in terms of this film and this character, it is utterly authentic.

Monroe is, small surprise, as much the center of *Niagara* as the falls themselves. This is what prompted the famous poster art showing a gigantic Monroe spread out across the edge of the falls, posing seductively while the water cascades over her in the shape of a low-cut gown. (In its screwball monumentality, the image is nearly as whacked out as anything in the movie itself.) Everything in the film connects with her character's actions, and yet Joseph Cotten (George) and Jean Peters (Polly), who are both excellent, are given more actual screen time. It must also be said that the proceedings aren't nearly as compelling after MM's departure, even with the brink-of-disaster scenes of Polly nearly going over the falls. Most egregiously, there are some gaps in continuity, as when Rose and George are suddenly reconciled in a "morning after" scene after she'd aggravated him to a state of near-psychosis. Something obviously happened to bring them back together, but it isn't shown. The responsibility for the deletion of this and several other scenes can be directed all the way to the top of Twentieth Century-Fox, namely Darryl Zanuck, who continued to advise on and doctor the scripts of many Fox films, quite often to the good. Unfortunately, there was also his famous immunity to Monroe's appeal, and producer Brackett would later recall the battles he had with Zanuck to retain what he felt to be "some of her best scenes." Zanuck won the war, and *Niagara* suffered as a result. The cuts were so ruthless that an image taken from one deleted scene even found its way onto many of the posters—a shot of the police inspector (Denis O'Dea) calling on Rose at the motel following George's disappearance. Zanuck's myopia regarding Monroe was a leitmotif throughout the first half of her career, and this was an instance when it was displayed most detrimentally.

Fortunately, neither Zanuck nor anyone else would remove the film's two best sequences: Rose's scene in the hospital and her final pursuit by her husband. The chase makes especially fine use of the locations on the Canadian side of the falls, with Hathaway bringing the entirety of his imagination and expertise to the final moments in the bell tower, with looming shadows and stark overhead views punctuated by shots of the bells themselves, serving as a silent jury for the twisted justice being executed beneath them. (And for an extra twist, George then spends the night with Rose's corpse, to whatever ends one can only imagine.) If Hathaway was working at maximum capability here, Monroe matched him in a scene just before it. Rose, having discovered that her plot has gone way wrong, lies in a hospital bed under heavy sedation. Then the bells play "Kiss" once again, and she starts to stir, waking to a realization that her death is the next item on George's agenda. At first, the soundtrack is the bells alone, and then a male chorus begins to sing "Kiss," at first almost subliminally. As the music gets louder, Hathaway holds Monroe in an extreme close-up as a confusion of feelings passes through Rose's mind: torpor, then awareness, then longing and remembered love, then extreme terror. Instead of her gimmicks—the overdone consonants or nudity or that show-off walk—Monroe here has the opportunity to show what she can do as an actor, charting the character's path through subtle gradations of her facial expressions. It is, in fact, a vivid example of creative screen acting and one of her single best moments on film.

Perhaps Monroe was aware, as she put her stamp on the vile yet compelling Rose, that she would not be visiting these dark precincts again. Her next character, Lorelei Lee, shared nothing with Rose except possibly a taste for luxury. There would be no more murder plots or luring men to their doom, and not simply because the whole genre of film noir was by now in its closing phase. Except for predictable outcries from prudes and churls, few would again be unsettled by Monroe's presence on the screen. Her change of direction would be so profound that even now, her work in *Niagara*, audacious as it is, is frequently denied its due. Rose's demise, portrayed so vividly on the screen, served not only as the end of a character but also as the last time audiences would be confronted by a malevolent Marilyn Monroe. What an electrifying way to make a final statement.

6
Tiffany's

Surely there isn't another movie musical that opens with quite the bang of *Gentlemen Prefer Blondes*. The self-validating blare of the Twentieth Century-Fox fanfare is only a meek introduction to the brassy intro that sounds as they appear. Against a dark stage background, Marilyn Monroe and Jane Russell, draped identically in the reddest of sequins, pop like Roman candles. The opening credits haven't even run—as they most commonly did in 1953 movies—and there they are, strutting out with almost preposterous assurance and tossing their white fur wraps toward the audience. "We're just two little girls from Little Rock," they sing, though neither of them looks little, or girlish, or Arkansan. This is the purest Hollywood va-voom, staged and designed and performed with the kind of confidence that can only come when all parties involved know that they're on fire. For audiences, beginning in the summer of 1953 and continuing to now, the dazzle quotient is off the charts. To those who had seen the show on Broadway or on its long and successful tour, this opening may have been something of a puzzlement, being nothing like what had taken place onstage. It was, in fact, a signal that the movie of *Gentlemen Prefer Blondes* had been transformed with such thoroughness and conviction that it could be considered a total reimagining. There was another metamorphosis as well: Marilyn Monroe, presented here in a completely fresh incarnation that would come to define her career. With this one film, as flanked by *Niagara* and *How to Marry a Millionaire*, she was reaching something that can only be seen as a summit.

Long before it made it onto the screen with Russell and Monroe (that was the order of on-screen billing), *Gentlemen Prefer Blondes* had become something of an American institution. Purely and solely, it was the brainchild of screenwriter and all-around wit Anita Loos, who penned a series of short sketches ("The Lorelei Stories") for *Harper's Bazaar* in 1924, then published the stories in book form the following year. *Gentlemen Prefer Blondes: The Illuminating Diary of a Professional Lady* was an immediate hit, and the lady herself, Lorelei Lee, quickly became a symbol of one kind of liberated woman: a dishy flapper who moves along a ladder of wealthy gentlemen from Little Rock to New York and Paris, asserting with some sureness (and, in her diary, misspelling) that "Kissing your hand may make you feel very very good but a diamond and safire bracelet lasts forever." With her more practical cohort Dorothy Shaw (somewhat of a Loos self-portrait), Lorelei cuts a wide and uninhibited swath while indulging in all manner of 1920s phenomena: drinking, gold-digging, psychoanalysis, Christian Science, and much else. Loos, with her husband, John Emerson, wrote a Broadway play based on the book, then worked on the screenplay for a now-lost silent film version. The book's popularity endured at a somewhat lower level during the Depression and World War II, and then, in 1949, came the musical, with songs by composer Jule Styne and lyricist Leo Robin. The show's rather ramshackle plot and a number of so-so songs ("Keeping Cool with Coolidge," "Mamie Is Mimi," etc.) mattered far less than its Lorelei, the charismatic and eternally quirky Carol Channing. With a long Broadway run followed by a hit tour, the show helped to spur a '20s nostalgia wave and gave Channing star stature and, in "Diamonds Are a Girl's Best Friend," a lifelong anthem.

It was all changed for the movie, all of it. The show had only recently embarked on its tour when Twentieth Century-Fox paid a healthy $150,000 for the movie rights. There were some vague initial thoughts about casting Channing as Lorelei, which were replaced quickly with the awareness that another musical blonde was already under contract to the studio. This was Betty Grable, queen of the box office in the 1940s and, like Lorelei Lee, something of an American icon. For Grable, *Gentlemen Prefer Blondes* would be a welcome upgrade from the so-so fare she had recently been doing, half-forgotten things like *Call Me Mister* and *Meet Me after the Show*. Then, as the film began to take form, several things became evident: (1) Grable, after twelve years as a top star, was beginning to seem a bit shopworn. (2) The grosses of her recent films, which were never inexpensive to produce, were taking a downward turn and could no longer justify her vast salary. (3) Monroe was exploding. Even before the filming of *Niagara*, it was clear where she was headed. The main question was about her singing, since apparently no one at Fox had seen *Ladies of the Chorus*. When it became clear that she could handle the music, she was cast as Lorelei. Grable, in the process of making an ill-fitting rural romance called *The Farmer Takes a Wife*, knew immediately that it was all starting to wind down.[1]

---

[1] Tough and hardened show-biz veteran that she was, Grable was well aware that the likes of *The Farmer Takes a Wife* would not turn things around for her. Perhaps that's why she was heard to refer to that new film as *The Farmer Takes a Dyke* and, reportedly, *The Farmer Takes a Dump*. But give her

The other defining choices with *Gentlemen Prefer Blondes* came with the decisions to scrap the 1920s setting in favor of slick modernity, completely reconfigure the script of the show—itself a major rewrite of the book—and scrap all but three of the original songs. Even that remaining trio underwent major surgery, since "A Little Girl from Little Rock" was doubled to two little girls, and line upon line of salty lyrics were ruled impermissible by the censors. (There was no way, in "Diamonds," that a movie Lorelei would refer to men as "Goddam liars.") There was also some more generalized caution related to the star duo. Russell had made her fame in the 1940s with the notorious and dauntingly asinine Howard Hughes "sex western" *The Outlaw*, which spent a fair amount of its time in contemplation over how well she filled out her blouse. Monroe, for her part, had just gotten a boost from that calendar business. The Production Code people decided that the combination of these two required extra vigilance. Normally, the Code administrators (then usually known as the Johnston Office, after Eric Johnston, president of the Motion Picture Association of America) would simply caution a film's producers before the film went into production that costuming judged too revealing or, heaven forbid, indecent would not be acceptable. For *Blondes*, they went further, mandating that every single costume in the film worn by a female performer, including the chorus dancers, needed to be approved beforehand. Both Monroe and Russell emerged from these directives tightly wrapped and, for the most part, covered up. The exceptions included one Russell outfit that almost entered dominatrix territory and a tight gold number for MM (seen only from the back and briefly) that would later cause a near-riot when she wore it to a public function. For the most part, the wardrobe, especially for Monroe, is sleek, even elegant, and so direct and uncluttered as to verge on the timeless.

As those first seconds make clear, *Gentlemen Prefer Blondes* is on a different wavelength from other movie musicals of its time. *The Band Wagon*? No. And not *Singin' in the Rain*, *Calamity Jane*, or, back at Fox, *Call Me Madam*. Having already deviated from its source material, it wears its genre with nonchalance, only casually spotting musical sequences within the overall framework. Some of this was due to its division of creative duties. Howard Hawks, who had already worked with both stars, worked on the non-musical "plot"

credit; some months later, when she starred alongside MM in *How to Marry a Millionaire*, she was the epitome of a friendly and supportive colleague.

scenes.[2] Having famously directed meditations on male bonding (e.g., *Only Angels Have Wings*, *Red River*, etc.), Hawks turned here, for the only time in his career, to female comradeship. More than anything else—gold-digging, the battle of the sexes, Americans abroad—*Gentlemen Prefer Blondes* is a loving examination of how well a pair of friends can get along. With the role of Dorothy boosted up from the show, Russell and Monroe share approximately the same amount of screen time and, under Hawks's leadership, work together in a fashion that can only be called blissful. Their camaraderie onscreen is so palpable that it could hardly be faked, and it's nice to note that the friendship extended into real life as well. Russell, eternally laid-back and unpretentious off the screen as well as on, was able to function as a go-between when Hawks and Monroe were functioning on divergent wavelengths. The presence and influence of Natasha Lytess remained a thorny issue, however, and when Hawks had her banned from the set, MM stayed away until she was reinstated.

The other directorial presence on *Blondes* was that of choreographer Jack Cole, who had near-total dominion over the musical sequences. Hard-driving and nervy, Cole had been working in film for approximately a decade, usually with his own troupe of trained dancers and also some stars—Grable, Rita Hayworth, Mitzi Gaynor—who had sufficient ability to realize his imaginative and often intricate concepts. For *Gentlemen Prefer Blondes*, he was confronted with the challenge of making two sedentary creatures look like they could indeed dance. The sturdy Russell could move well but, like MM, had next to no experience. Cole's solution was, essentially, to have them dance from the waist up, constantly using gestures that coordinated with the music while, when necessary, strolling around. In the words of Cole's assistant, Gwen Verdon, "The ladies basically walked everyplace or they were carried everyplace, so they didn't really have to do dance steps." Even so, both stars worked hard during rehearsals, and when Russell was done for the day, Monroe would keep practicing. Not that it's difficult to look at them performing in the film and see that, no, they're not really dancing. They point and shimmy, with Monroe in particular doing something she would reprise in later films and also when she entertained the troops in Korea: both hands rise up to a position between the collarbones, followed by a quick twitch of

---

[2] Hawks was the initial director of *The Outlaw*, at least until he wearied of Hughes's constant meddling and quit, or was fired, or something in between. He and Russell got along famously, even though, as with MM, she was far from his ideal of on-screen feminine allure. "I never thought of either of them," Hawks later remarked, "as having any sex."

the shoulders that accentuates the breasts without being either too obvious or too vulgar. She does it in "Little Rock" and "Diamonds" and "When Love Goes Wrong," usually punctuating it with a sexily impish expression. "When Love Goes Wrong" also demonstrates some of the differences between the two women and their appeal. When they begin to shimmy side by side, Russell's moves and expressions are sunny and energetic. MM means it to be sexual.

Monroe and Russell each feature in a large production number with chorus, both quintessential Cole and, in quite different ways, classic. For MM, it's "Diamonds Are a Girl's Best Friend," in a staging added to the film very late in the day. Cole's initial concept was to have her in a Versailles kind of setting, seemingly draped in diamonds and little else as she fondles her jewels, with Verdon playing her attentive maid. The wardrobe tests show Monroe circled with bands of "rocks" over what appears to be a transparent layer of net. Ultimately, this was rejected, again due to all the post-calendar caution, and both Cole and designer Travilla were compelled to go back to the drawing board. The final concept put MM in a column of well-anchored pink satin (with a big bustle-like bow) against a fiery-red background. Cole's new staging employed a motif he had used a year earlier in MGM's *The Merry Widow*: a group of women in pink ball gowns with veils over their faces who back Monroe as she struts around with men in tuxedos. It's so vivid, and so definitive, that it's difficult to picture how that original concept might have worked, and MM holds the screen with possibly the most authority of her entire career. Coached rigorously by Cole and Verdon, she connects so completely with both the music and the wittily cynical words that more dancing on her part would likely have been superfluous, perhaps even detrimental. It's no wonder at all that this sequence has come to be the ultimate statement of who she was as a performer.[3]

The same is true—if in a somewhat baroque way—for Russell's big number, "Ain't There Anyone Here for Love?" The black-clad Russell saunters in the midst of a group of skimpily clad Olympic athletes who are far more

---

[3] Although the original "Diamonds" number was not shot, the banned dress itself did turn up in a later film. Well, sort of. The top section of the outfit was put on a darker and less provocative lower portion and worn by someone Fox was grooming to be an MM replacement, Sheree North, in *How to Be Very, Very Popular*. (North was playing a role that Monroe rejected. Strange are the currents of film history.) One of the "Diamonds" chorus boys, very prominent on-screen next to Monroe, is future *West Side Story* star George Chakiris, who later recalled how hard MM worked in rehearsal. This would be the first of three appearances he made in her films, the other two being in a dream sequence in *How to Marry a Millionaire* and in the gargantuan finale of *There's No Business Like Show Business*.

intent on working out with each other than in paying attention to her. The homoeroticism is about off the charts, and as always, Russell takes to her chores with bountiful and all-encompassing good humor. Such humor extended off-screen to her interactions with MM, Hawks, and Cole, all complex personalities in their own ways. She and Monroe always regarded their collaboration fondly, and many years later, she shared a singular memory about Cole. When she visited him at his home, she soon discovered, to her eye-rolling bemusement, that one of his hobbies was creating gay-porn needlepoint.

Russell's vocal style was as likable and relaxed as her demeanor, and she had already sung in films and made a number of studio recordings. Monroe's previous experience was a matter of *Ladies of the Chorus*, "Kiss" in *Niagara*, and some work with vocal coaches Fred Karger and Phil Moore (plus that well-liked performance in the Fox contract player revue in 1948 and her unreleased single). As it happened, she was an instinctively communicative vocalist, and she worked as hard with vocal coach Hal Schaefer as she did with Cole. It didn't hurt that her singing idols were Frank Sinatra and Ella Fitzgerald; she could and did borrow from both of them, especially in matters of phrasing, and she was always conscious of the connections that could be made between vocalism and characterization. In "Bye Bye Baby," shot by Hawks with notable interference from Lytess, she carefully molds the lines to coordinate with the dramatic situation and with Styne's music. In "Diamonds Are a Girl's Best Friend," she is constantly varying her tone to fit the changing moods of the piece. (And no, that's not her doing those operatic "No, no, no" roulades at the start of the number. That voice belongs to singer Gloria Wood.) As shot, the film had a couple of other numbers: "Down Boy," MM's admonition to Charles Coburn, and an elaborate French version of "Little Rock" performed by Monroe, Russell, and the chorus, with Verdon as lead dancer. In the great tradition of big musicals that shoot too many numbers and the even greater tradition of Darryl Zanuck exercising his often myopic power as an editor—too many musical numbers, he deemed—they were both removed. The recording of "Down Boy," surfacing after more than half a century, proved to be a delight, with MM effortlessly swinging up and down the scale like a seasoned pro. In the case of the "Little Rock" reprise, a few seconds can be spotted in the coming-attractions trailer. While many of Fox's cut sequences survived complete, these did not—unless they were spirited away into a private archive, where some jerk of a collector might savor the idea of having something that nobody else can see.

As important as Monroe's singing is to the success of *Gentlemen Prefer Blondes*, it's her comedy playing—alone and with Russell—that is the film's primary glory. Finally, the overdone diction finds a hospitable resting place in Lorelei's very deliberate way of speaking. "It's *Mine*, and I'm GoinG To *Keep* iT," she declaims about that tiara that's causing so much trouble, and her pronunciation is a perfect choice in its determination and in the careful overlay of "refinement." As can be seen over and over again, Lorelei has both a heart—she loves her millionaire as much as she loves diamonds—and a brain (albeit a brain that functions quite idiosyncratically). Except in a couple of low-comedy moments such as getting stuck in a porthole or trying to put the tiara around her neck, Monroe plays Lorelei as a woman completely in control of her life. In the next-to-last scene, she explains Lorelei's ethos to her prospective father-in-law with such clarity that the old man gawks in amazement at how smart she is. Money, she declares, isn't the main thing, but it's not chopped liver, either. And since autobiography can sometimes turn up in curious places, it's worth noting that tucked into Lorelei's reply to him is something Monroe herself apparently added to the script: "I can be smart when it's important. But most men don't like it."[4] Anyone who tags either Lorelei Lee or Marilyn Monroe as any sort of "dumb blonde" is trafficking in a rather bad case of projection. When Malone, the private detective tailing her, terms Lorelei "a mercenary nitwit," he's the fool, not her—and we've already seen Lorelei and Dorothy making an absolute laughingstock of him (in his boxers and wearing a frilly negligee, yet). Only compare the character Monroe plays here with that other "LL" she'd done for Hawks a few months earlier in *Monkey Business*. Lois Laurel truly was, to put it rudely, a dummy, and Monroe had no opportunity to do anything else with it. As Lorelei, with a substantial role and fine auspices and far greater self-confidence, MM comes into her own as an accomplished comedy performer. (Certainly, Lorelei's "mother," Loos, thought so when she saw the film.) No question about it, some of the attitudes in *Gentlemen Prefer Blondes* can seem dated after seven decades. How could they not? And some viewers will find a cringe or two somewhat justifiable. But don't weigh down this merry carnival as something

---

[4] Monroe's own wit and wisdom put her in good stead when, quite properly, she compared her own salary (probably somewhere south of $15,000) for *Blondes* to the $200,000 (or so) that the studio paid RKO and Hughes for Russell. Her irked comment was something along the lines of "After all, gentlemen, *I* am the blonde." Back in the fading glory days of the big studios, the denial of "equal pay for equal work" could even extend to sex symbols.

akin to a chauvinist victory. It's the women here—Monroe and Russell as well as their characters—who emerge in utter, absolute triumph.

Success—and overwork—can beget more of the same, and Monroe was rushed into another big film just a few days after finishing *Gentlemen Prefer Blondes*. A huge hit for Monroe and for Fox, *How to Marry a Millionaire* is one of those films that is airily enjoyable on its own terms yet acquires importance, even gravitas, with all its connections to history. It's rather odd how a slight, glossy piece like this can end up bearing so much weight and significance, for its studio, for its stars, for technology and sociology, and even, ultimately, for the history of television. First of all is its pedigree, which began with two Broadway comedies—*The Greeks Had a Word for It*, a hit in 1930, and *Loco*, a flop in 1946. *Greeks* (filmed in 1932, with "Them" substituted for "It" to keep the censors at bay) centered around a trio of high-class modern courtesans, while *Loco* made comparable use of one similar young woman, loose of morals and good of heart. *Greeks* would provide an equation that would be used again and again in the 1930s and '40s, most conspicuously at Twentieth Century-Fox: three women hunting for wealthy protectors and, for the most part, settling for love. At Zanuck's Fox, the scheme turned up over and over, sometimes with *Greeks* as the cited source material: *Ladies in Love*, *Three Blind Mice*, *Moon over Miami*, *Three Little Girls in Blue*. The details varied even as the basic premise stayed the same. It was, in this realm of popular cinema, a bankable proposition.

An even more time-honored trope came in the early 1950s with a determined move by the American film industry to lure audiences into movie theaters. While there had been lulls before, particularly during the Depression, an even greater threat was keeping audiences at home in 1952. Television had made alarming incursions into the viewing public, and grosses—already decimated after the breakup of the studio-theater monopolies—were taking a dive. To combat the drift, moviemakers resorted to several things not possible on those seventeen-inch screens: size, spectacle, color, plus, as with something on the order of *Niagara*, something too naughty for the tube. Spectacle had always been a go-to for producers, whether historical, musical, biblical, or simply scenic. The concept of size had usually applied to the scope of the production, but in the 1950s, it also began to refer to the actual movie screen itself, which in many cases doubled its dimensions in various formats. Cinerama was the first (and most technically complicated); then would follow CinemaScope, VistaVision, Todd-AO, and all the others. Plus, in a brief and somewhat illusory heyday, there was 3D. At Fox, studio president Spyros Skouras embraced a French photographic process that was promptly christened CinemaScope and had it hawked—with a nod to 3D-induced eyestrain—as "The Modern Miracle You See WITHOUT Glasses." Two productions were tagged to introduce the process: the religious spectacle *The Robe*, which had already been planned for the standard screen ratio, and *How to Marry a Millionaire*. The choice of these two projects was especially canny, since CinemaScope would not be their sole inducement. For *The Robe*, there would be all the Roman-epic trappings plus, well, God, and for *Millionaire*, there would be the movies' latest supernova, Marilyn Monroe.[5] The production of the two films, in spring 1953, was concurrent. *The Robe*, because of its size and the logistics of filming it twice (CinemaScope and "flat"), took longer to shoot. *Millionaire* was the first to wrap filming although the second to be released.

In addition to that new super-wide screen, both of the new CinemaScope features were demonstration pieces for another only-in-the-theater innovation: spacious multichannel stereophonic sound. This is what accounts for a part of *Millionaire* that has caused numerous heads to be scratched. Why on earth would this slick romcom start off with an elaborate on-screen overture? It is, specifically, Fox musical master Alfred Newman conducting a new arrangement of his *Street Scene* theme, originally written for the 1931 film. Newman had used it in a number of subsequent films to create a New York City ambience, and this was the biggest exposure it would ever get—specifically, to show off the stereo scope and clarity complementing the new twice-as-wide screen. There are myriad other inducements as well in this flashy display piece: vistas of Manhattan and snowy Maine, a couple of you-are-there moments that try for a 3D feeling, and an extended fashion show. Director Jean Negulesco handles his wider aspect with reasonable competence, more so, in fact, than that which his cohort, Henry Koster, was able to effect with the sanctimonious pageantry of *The Robe*. In unimaginative yet efficient fashion, Negulesco generally keeps the three stars (MM, Betty Grable, Lauren Bacall) lined up horizontally with a minimum of dead

---

[5] Monroe's introduction to CinemaScope actually preceded her appearance in *How to Marry a Millionaire*. During the production of *Gentlemen Prefer Blondes*, it was decided that "Diamonds Are a Girl's Best Friend" would be an effective way to demonstrate the glories of CinemaScope to theater owners. Accordingly, Monroe and the chorus were filmed doing "Diamonds" twice, once in the standard ratio and again in CinemaScope. The sequence was intended only to sell exhibitors on the new process, but it reached the public a year after MM's death as the finale of the Fox-produced (in CinemaScope) documentary *Marilyn*. Some have argued that the sequence is only a cropped version of the original number, which they say wasn't filmed twice, but no, it was. There are small, but detectable, differences between the two.

space on either side of the screen. While not an artist on the level of Hawks, he keeps things moving at a reasonably good pace, and he worked well with Monroe. At least, he did until there was the predictable brouhaha over the ever-present Lytess, who was dismissed and then reinstated after a Monroe bout of "illness."

In some ways, *How to Marry a Millionaire* could be seen as a trifecta, *Gentlemen Prefer Blondes* with three gold diggers instead of one. Truly, however, there's an entirely different vibe. Bacall, as the ringleader, is tough, sophisticated, and rather cold in ways that Jane Russell was not. This was, in fact, Bacall's first comedic role on-screen, and her skill with the sharp dialogue set the tone for much of her subsequent career. Grable, playing the role that Monroe had wanted, is a genial, come-what-may party girl, while MM's Pola is, again, less dim than she seems, her own personal haze coming less from ignorance than from naivete and, literally, myopia. She is, she explains, blind as a bat, and outlines her ethos by misquoting Dorothy Parker as "Men aren't attentive to girls who wear glasses." It was the spectacles, not surprisingly, that prompted Monroe's initial resistance to the role, and she was persuaded otherwise only after being shown the role's comic possibilities. The fog through which Pola perceives the world is, of course, figurative as well as literal, and it's only when she takes ownership of her own limitations—and keeps those specs on—that she finds fulfillment. The running gag about Pola's eyesight presented Monroe with some opportunities for physical comedy, and in typical fashion, she set about preparing for it as thoroughly as possible. She enrolled in classes given by the famed mime and eccentric dancer Lotte Goslar, who—as with most of MM's instructors— was impressed by her willingness to work hard and also her imaginative approach to building a character through movement. The results are there on the CinemaScope screen: Monroe moves with even more smooth assurance than she had in *Gentlemen Prefer Blondes*, and she makes a meal of Pola's running battle with clarity. One moment for the ages comes in a nightclub dressing room, as Pola—wearing a rather insane satin creation by Travilla— preens in front of a wide expanse of multiple mirrors. The effect, naturally, is to ratchet up Monroe's blatant appeal to near-infinity—and then Pola puts away her glasses, starts to head out, and, with a thud, runs straight into a wall.

An extended scene in the middle of the film sealed her triumph. Pola thinks she's on a plane to Atlantic City and, when her fog clears, finds out that it's headed instead for *Kansas* City. She strikes up a conversation with fellow passenger David Wayne, who encourages her to keep the glasses on.

The comedic give and take is outstanding, and it's especially significant for Monroe in that she's doing it in such a confined space. Compelled to act only with her face, voice, and hands, she uses all of them to bestow warmth and dimension on a limited character. She truly interacts with Wayne, and the business of putting on her glasses makes for one of her best comedic moments in any film. Pola's liberation when she realizes it's OK to wear them is both hilarious and rather touching, especially with the detectable glow that comes over Monroe's face. As she knew, she looks fairly terrible in those drab mid-'50s specs, but, like any accomplished comedian, and especially like Marie Dressler, she is able to turn away from personal vanity. Wayne later recalled that the scene was torturous to film, due both to MM and to CinemaScope. None of that shows.

"The Most Glamorous Entertainment of Your Lifetime," blared the ads for *How to Marry a Millionaire*, and in this case, the lack of understatement was at least comprehensible. The film was a massive hit, and it was noted at the time, and afterward, that Monroe had as much to do with this success as CinemaScope. She, not Grable, was the studio's new juggernaut, and while Grable's contract mandated that she be billed first on the screen, all the advertising gave MM the top spot. With less screen time than Grable and Bacall, she had no problem whatever pulling in the greatest attention. In truth, Grable handles the role of Loco with professional ease and good comedy timing, yet she lacks both Monroe's dazzle and Bacall's tart magnetism. Nor does it help that her hairstyle and wardrobe seem to hark back to her 1940s heyday, whereas those for Monroe and Bacall are more chic and forward-looking. Though not ready for retirement, Grable knew what was going on, and she famously passed her crown to MM by telling her, "Honey, I've had mine—now go get yours."

Since *How to Marry a Millionaire* was conceived specifically to show the world what television could not deliver, it's perversely fitting that it would later have a major connection in that very area. Eight years after it opened, *Millionaire* was the catalyst for something of a small cultural revolution: it was the opening-night lead-off for NBC's long-running series *Saturday Night at the Movies*. Until 1961—that now long-ago time of three major networks plus a handful of independents—movies were a commodity for local stations. A few films (notably *The Wizard of Oz*) had special network runs, and otherwise films were mainly fodder for the likes of afternoon and "late late" slots. NBC changed that by diverting recent films, all (in the first two seasons) from Twentieth Century-Fox, from local distribution to a far larger and more consequential national platform. The ballyhoo surrounding the first TV showing of *How to Marry a Millionaire* on September 23, 1961, nearly matched what it had gotten in 1953, and NBC's ratings were immense. Few of those many watchers, it might be mentioned, commented on how the limitations of the pan-and-scan format guaranteed that Monroe, Grable, and Bacall would seldom all be seen on the screen at the same time. (Nor, despite the network's "In Living Color" tag, was the film's Technicolor able to carry much weight in America's primarily black-and-white households.) NBC continued its MM-headlined streak over the next two years by starting off the show's second and third seasons with, respectively, *Gentlemen Prefer Blondes* and *The Seven Year Itch*, with her other major Fox titles, from *Monkey Business* to *Let's Make Love*, figuring in the lineup as well.[6] In her lifetime, the small screen could not contain her; after she died, it contributed vastly to her legend.

Crossover between film and its hated home-screen rival was still in its infancy when, on September 13, 1953, Monroe made her only "dramatic" television appearance, in the season premiere of *The Jack Benny Program* on CBS. In a sketch titled "Honolulu Trip," MM played Benny's dream-girl-made-flesh, singing "Bye Bye Baby" and using her Lorelei Lee whisper, complete with deliberate consonants, in an amusing mock love scene. Her warm rapport with Benny is especially noticeable when she comes back out for a post-sketch chat—still affecting the Lorelei voice—and plugs both *How to Marry a Millionaire* and CinemaScope. Looking especially slim in the same lace Travilla gown she would wear for the *Millionaire* premiere some weeks later, she manages enough professionalism to conceal almost every vestige of the terror she felt over appearing on live television. No coach alongside the camera, no possible retakes, and she gets through it beautifully. She does, however, run off the stage with undue speed when she's done, obviously relieved that it's all over. Unseen for many years, later resurrected on YouTube, this show is an irresistible souvenir to cap what, for her, had been a dazzling year. The acclaim was finally matching the ballyhoo, even as she herself was embarking for a long, sometimes frustrating quest for something more.

---

[6] Monroe died seven weeks before the second season kicked off with *Gentlemen Prefer Blondes*. The world was still processing the news, and NBC delicately framed the showing as a memorial tribute. Following the feature, Jane Russell reminisced about the film, and about Monroe, with as much commonsensical warmth as she had displayed in the movie itself.

1. 1951 star ascendant: A triumphant Monroe poses alongside her likeness on a billboard for Fox's *As Young As You Feel*. It doesn't bear a great resemblance to her, and she doesn't wear a gown like that in the film, yet it still must have been a good feeling.

2. Making a living: A slightly out-of-focus Monroe makes her first known film appearance in *Scudda Hoo! Scudda Hay!*, released in 1948. Natalie Wood and June Haver, in the foreground, were obviously primed to get the lion's share of the attention.

3. Ladies of burlesque: Monroe (age twenty-one) and Adele Jergens (age thirty) as mother and daughter in *Ladies of the Chorus*. In the buttoned-up-by-the-Production-Code time of 1948, stripper attire was more a matter of implication than actual hot-cha.

4. Having already spoken her thirteen words of dialogue, Monroe comes between Otto Waldis (being sinister) and Groucho Marx (lecherous, as always) in *Love Happy* (1949).

5. In *The Asphalt Jungle* (1950), Monroe enjoyed a host of blessings: great direction, a fine script, a superior cast, and, not least, outstanding photography and lighting. Here a luminous Angela Phinlay greets tough copper Andrews (Don Haggerty).

6. Appearing briefly: In *Love Nest*, Monroe was seen in her swimsuit little more than momentarily. However, for the still camera, she manages to make the sight a bit more revealing; no way, in 1951, would an actress in a studio film be permitted to expose her navel.

7. Monroe, in her blue jeans, with Keith Andes on the set of *Clash by Night* (1952). "Both are quite handsome but neither can act," griped the *New Yorker* critic. He was half right.

8. Upgrades: The disturbed babysitter in *Don't Bother to Knock* (1952) gave Monroe her largest and most challenging role to date. Here Nell plays dress-up with her employer's jewelry.

9. For *Niagara* (1953), Monroe was given top billing as well as an advertising concept that could fairly be termed monumental. Note the photo at bottom left, with Monroe and Denis O'Dea in a scene cut from the film.

10. On New Year's Eve 1952, more than halfway through the shooting of *Gentlemen Prefer Blondes*, this was still the Travilla gown in which Monroe would be performing "Diamond's Are a Girl's Best Friend." Weeks later, a new concept and design resulted in a more covered-up MM.

11. Just two little girls: Jane Russell and Monroe, as coached by Jack Cole and Gwen Verdon, make their moves in the opening scene of *Gentlemen Prefer Blondes* (1953).

12. Monroe with Jack Benny and Eddie ("Rochester") Anderson on the "Hawaiian Vacation" set for Benny's television show. While not exactly her television debut, it was her first appearance in that medium as a bona fide star—which, by September 1953, she indubitably was.

13. A film that never was: Monroe (in a *River of No Return* pose and costume) with Frank Sinatra, Van Johnson, Mitzi Gaynor, and Dan Dailey in an optimistic advance ad for the musical comedy that she refused to do.

14. Coda for "Chopsticks": Monroe and Tom Ewell in *The Seven Year Itch* (1955). It happens to her, the Girl Upstairs claims, all the time.

15. In *Bus Stop* (1956), Cheri (Monroe) and Bo (Don Murray) travel a long road to find mutual respect and understanding. On the screen and off, Monroe understood that very well.

16. In one of the most ebullient moments in *The Prince and the Showgirl* (1957), Elsie Marina (Monroe) does her "Coconut Girl" routine while the young, delighted King Nicolas (Jeremy Spenser) looks on.

17. Girlfriends: Daphne/Jerry (Jack Lemmon) and Sugar Kane (Monroe) share a drink in an upper berth. As familiar as we all are with *Some Like It Hot* (1959), it's still a little odd to see how it would have looked in color. Billy Wilder was right: those guys made more convincing women in black-and-white.

18. As George Cukor looks on enthusiastically, Jack Cole shows Monroe her moves for "My Heart Belongs to Daddy." If only the rest of *Let's Make Love* (1960) had been half as good as this number.

19. Parting shot: Monroe, Clark Gable, and Tom Dooley the dog. It's the final scene of *The Misfits* (1961) and of both their careers. Not even a better film than this could have ended on a more poignant note.

20. Monroe as Ellen Arden in the unfinished *Something's Got to Give*, on the set in May 1962. She's slim, elegant, hopeful, and a little fragile. Above all, she's quite beautifully sad.

7

Due Diligence

The three Marilyn Monroe films released in 1953 marked her breakthrough and, in significant ways, her peak. Both she and her studio reaped ample rewards, Fox with high grosses and Monroe with an almost unprecedented amount of fame and attention. Consequently, and small wonder, Fox was eager to keep her working—nonstop, if need be. She would star in two films released the following year, both of them expensive and, largely because of her, widely attended. If that sounds similar to what had come before, there was a difference. Her three hits of the previous year, including the flamboyant, outré *Niagara*, had been meticulously tailored to her needs, qualities, strengths, and appeal. They also showed that her approach and style owed very little to conventional acting methods (small "m") as they were understood in the early 1950s. A crucial reason they all succeeded was the fact that they paid attention to a verifiable truth: as an actor, Monroe was in her own sphere. *Niagara* pushed the blowtorch sex-bomb premise as far as it could go, and then, in *Gentlemen Prefer Blondes* and *How to Marry a Millionaire*, she created a defining persona that was unique and effective. The "Marilyn" she played in those films had been forged from her own study and hard work, plus the attentiveness of writers who understood her gifts, capabilities, and potential. She could do more than be Lorelei Lee, of course, but neither her studio nor even she always understood what might and might not be possible. Her two 1954 films demonstrated this in definite and somewhat unsettling ways, and she was by then a sufficiently astute judge of material to have not wanted to do either of them. The studio prevailed both times, and she suffered because of it.

River of No Return was designed to celebrate, or at least cash in on, a confluence of high-profile circumstances. There was Monroe herself, by now the most talked-about star in film; the sexy danger of Robert Mitchum, also near a career high point; some spectacular location footage, courtesy of an extended shoot in the Canadian Rockies near Banff, Alberta; and, once again, CinemaScope, whose wide vista was uniquely suited to capturing views of a stream that ran, in the words of the movie's title song, "wild and free."[1] Unfortunately, this collection of surefire ingredients was offset by some glaring deficiencies: a mediocre screenplay lacking clear character development; a director with little affinity for westerns or, really, any conventional action film; and, sadly and truly, Monroe herself. The lessons learned in her three previous films were either forgotten or disregarded here, where she's given a conventional gold-hearted saloon singer role far better suited to Maureen O'Hara or Yvonne De Carlo. No wonder, later on, she referred to *River of No Return* as a "Z cowboy movie, in which the acting finishes third to the scenery and CinemaScope."

Under any circumstances, it was debatable how well she would fit into something like this, and then the deal was sealed with the choice of director. Otto Preminger was, in a way, as idiosyncratic and uneven a talent as Monroe. Some things (like *Laura*) he could do abundantly well, while others, especially traditional genres such as musicals and comedies, might fall apart due to his unsuitability. Like MM, he had not been a willing participant in this particular exercise and, in his case, was working off a preexisting commitment with Fox. After this experience, he apparently vowed never again to direct a film that he did not also produce, and with only a couple of exceptions, he kept that promise.

Monroe, for her part, had been quick to voice her objections to the script. To placate her, Fox offered some empty assurances that rewrites and changes would make things better. She was finally persuaded to do it because of the four songs she would be performing, for which she demanded and got Jack Cole as choreographer. There would also be, of course, the by now inevitable, and problematic, presence of Natasha Lytess. Preminger, even more than others before him, found Lytess's presence disruptive and unnerving, which resulted in clashes between him and Monroe that were as predictable as anything in the script. (Once more, Lytess was banned from the set and then, at MM's insistence, reinstated.) When Monroe sprained her ankle during the river shoot, there were many who thought it was actually a ploy to defeat

---

[1] In the grand tradition of location shooting, multiple rivers were called on to play the title role—four in Canada plus the Salmon River in Idaho. The scenery really is thrilling—at least, when it's not being undercut by the exceptionally obvious closer shots made on a soundstage in front of a process screen. Using a process screen was standard procedure in those days, as anyone watching *The Ten Commandments* can testify. In this case, the bracing beauty of the location work shows up the trickery pretty badly, as when Monroe, Mitchum, and Tommy Rettig are out on an untamed river in the middle of the wilderness, and neither the light, the wind, nor the water seems to be coming from quite the right direction.

Preminger. Apparently, there genuinely had been some kind of injury, at least enough to summon Joe DiMaggio up to Canada for consolation.

After all the scenic grandeur and personal conflict in Banff, *River of No Return* resumed filming at Fox—repeatedly, in fact, since some of Preminger's original footage was so lifeless and disconnected that Darryl Zanuck ordered Jean Negulesco to shoot extensive retakes several months later. When released in the spring of 1954, it made a good deal of money—though not as much as MM's previous three films—and most reviewers were content to comment on the scenery, both natural and human. For her part, MM had by then been assured by her agent and studio people that her work on the film had been outstanding. Thus, it was an awful surprise for her to see a review in the high-visibility *Hollywood Reporter*:

> If *River* proves anything at all, it is that Marilyn Monroe should stick to musicals and the type of entertainment that made her such a box office lure. If the film fails to bring in smash returns, 20th-Fox can attribute it to Marilyn's inability to handle a heavy acting role.

Reportedly, she screamed when she read it. What meager compensation it was for her to know that her initial feelings about the script had been correct. And what was worse, her performance deserved every harsh word of it. Except for her songs, some byplay with talented kid actor Rettig, and a few sequences where she doesn't speak, this is the worst performance of her career.

Granted, she had not always been successful with serious drama before this; her moments of overdrive in *Don't Bother to Knock* had shone a light on her inability to handle conventional melodramatics, as had her long-ago test for the aborted *Cold Shoulder* and that one overdone moment on the telephone in *Niagara*. Monroe simply did not have those particular skills at her disposal. Here she relied heavily, and wrongly, on help from Lytess and on her own misguided instincts. It's easy to see why she was compelled to do this, since the script—which began as a kind of frontier version of *The Bicycle Thief*—was more a random collection of scenes and notions than a coherent narrative. Kay, the character she played, seems to have almost no backstory apart from her "career" as a saloon singer and her romance with a worthless gambler (Rory Calhoun). Otherwise, mainly and literally, she's along for the ride, sporting a shirt and jeans that fit her as snugly as any of her dance-hall costumes. Some of the inconsistencies in the narrative—as when Mitchum suddenly attempts to rape her (yes, really)—came as a result of retakes and rewrites, done with an eye less toward conviction than toward commerce.[2] This is also one of those dreadful Hollywood movies that portray indigenous people as a faceless band of marauding, subhuman savages; when they finally make their way to the raft bearing Mitchum, Monroe, and Rettig, the very first thing one of them does is to rip Monroe's shirt off her body.

Shooting a Preminger film frequently meant that the director would single out one actor, male or female, for special treatment of an especially brutal sort—Jean Simmons in *Angel Face*, Tom Tryon in *The Cardinal*, Dorothy Dandridge in *Porgy and Bess*, and on and on. For *River of No Return*, it was Monroe, whose amorphous mien and reliance on Lytess triggered some notably violent directorial outbursts. Perhaps, then, the low spots of her performance might be seen as conscious attempts to undermine the work of a hated taskmaster. That was obviously the case at one point on location when, in the midst of an exhaustively meticulous camera setup, she stopped in mid-shot to announce that she had to go to the bathroom, a stunt that left the normally explosive Preminger speechless. Generally, her performance seems to have been the result of a rather desperate and misguided attempt to add substance—any kind of substance—to an underwritten role. She careens constantly between wooden, heavy-voiced stolidity and eye-popping over-statement, and it goes without saying that the overstressed consonants are in full flower. One moment in particular is so wince-worthy that it has become something of a rallying cry for those jerks who still try to insist that she couldn't act. When Mitchum asks her how she could hook up with a creep like Calhoun, she enunciates the reply, "He didn'T treaT me like a tramP. He treaTeD me like a WOMAN." Her facial expression here is as unnatural as her diction, and the wonder is that this wasn't reshot along with the rape scene.

Monroe does connect with the role—or, at least, with being a resourceful performer—when she sings. *Gentlemen Prefer Blondes* was opening just as production was starting, and her reviews may have buoyed her with far more self-assurance in handling music rather than dialogue. (This was certainly the case a couple of months later, when she was able to overcome her terror

---

[2] Talk about adding insult to injury: upon Zanuck's directive, the almost-rape scene was shot months after the rest of the film. Then he decided that it needed to be reshot to make it hotter and more violent. (Perhaps he thought of those two things as one and the same.) By way of suggestion, he sent a memo musing that "Maybe we could suggest that she gives him the knee in the crotch." Then, when it came time to make up the posters and ad art, guess which scene was featured most prominently?

of live performance to entertain the troops in Korea.) She projects wistful drama in two ballads ("One Silver Dollar" and the title song), folksy charm in "Down in the Meadow," and lusty extroversion in "I'm Gonna File My Claim." Like Jack Cole, vocal coach Hal Schaefer worked patiently with her, and in this case, the closeness of the relationship eventually spilled over into so personal a realm that he attempted suicide over her. The professional aspects of the collaboration, at least, were quite positive, and her singing is more varied and communicative than ever. Under Schaefer's tutelage, she learned to employ the breathy whisper of her comedy playing to punctuate the slower numbers, while for a boisterous piece like "I'm Gonna File My Claim," she cultivated an amusingly rowdy belt and, for good measure, a few Mae West inflections. One of her most distinctive vocal attributes was a quick vibrato on sustained higher notes, used subtly here and more frequently later on, especially in *Let's Make Love*. For a perpetually insecure performer, she seems to have built up a fair amount of confidence about her gifts as a singer, and it should be noted that after shooting *River of No Return*, she signed a recording contract with RCA Victor. As it turned out, her only discs for RCA would be her studio tracks of "I'm Gonna File My Claim" and the title song and, a few months later, an "extended-play" disc of songs from *There's No Business Like Show Business*. Several more cuts were not released until after her death, and the pity is that she did not lay down enough tracks for RCA to make up an entire LP. In particular, the Irving Berlin oldie "You'd Be Surprised" is sly and, in both senses of the word, quite fresh. Those Frank Sinatra and Ella Fitzgerald records she liked to play were quite a good influence.

Apart from her songs and the well-shot scenery, *River of No Return* manages some good moments amid the mediocrity. Mitchum was one of the few Monroe leading men with any kind of sexual smolder, his laconic sensuality counterpointed intriguingly with her more blatant presentation. In a better-realized script, without an attempted rape thrown in, they might have made an interesting team. Tommy Rettig was one of the more talented child actors around this time, and his rapport with MM, on-screen and off-, was relaxed and positive. She genuinely enjoyed being around children and had already done good work with little George Winslow in *Gentlemen Prefer Blondes*. Rettig would remain one of her best on-screen acting partners, and she even served as his sort of date a few months later for the premiere of his film *The 5,000 Fingers of Dr. T*. It remains that, for the most part, *River of No Return* would always be for her the model of the kind of work she did not want to do. In her entire filmography, it may be the single entry that shows most starkly both the things she did really well and those she could not handle.

It was a long ten months, following the main shoot of *River*, before Monroe began making another film. For a star under contract to a big studio in those days, that could constitute a make-or-break gap for a career. In this case, it was hardly a time of idleness, let alone anything like a vacation. Indeed, it was one of the pivotal times of her life, with major moves and decisions on both professional and personal fronts. There were, most famously, her marriage to DiMaggio in January 1954 and her appearance before the troops in Korea the following month. Just as important, this was the time of her decision to wrest control of her career away from her studio. From early on in her Fox contract, she had been frustrated by the stark contrast between her burgeoning fame and the desultory, even demeaning treatment the studio seemed to constantly give her. This, it seemed to her, was an indicator that Zanuck and the other decision makers did not believe in her ability, while at the same time being quite willing to cash in on her name. *Don't Bother to Knock*, equivocal success that it was, had been a meek demonstration that the situation might possibly be getting better, and she had finally proven herself with the three major successes of 1953. But then came *River of No Return*, which—even before the bad reviews—she felt did not indicate a fitting direction for her acting career. The financial component was a major factor as well. DiMaggio and agent-producer Charles Feldman were chief among those advising her that she was worth more, and deserved better, than what she was getting. Accordingly, around the time that *How to Marry a Millionaire* opened, Monroe began to confront some situations and resolve to make some changes. It was, for her, a kind of rebellion, and much of it centered around a new film that seemed to epitomize her entire situation.

Although posterity and biographers have given this film the title *The Girl in Pink Tights*, surviving evidence shows that it was generally called, simply, *Pink Tights*.[3] The title alone seemed to carry connotations of tawdry things, the precise kind of exploitation that she was now seeking to move past. Nor was the situation improved with the awareness that this was going to be Fox's newest manifestation of its time-honored and timeworn practice of recycling. In this case, it was a matter of Fox taking shards and splinters from

---

[3] *The Girl in Pink Tights* was actually a current title at that time—just not for the new Monroe project. Instead, it was a short-lived 1954 Broadway musical featuring the piquant Zizi Jeanmaire. It's even been written that Monroe was set to star in a film version of the show—which, given that her film was due to shoot months before the show even opened, would have been quite a feat.

its old films and assembling them into a new (yet not really) entity. Again, the accepted historical account is in error, because it's been frequently stated that *Pink Tights* was intended as a remake of Betty Grable's 1943 hit *Coney Island*. But the *Pink Tights* plot was quite unlike that of *Coney Island*, which Grable herself already had remade seven years later as *Wabash Avenue*. Instead, *Pink Tights* was less remake than reiteration, a continuation of the basic formula that Fox used with Grable (and occasionally with others) through most of the 1940s and into the '50s. Call it *Coney Island* or *Mother Wore Tights* or any of the others, it was a retread of the same routine that made audiences love Grable until they grew tired of the legs-and-songs standardization that marked so many of her films. The plot devices in *Pink Tights* were lifted all but verbatim out of the Grable/Haver playbook: Jenny, a straitlaced Boston schoolteacher, is engaged to a stuffy medical student whose family is status-rich and cash-bereft. Taking matters into her own hands, Jenny casts aside all apprehension and goes to New York to earn money for his schooling. She ends up, clad in the title garment, shimmying in a Bowery dive managed by Frank Sinatra, alongside a song-and-dance team (Dan Dailey and Van Johnson) and a soubrette (Mitzi Gaynor). She quickly becomes a scandalous success and, by the end of it, has thrown aside her disapproving fiancé for the pugnacious but sexy Sinatra. It was a frayed and seedy thing, albeit decked out with new songs by Jule Styne and Sammy Cahn, including "Run for Your Life," "The Hottentot," and "I've Got the Best Shoulder in Town."

Fox had announced *Pink Tights* as Monroe's next film in July 1953 and ordered her to report for rehearsals beginning on December 7. At no time during that entire period did the studio send her a script or indicate anything more than some bare outlines and credentials: it was to be a period musical shot in CinemaScope, produced by Sol Siegel (from *Gentlemen Prefer Blondes*), and directed by Henry Koster. She did, however, get a grapevine report that it was a Grable redo with all the clichés intact, emblazoned with an even crasser title than anything Grable had been handed. There was also the matter of salary. Monroe would be top-billed and paid her contracted $1,500 per week; Sinatra, newly resurgent after *From Here to Eternity*, would be getting a weekly salary of $5,000. None of this, for Monroe, portended anything in the way of respect or regard. She also knew what would happen. "It's just not in the same league as *Gentlemen Prefer Blondes*," she told a reporter, after finally having had the opportunity months later to see the script. "If I'd done *Pink Tights*, there would have been 'Yellow Tights,' 'Blue Tights,' and 'Green Tights' afterwards."

The entire *Pink Tights* business coincided with a Fox film that Monroe did want to do. *The Egyptian* was to be the studio's main prestige project for 1954, with an even starrier cast than *Pink Tights*. The title role in the ancient world epic was to be played by Marlon Brando, as hot a name as Monroe and with a great deal more critical esteem. Monroe was eager to be cast as Nefer, literally a whore of Babylon who drives said Egyptian to a sizable amount of personal degradation. A (putatively) serious role alongside Brando indicated the kind of career direction she was actively seeking, and she offered to play Nefer in a screen test. Zanuck refused to give this any consideration, having already earmarked the role for his own protégée-slash-mistress. Bella Darvi was a Polish-born adventuress with a fair amount of physical allure, an addiction to gambling, and no vast dramatic ability. It was her casting, as much as anything else, that caused Brando to walk off *The Egyptian*, and it also helped Monroe to wake up and smell the coffee. Fox and Zanuck wanted her only for projects that were cheap in spirit if not in budget, and it was a simple and logical thing to focus her dissatisfaction on Zanuck, who plainly had next to no regard for her as an actress and, likely, a person. It's hard, in any case, to imagine her in a film like *The Egyptian*, vamping men to their doom while decked out in gold lamé, several pots of eye shadow, and a big blue wig. Whether she would have been less ridiculous a Nefer than Darvi—not that high a hurdle, granted—may be irrelevant. What is incontestable is that *The Egyptian*, along with *Pink Tights*, marked a turning point.

Monroe's conflict with her studio was—along with pressure from the gentleman himself—a leading part of the impetus that convinced Monroe to marry DiMaggio. One salient factor in this famously ill-starred union was that he had no interest whatsoever in her film career, although he did give her advice in her rebellion against Fox. On their trip to Japan in February 1954, they were both handed a graphic indication, in the near-riotous reception she was given, of just how famous she was. This irked DiMaggio and at the same time showed Monroe how much more she deserved than the treatment she was getting at Fox. The adulation was multiplied when she gave ten performances before the troops in Korea. Enough footage of those performances survives to demonstrate both the enthusiasm (a weak word, certainly) of the soldiers and her own professionalism. It might have been sufficient for her simply to show up, especially in that flimsy cocktail dress that did nothing to protect her against bone-chilling temperatures. Yet she did more, putting on a show with improvised comic patter and songs and some Cole moves recycled from *Gentlemen Prefer Blondes*. "Diamonds Are a Girl's Best Friend" was naturally on the program, as were "Bye Bye Baby" and George Gershwin's "Do It Again," which was judged so provocative that the lyric had to be changed to "Kiss Me Again." (Her contemporaneous recording of the song, studded with gasps and heavy breathing, demonstrates that the army brass was not being totally unreasonable in wanting to keep a lid on things.) However terrified she may have been about live performance, however difficult the logistics, and whatever she may have felt about doing it all without the guidance of Cole or Lytess, she was triumphant.[4] She returned to the States physically weakened by pneumonia but feeling professionally emboldened. The suspension by Fox only strengthened her resolve to change her path, and the studio finally appeared to yield to her demands. *Pink Tights* went away for good, and she was lured back to the studio with a constellation of inducements: a bonus, the possibility (later denied) of director and script approval, the right to make only two films per year, and, potentially, the opportunity to star in the Broadway hit *The Seven Year Itch*. These maneuvers account for why, in the spring of 1954, she was called upon to participate in what is likely the most peculiar film of her career.

It's always been recounted that Monroe was coerced into doing *There's No Business Like Show Business* solely because of *The Seven Year Itch*; in other words, if she did one, she would get the other, essentially bribing her into something hardly less onerous than the detested, ultimately defunct *Pink Tights*. If there is some accuracy in that account, there's more to the story. By 1954, Irving Berlin had been working in film for a quarter century, since the very beginning of movie musicals. This, of course, was in addition to his other fields of triumph, which included the theater, the world of popular song, and, by extension, the whole of American pop culture. For Berlin, movies were an especially gainful endeavor, since he could be paid upfront (plus, sometimes, a percentage) for his songs—and the use of his name—and then there would be radio play and high sales numbers from sheet music and records. While he didn't care for the comparative loss of autonomy in dealing with studios, the association could be massively beneficial. This had been the case in 1938 with Fox's *Alexander's Ragtime Band*, the first of several Berlin-oriented films that spotlighted a cluster of old and new songs under the umbrella of a slim

---

[4] The entire *Pink Tights* debacle had marked a change in her relationship with Lytess, whom DiMaggio loathed (the feeling was mutual) and from whom MM had been growing somewhat distant personally. Following instructions from Fox, Lytess urged MM to bite the bullet and show up for the *Pink Tights* rehearsals. Monroe viewed this as a betrayal, and in less than a year, their association was kaput.

plot. *Holiday Inn*, in 1942, had given the world "White Christmas," and *Blue Skies*, four years later, was a sizable hit despite some glaring faults. Then, in 1948, came perhaps the most popular of all the Berlin "medley" shows: *Easter Parade*, with an unusually good musical program and natty performances by Judy Garland, Fred Astaire, and Ann Miller.

By the 1950s, the Berlin formula was beginning to wind down, yet he still had the clout to wangle lucrative deals for two final ventures. At Paramount, there was *White Christmas*, something of a reworking of *Holiday Inn*, while at Fox, Berlin's music was the focus, if not the entire cause, of *There's No Business Like Show Business*. That upbeat anthem had been featured in Berlin's *Annie Get Your Gun*, and now it would be the motto for a grab bag of sentimental family drama, musical numbers, and exhausting production values. Even in 1954, a year or so before the explosion of rock and roll, such a configuration was on the passé side of the movie equation, which hardly deterred Berlin and Zanuck from seeing some lucrative possibilities. So did Paramount with *White Christmas*, but that was something of a contained, prepackaged item; *There's No Business Like Show Business*, with all its CinemaScope, DeLuxe Color sound and fury, strayed close to dementia. The fact that Monroe came to be part of it made it, of course, even wilder. She's so far from backstage-movie tradition that her presence in the film becomes as disruptive as her character is to the show-biz family at its center. And as if that weren't enough, things are thrown even further off-kilter with the presence, in the bosom of said family, of Johnnie Ray. Among 1950s pop singers, Ray was a bizarre comet, singing weepy ballads while giving the impression that a nervous breakdown might kick in before he reached the coda. This would be his only major film appearance, though it had been Zanuck's stated impression—and remember, this is a work of nonfiction—that Ray's acting talent might be every bit as abundant as that of Bella Darvi.

Berlin, whose name was emblazoned above the title of *There's No Business Like Show Business* (as was Zanuck's, at least in the screen credits), was not only the main reason for that film's existence, but was largely the cause of Monroe being in it. While claiming not to be familiar with her film work, he knew who she was and how she looked, and he insisted that the script be changed to make her part of the show. Thus, by December 1953, a screenplay already long in the works had been reconfigured to allow for the presence of Monroe in what was essentially a supporting role. A little later, during that shaky time when Fox was still intending to make *Pink Tights* with or without MM, the studio's new contractee, Sheree North, was announced for

Pink Tights and under serious consideration for *Show Business*, which was scheduled to roll after the completion of *Pink Tights*.[5] Then, with *Pink Tights* being put on the shelf, Monroe was persuaded to do *Show Business* as, essentially, a kind of good-faith gesture, with her contract demands and *The Seven Year Itch* as unofficial incentives. Although many of those demands were ultimately not met, Fox did accede to her stipulations regarding her participation in the Berlin project. The ubiquitous (if increasingly problematic) Lytess would be allowed on the set, and although the remainder of the film would be choreographed by Robert Alton and costumed by Miles White, Monroe insisted that she be dressed by Travilla and have her musical numbers staged by Jack Cole. None of this gave her much satisfaction, and it is hardly a coincidence that *There's No Business Like Show Business* would end up as the first Monroe film made in an atmosphere of near-constant crisis. There were, as there would be later, a network of causes for this: dissatisfaction with the material and with director Walter Lang; anemia and other illness, some of it a remnant of the Korea tour; increasing reliance on medication; and a marriage moving rapidly toward its unhappy end. All these manifested themselves in delays more incessant than ever before. Costar Gaynor, a show-biz pro from an early age, would later recall the constant waiting for Monroe to make it onto the set and the unending retakes needed after she blew her lines.

Surely this movie can be seen as an outlier, even a white elephant, in the Monroe canon, yet even taking into account its intrinsic strangeness, it's far from a total loss. First, and most famously, there are her musical numbers, which inspired the only enthusiasm she could muster. Having continued her vocal coaching with Schaefer, she had become—even in a film that gives Ethel Merman top billing—a more assured singer than ever. Perhaps it's best to listen to the recordings separately, given the lurid and occasionally overly busy things Cole gave her to do. More so than in *River of No Return*, her singing is both vivid and compelling, if notably outside the "conventional" Berlin mainstream. "Heat Wave" is wittily arranged to spotlight personality over vocal chops, and when called on to move past her trademark breathiness to produce some vocal heft, she does so quite ably. "After You Get What You Want, You Don't Want It" is a real Berlin curio, a kind of ricky-tick ragtime piece from 1920 that almost everyone had forgotten. For Monroe, it's taken at

---

[5] North, a gifted dancer who was not happy being seen as a clone of MM, eventually found her own path, including a worthy latter-day career as a character actor. Art sort of imitated life when, in 1980, she played Gladys Baker, Monroe's mother, in a TV movie.

a flexible tempo that gives her a chance to swing out, and several biographers have observed that she may have found a good deal of private resonance in some of the Berlin lyrics. Among a number of attractive details, perhaps the most striking is the way she starts the second chorus, a wry downward slide on "'Cause" that seems to distill the meaning of the entire song into one measure. If anything, "Lazy" is even more effective, a slow glide in which her sophisticated languor confidently reminds the listener that Ella Fitzgerald is an excellent role model.

In her insistence on Travilla and Cole, Monroe was exercising some clout for one of the first times in her career, at least apart from her ongoing insistence on Lytess. Unfortunately, Travilla's gowns have little of the uncluttered smartness of her clothes in *Gentlemen Prefer Blondes* and *How to Marry a Millionaire*; it appears that every surface required some kind of decoration or enhancement. This was hardly an accident, since the reigning aesthetic of the production was to make everything big, ornate, and conspicuous. In the final number, Merman wears an oversized white concoction fitted out with a bodice that has something resembling tentacles. When asked about the over-the-top nature of the clothes, Miles White recalled, "That was how Zanuck wanted it."[6] Travilla followed suit with Monroe. In one scene in which she's ostensibly wearing street clothes, Monroe has a pair of triangle-shaped earrings so outsized that they seem to be signaling to the Masons in the audience. The supposedly rented gown she wears for "After You Get What You Want" is less suited for an unknown chanteuse than for a top-billed showgirl, with sequins, starbursts covering her breasts, and an enormous bird-of-paradise headpiece. Even her rehearsal outfit for "Lazy" is accessorized with a *big* blue bow around her waist that would have been more at home on a birthday gift. Most famous is her "Heat Wave" ensemble, which can best be described as Carmen Miranda on hallucinogens and becomes even more blatant because of the way Cole instructs her to move in it.

Any moral fire Monroe had drawn before this film paled in comparison with the outcry that would greet her musical numbers here, particularly "Heat Wave." Some of the outrage seems pretty quaint, all in all, particularly a heated declaration from Ed Sullivan that she had no business doing such

---

[6] Quite likely, it was White's longtime association with Ringling Bros. and Barnum & Bailey that led to his hiring, since Merman frequently looks like she's part of the circus. Gaynor fares a bit better, especially in the last scene, where her timeless red sheath contrasts blatantly with Merman in that white monstrosity and Monroe, whose dress looks like it could stand up on its own, without a person inside.

performances in a movie that included a priest—as played by Johnnie Ray, yet—among its leading characters. (A concept for further examination might be MM as a catalyst of sacrilege.) Some of it is the song itself, which was always considered somewhat, if you will, steamy. A few years after Monroe did it, Gale Storm performed "Heat Wave" on her *Oh, Susanna!* sitcom and ran into a few protests for an interpretation that was actually rather genteel; perhaps people were still reeling from what Monroe and Cole had conjured up. It's clear that both of them were working hard to pull the focus away from Merman and all that music and production. Lacking Merman's decibel power and the dance skill of Gaynor and Donald O'Connor, they opted for a piquant combination of wit and shock. With its leaping, lightly clad chorus boys and its fire and smoke, it starts hot, and then Monroe enters, constantly manipulating her open skirt to make it look like she's flashing the audience. At one point, she even—and it can only be phrased this way—humps a tree. It's fun, certainly, even as something about the way she performs doesn't quite connect. Her eyes seem glazed and almost dead, as if she's not quite present despite her vivid physicality, and it's also worth noting that there was a rather unpleasant on-the-set scene with DiMaggio while she was filming the number.[7]

"After You Get What You Want, You Don't Want It" is a solo number, which means that Monroe is far more exposed. She had worked solo in *River of No Return* as well but in confined spaces. Here she has a large performance area, which compelled Cole to make her move excessively in a way that undercuts the song. As usual, Cole gives her gestures in place of dance moves. These are less effective here than in *Gentlemen Prefer Blondes*, especially a kind of shadow-boxing motion that is repeated so often that it becomes tiresome. It all seems more a collection of mannerisms than a truly cohesive performance, busy and even aggressive in a flashy way that corresponds too well with that beplumed and overdone getup she's wearing. If she's playing a hopeful near-unknown, she's comporting herself more like an over-the-hill diva who's trying too hard. Even as no one would expect this film to display

---

[7] Call it iconic or lewd or plain weird, "Heat Wave" has any number of odd aspects. Due to her recording contract with RCA, Monroe was not on the original soundtrack album released by Decca, in which her songs were taken by Dolores Gray. MM's own released version of "Heat Wave" is in part an alternative take using a more kittenish kind of Lorelei voice. As heard in the film, her "What's your name, honey?" is possibly her most aggressive delivery ever. Jack Cole was never opposed to borrowing from himself, and just before he staged "Heat Wave" with MM he choreographed the Betty Grable musical *Three for the Show* for Columbia Pictures. Sure enough, Grable's "How Come You Do Me?" is, at points, a dead ringer for "Heat Wave," especially in its design. Monroe's film was released first, so it appeared that Grable was doing the knock-off, instead of the other way around.

recognizable human emotions, something like this is exceptionally false. The contrast between the look of her performance and her suave, coolly assured vocalism is odd and, it must be said, perversely fascinating. (Much in this movie is either perverse or fascinating. This is both.)

"Lazy" is better, primarily because it's conceived, with witty resourcefulness, in such a fashion as to allow O'Connor and Gaynor to dance rings around her. In fact, when she rises from her chaise to join them, the camera cuts away, giving the impression, possibly accurate, that her section of the dance was eliminated because she couldn't handle it.

Even as her three numbers constituted her main participation in this oversized bash—the costliest Fox film, in fact, in a long while—she was also given a character to enact. (Sort of.) Vickie Parker resembles Marilyn Monroe in ways that are hardly a coincidence: she changes her name and her agent, she has improbably lofty dramatic aspirations, she works hard on her diction, and, most onerously, she's an opportunist who is suspected of sleeping with those who can benefit her career. There's enough autobiography, in fact, to create a bit of anticipation that a baseball player might be coming through the door. With little help from director Lang, Monroe handles most of this with sturdy professionalism—except when she overdoes the consonants—but it's rather apparent that parts of the role have been molded to exploit many of the worst things people (and Zanuck) were thinking about her. As was noted at the time, and forever afterward, her romantic chemistry with O'Connor is odd, to say the least, though they both try gallantly to seem interested in each other. The Merman character has the most animosity toward her—which was not in total contradiction to how things played out off camera—and when Merman and Monroe finally have a scene together, it's quite the dazzling mismatch of personalities. One has her take-charge-and-just-say-the-lines attitude, while the other seems to be feeling her way into the moment and thinking about motivation. Two startlingly disparate planets pass each other without quite making contact. It's really mesmerizing.

Monroe had done something of a good soldier turn to play Vickie Parker, and for her trouble, she did get rewarded. More, possibly, than Fox, since the grosses for *There's No Business Like Show Business*, given its huge cost, were disappointing. MM went immediately—as in overnight—into *The Seven Year Itch*, and since she had been judged responsible for the delays that caused one film shoot to run without a break into another, there was little to be done other than show up and do the work. The difference would lie in the material, the director, her own engagement, and, ultimately, the achievement.

8

No Name Required

It is quintessential Marilyn Monroe, as well as the pivot point for her entire career. Everything changed with, and after, *The Seven Year Itch*, as much because of what it wasn't as because of what it was. *There's No Business Like Show Business* was completely devoted to looking back at the past, which was why Monroe's participation in it was so transgressive. In contrast, *The Seven Year Itch* looked forward, albeit with propriety, caution, and a leer or two. Its contradictions were so plentiful that it gave MM ample license and validation even as she came to feel that it hindered her. She had wanted to do it, desperately, and yet she soon believed that it would not be, or provide, what she needed. In this, it set the tone for most of her later work, where the highest of hopes would frequently come crashing amid a great deal of disillusionment. (Cue, perhaps, her recording of "After You Get What You Want, You Don't Want It.") Part of the problem, for her, was that, as with so much of her work, the iconography—all swirling white skirts and parted lips—seemed to obscure what she had tried to achieve. For neither the first nor the last time, the sensation concealed the art.

While it would have been enough that *The Seven Year Itch* provides us with Monroe at her most intrinsic, it does far more. On stage and on film, it is a wry summation of what much of the 1950s was about. From first to last, it is a work about sex and everything that was thought at that time to pertain to sex—up to and including Marilyn Monroe, who is mentioned by name in the course of the movie. The play, naturally, had been permitted to be a good deal more frank, not a surprise given the operatives of censorship in the Hollywood cinema of 1954. The most troublesome aspect came with the fact that the sex it proffered was connected solely with adultery. Even Broadway, in 1952, had been startled by a comedy that dealt head-on with a husband who yields to temptation while his wife and son are out of town. Moreover, the husband was such an ordinary specimen of randy manhood that the play was able to assume a universality that made adultery seem an everyday kind of thing. (It was, and it is. Just don't talk about it.) This schlub, with his daydreams and suspicions and baggage, was American Everyman, a true son of the paternalistic Ike then occupying the White House. (And, as was learned later on, Eisenhower himself had not been immune from adulterous impulses.) In both the play and the film, the concept of an unexceptional protagonist was underscored with the casting of Tom Ewell, surely one of the most nondescript-seeming actors who ever lived. In his look and manner and voice, Ewell seemed to embody manhood in its least memorable form, the sort of person many might prefer to think of as asexual, save for the fact that sex would never be off-topic in his own mind.

The character Ewell played, Richard Sherman, obviously had a fair amount in common with George Axelrod, who wrote the play and co-scripted the movie. (Sherman observed his fantasies as if they were movies; Axelrod put his down on paper and dramatized them.) The playwright seems to have understood a good deal less about women, which is one reason the young woman who creates such a fuss in the play and in the film does not have a name. Axelrod later claimed that he couldn't come up with the right name for her, which helps give her so evanescent a quality that people often wonder if, in fact, she's a real person. Or is she, in fact, simply the most fleshed-out of the Sherman fantasies that run all through the play? On Broadway, the role of the Girl Upstairs had been taken by Vanessa Brown, a pert and attractive young brunette who, despite her appeal, did not seem impossibly unattainable. On film, in CinemaScope and DeLuxe Color, it becomes Marilyn Monroe, so terminally a bombshell that she often seemed to be something other than simply human. Thus did the balance of the dynamic begin to shift from what it had been on Broadway. Some critics in 1955 felt that MM's Girl was too real (some would have said fleshed-out) to fit Axelrod's concept. Accordingly, there then followed a fair amount of the condescension that she was prone to get from those who didn't quite understand her talent. The *New Yorker*, for example, accused her of reducing the proceedings to the level of a burlesque show, as if some of that hadn't already been baked into the Axelrod cake. The fact was that at this point, she had so perfected that character—naive, wise, carnal, innocent—that the uncomprehending could delude themselves into believing that she was simply doing mechanically effected shtick, rather than demonstrating the product of hard and intensive work. Her previous two films had not offered her enough opportunity, let alone leeway; here, though, with the guidance of a sharp and resourceful director, she was able to recreate and reimagine someone else's character in terms of her own gifts and ideas.

It was in *The Seven Year Itch* that Monroe found perhaps her most astute collaborator. Brilliantly gifted and maddeningly erratic, Billy Wilder had already directed and cowritten some of the prime works of mid-century cinema: *Double Indemnity*, *The Lost Weekend*, *A Foreign Affair*, and, above all, *Sunset Boulevard*. Those, along with the coruscating *Ace in the Hole*, were all projects that he had helped conceive and, consequently, were infused with his own endlessly cynical take on the role opportunism plays in the human condition. *The Seven Year Itch* would not be one of Wilder's more personal projects, which is part of the reason, much later, he all but disowned it. Instead, he was part of the package assembled by Charles Feldman, one of Hollywood's most accomplished dealmakers. As an agent, Feldman had represented Marlene Dietrich, John Wayne, and many others, and he had produced the superb film version of *A Streetcar Named Desire*. He was also one of the less known major players in the MM saga, giving her copious professional advice in her dealings with Fox. Often suspecting that he favored the studio's interests over her own, she never trusted him completely yet could respect his accomplishments. She also knew what a boon it would be to have Wilder directing her in the film version of a hit Broadway play. That awareness, as fostered by Feldman, would serve as a beacon for her as she trudged through the rigors of *There's No Business Like Show Business* while, at the same time, preparing to star in *The Seven Year Itch*.

Even if it had not turned out as well as it did, *The Seven Year Itch* would still be something of a legendary cultural (or is it sociological?) event. Seldom in film history has there been such a complicated manifestation of stardom as that which occurred early in the morning of September 15, 1954, on East 52nd Street in New York City. It was part film production and part publicity stunt, along with an overlay of interpersonal melodrama. Monroe, wearing a white Travilla halter dress with a pleated skirt, walked with Ewell outside the Trans-Lux Theatre, which was decked out with posters for *The Creature from the Black Lagoon*.[1] The gimmick, of course, was that she would stand over the subway grate, and the passing trains would blow her skirt up around her face. Apparently, there were fans placed under the grate, since seldom—if ever—do real subway trains produce such forceful winds. This, incidentally, is a fact that has not subsequently deterred the curious or the MM-obsessed from standing on a grate to feel whatever breeze there might be. Not all of

---

[1] Normally, such conspicuous product placement would have been done for a Fox film, not one produced (as *Creature* was) by Universal. *Creature*, however, had been such a popular touchstone (and in 3D) that Wilder could appropriate it for some surefire humor. As it happened, the actual film on the Trans-Lux bill that night was MGM's *Lili*, whose gentle whimsy would not have fit in here at all.

the Trans-Lux footage ended up in the film, as the scene was partly reshot at the studio. But what a summit meeting of the public and private aspects of Monroe's life. There she was, luxuriating in attention and exhibitionism as a massive bunch of onlookers shouted "Higher! Higher!" while the skirt blew up around her face and her panties were in clear view. (Two pairs of panties, actually, in deference to the bright lights.) And there stood Joe DiMaggio, watching on in silent frustration and fury in the knowledge that something this phenomenal could never be made to fit into his concept of marriage.

That marriage ended officially in California a few weeks later, with images of a tearful Monroe making a vivid contrast to the joyful pinup straddling the subway grate. If there is absolutely no indication that anything inauthentic lay in her anguish, as photographed by many cameras, the entire divorce business had been carefully managed for maximum exposure and sympathy. She was not giving a "performance" as the miserable Mrs. DiMaggio, and yet she was, by that point, extremely hip to how it all played to a massive and worldwide audience. Given her shrewd attitude about her public image, and having already seen the furor over the subway pictures, Monroe was very aware that everything she did would further her status as one of the most famous people on the planet—who was, let it not be forgotten, married to another person of extraordinary renown. The truth of the matter is that, for all its brevity, the Monroe-DiMaggio marriage had been on the rocks for months. Quite likely, the subway scene drove it to the breaking point, and there were reports of a loud, perhaps physical, fight going on in the couple's hotel suite after the shoot. None of this means that there was anything manufactured about this confluence of private anguish and public glory, even as the resulting cacophony could be—and was—managed in masterful fashion.

In light of the personal crises that hobbled most of her subsequent films, it needs to be said that Monroe's marital dramas did not deter her from getting through the Seven Year Itch shoot with what was, for her, surpassing professionalism. The comparative ease of the filming was in notable contrast to the difficulties and delays that had marked her previous two films. In River of No Return and There's No Business Like Show Business, she had been compelled to cope with unprepossessing scripts and unsympathetic directors. Here, with a project she had fought to do and a director she respected, the difference was plain to everyone. Even with the multiple takes, forgotten lines, and endemic lateness, a synergy quickly developed between Monroe and Wilder that was enormously beneficial to both the performance and the film. They shared a congruent take on the character of the Girl Upstairs—as markedly

"Monroe-ized" from the original play—and Wilder understood how to handle her as she worked to personalize a role that could seem, on paper, so insubstantial. He encouraged her, maintained patience during her lapses, and was even hospitable toward Natasha Lytess. As a longtime veteran of the Hollywood wars, he knew quite well that the more grace he showed toward Lytess, the more responsive Monroe would be to his direction.

As the Girl Upstairs, Monroe gave her fullest demonstration yet of the character she had been burnishing in *Gentlemen Prefer Blondes* and *How to Marry a Millionaire*—a shrewd naïf flouncing along to her own beat, utterly true to her own moral code, and totally incapable of unkindness. The Lorelei whisper has been filled out with a bit more tone, and her movements are somewhat smoother and more coordinated, showing the benefits of those mime classes. The consonants are under control, and her self-consciousness is at a minimum. Her vivacity has acquired a slightly more sophisticated sheen, the effect of which makes her "wowzer babe in the woods" characterization seem all the more credible. Her clear understanding of this character means that she is able to embrace both Axelrod's original concept and Wilder's retooling. She finds the bridge between the two and happily skips along it for the entirety of the film.

Unlike *Gentlemen Prefer Blondes* and *How to Marry a Millionaire*, her work is entirely alongside a male actor, so the vibe is different from what she'd shared with Jane Russell, Lauren Bacall, and Betty Grable. Her pairing with Robert Mitchum had not really worked, and putting her next to Donald O'Connor had been little short of whimsical folly. Here, though, she expresses such warmth and enthusiasm toward Ewell that it lifts him almost visibly, making him seem less drab and more of a plausible, if not appealing, candidate for adultery. Anyway, the whole point is that the Girl's feelings toward Sherman would be appreciation, not lust.[2] The contrast in acting styles between Monroe and Ewell is quite intriguing, since her work here is essentially timeless, while his is firmly rooted in a specifically Eisenhower-era maleness so nondescript and devoid of conventional appeal that it appears to take Axelrod's premise further than it can bear. It must be said that the disparities between the two actors do, for the purposes of the movie, come together

---

[2] It's debatable if anything, or anyone, could make Ewell seem truly desirable, although in 1956, there were two Monroesque figures who came close: Jayne Mansfield in *The Girl Can't Help It* and Rita Moreno in *The Lieutenant Wore Skirts*. While Mansfield's channeling of Monroe (through a coarse, cuckoo sieve) was, of course, well known, Moreno—still very much in her "peppery Latina" phase—was surprisingly able to do her own successful interpretation of a daft MM-style charmer.

quite well, and it is also worth noting that there were no reports of off-screen conflict. Later on, Ewell would share glowing memories of working with her. "She was wonderful," he said, "oh my God, she was great; so professional and so polite." While a healthy rapport with a fellow actor isn't a necessity, it can be an extremely positive way to take one's mind off private difficulties.

Even with the warm cordiality that existed between Monroe and Ewell, the gap between the two of them—however it may be tied to the overall scheme of the play and the film—seems unavoidably glaring. Thus, it must be wondered how Monroe would have done opposite the runner-up for the role of Sherman. At the time he was up for *The Seven Year Itch*, Walter Matthau was a little-known actor with a number of middling credits on Broadway and television. Alongside another New York–based up-and-comer, Gena Rowlands, Matthau made a screen test that was judged extremely successful. So much so, in fact, that Wilder decided that he should play Sherman. Darryl Zanuck, however, opted for Ewell, who was closely associated with the play and had already appeared in films, most memorably in *Adam's Rib*. Considering the success of the Wilder-Matthau collaboration later on, Matthau's almost-casting remains a piquant what-if. The test footage shows a different, more energetic take on the role that likely makes Sherman seem more viable as a sexual aspirant. Monroe would probably have worked well with him; even in those pre-stardom days, he had a gnomish appeal that could well have made him come across more compellingly than Ewell. Not surprisingly, a number of reviews of the film—especially in the *New Yorker*—held that Ewell's was a more accomplished and authentic performance than MM's, which is at the very least an indicator of both a pro-Broadway snobbery and the anti-Monroe bias to which many critics were prone. For many more observers, the more accurate observation came in hindsight: hers is incontestably the most effervescent and vital part of the film, on its own and even more so alongside Ewell.

Monroe's casting and her performance also soften the bitter pill the filmmakers had to swallow about the central premise: the screen Girl Upstairs, unlike her stage counterpart, does not have a sexual relationship with the man downstairs. Such blatant adultery would not be countenanced under the strictures of the Production Code, and so the sex ends up being dreamed about and elusive. Wilder was especially angry with this compromise, not surprisingly, since adultery had and would figure prominently in *Double Indemnity* and *The Apartment*. *The Seven Year Itch* was hardly the only stage-to-screen transfer to undergo such surgery, but in this case—and mainly because of Monroe—it has to be said that the damage does not seem terminal. MM's Girl *is* too good for Sherman, and not simply because of the vast discrepancy in physical appeal. Unlike him, she's not devious or suspicious or hemmed in by guilt. (His own wife, nicely played by Evelyn Keyes, also seems to deserve better.) Wilder's protests, for all their validity, sidestep the fact that the premise and the play and the film are all too lightweight to be irreparably hindered by the adultery being imagined instead of genuine.

One of the backbones of the Axelrod play was a series of fantasies in Sherman's head, by turns lustful, self-deceiving, and paranoic. Wisely, Wilder reconfigured them for film, expanding them just enough to allow for an amusing *From Here to Eternity* parody with the television model Roxanne and another featuring Carolyn Jones as a sex-crazed nurse. The most extended of these forms one of the film's best set pieces, which can be summed up in one word: "Rachmaninoff." With its soaring music and Ewell's clipped accent, it's an obvious spoof of David Lean's *Brief Encounter*, and there's more subtle recycling going on as well. Gowned gloriously in sequined tiger's skin, Monroe glowers and overreacts in much the same way she had done, in all misplaced seriousness, in *River of No Return*. Even the overarticulated consonants make an appearance. Perhaps this wasn't totally deliberate on the director's part, but then again, Wilder would always be irreverent about something he found to be ludicrous.[3] Monroe also gets to be faux-serious in another dream parody, a TV commercial that quickly becomes a public-service announcement against the lecherous Sherman. The mock-horror of her line reading of "like . . . The Creature from the Black Lagoon" is an ace comic moment that shows Monroe completely on top of her game.

Considering how well Monroe does in the fantasy sequences, it's a pity some of that footage ended up on the cutting-room floor. The most prominent of the deletions had Ewell trolling the depths of paranoia to imagine the Girl Upstairs as Tiger Lil, thieving mistress of a gangster played by Sherman's carpet cleaner, Mr. Kruhulik (Robert Strauss). All that is known to survive of it are some amusing stills showing Monroe decked out in slink and feathers, deploying a long cigarette holder and a tough-gal attitude. In another cut fantasy moment, this one sans MM, news of Sherman's adultery reaches Yankee Stadium, where it is discussed by catcher Yogi Berra and pitcher "Steady"

[3] There was recycling of a different sort in Alfred Newman's musical score, since his "Girl Upstairs" theme had originally been heard six years earlier under the opening credits of *A Letter to Three Wives*. Here its distinctive "up and down" striding melody gives Monroe's scenes some light, jazzy grace.

Eddie Lopat. This one, it can be noted, was shot while Monroe's marriage to "Yankee Clipper" DiMaggio was yet somewhat intact. One more little fantasy snippet does survive, evidently because its deletion from the film was done to appease the censors, not the studio: as plumber Victor Moore works to get MM's toe out of the faucet, he drops the wrench into the tub, and she smiles sweetly while he apologetically fishes it out.

Throughout the movie, Monroe's performance is a deft blending of real and ersatz innocence overlaid with a complex interweaving of the wise and the oblivious. The Girl Upstairs is not, emphatically, another dumb blonde, and none of the Monroe imitators would ever be able to negotiate such a twisty path between what may be a person's ignorance and what is definitely her awareness. This deftness finds perhaps its most perfect manifestation at the moment when she says she knows the Rachmaninoff recording is classical music because "there's no vocal" and, somehow, makes it come across as hip instead of simply dim. And who among her emulators would have been able to project the exuberant delight with which she plays "Chopsticks" or the implicit, layered way she forgives the clumsy pass Sherman makes at her? Nor, unquestionably, could any of them have managed the genuine warmth that makes the character so human and endearing. Whatever her vagaries, the Girl Upstairs, as Monroe plays her, projects a sense of overwhelming kindness that governs both her moral code and her sense of logic. Even when she's discussing a crackpot notion like keeping her underwear refrigerated, she seems comprehensible and even possible. It is surely that air of plausibility that serves as one of the most complex and successful parts of this lovely performance.

For a few minutes after she finished shooting *The Seven Year Itch*, Monroe was able to take some pride in what she had achieved. Then came the rumbles from the East, the new faction of associates who would become her companions in her rebellion against Hollywood. *The Seven Year Itch*, with its commercialism and leers and skirt blowing, was for them Exhibit A of the fashion in which Monroe's talent was being diminished, cheapened, depleted. Insecure as she was, Monroe took these words to heart, especially after she began, worshipfully, to seek the counsel of director and teacher Lee Strasberg. If it was good that she was encouraged to deepen her commitment and refine her craft, it was far less so that she became unable to see just how much she had already accomplished. In 1956, a book came out with the title *Will Acting Spoil Marilyn Monroe?* If one puts either "acting" or "spoil" in quotation marks, that question can make for a lively debate. Certainly, there would be some major changes in her approach as she moved forward, among them a heavy emphasis on psychoanalysis that many would come to think shattered Monroe's already delicate sense of professionalism. In all the films she made after *The Seven Year Itch*, she approached her roles with a greater seriousness that both reaped rewards and wreaked havoc. This was a high price to pay, which makes it especially worthwhile to look closely at her work as Axelrod's (and Wilder's, and especially *Monroe's*) Girl. If anything, the performance improves under that microscope. In the midst of personal stress, marital crisis, and professional uncertainty, she created something irresistible, graceful, valid, and permanent. It was a triumphant way to close out the first phase of her stardom, and the great pity is that she wasn't allowed or inclined to see and savor just how sweet a victory she had earned.

9

Course Correction

It was an audacious move on her part, not least because it was done with a level of conviction and determination that could only be called absolute. Many observers thought it hasty, intemperate, even phony. After all, how often does the world's biggest star—for by that time, she was that—see fit to leave everything behind? Not for marriage, as Grace Kelly would do, but for a crash course in rebellion and reinvention? In a time when movie studios were still large and powerful and had numerous actors under contract, Marilyn Monroe abandoned Twentieth Century-Fox and California to move to New York to study acting, realign large parts of her life, and consider the future. Cynics and detractors, of which there were many, saw it as a bid for attention and a ploy to get more money. That last was not inaccurate, for Fox was still paying her an amount that, considering her popularity and accomplishment, was laughable. Mainly, though, this was less about financial recompense than about artistic freedom: the right to have approval of scripts and directors, the right to say no to something like *Pink Tights*. Perhaps, even, the right to obtain some earned respect.

Monroe, who embarked on this journey shortly after completing *The Seven Year Itch*, had been considering drastic measures for a while. One of her key allies in this was the photographer Milton Greene, who discussed with her the possibility of an independent production company making the kind of films she felt she should be doing. It was certainly a tempting notion, even though Greene had far less film experience than she did, in fact, none aside from taking pictures of actors. It was also a trendy notion to be considering. Stars such as Burt Lancaster, beginning to assert their power in the mid-1950s, initiated their own production companies as a way of having more control and a larger share of the profits. So, Greene told MM, why not her? Monroe herself, not Fox, had been largely responsible for her remarkable ascension, and everyone knew how little Darryl Zanuck thought of her as both an actor and a person. She, for her part, could only look at a *River of No Return* as a vote of next-to-no confidence, and while *The Seven Year Itch* was certainly a major upgrade, it was, in her view, not enough. There was also the response to *There's No Business Like Show Business*, in which the un-abashed nature of her musical performances drew some of her heaviest fire to date, such as that clobbering by Ed Sullivan. The reviews for *River of No Return* had criticized her performance on aesthetic grounds; the objections to *Show Business* were frequently moral, which was another matter entirely. Even as she avoided *Pink Tights*, it seemed that Fox was determined to market her as a crude exhibitionist.

Another nail in this particular coffin came when, as with *The Egyptian*, she actively pursued a role. In this case, it was Miss Adelaide, the nightclub tootsie in *Guys and Dolls*. The film version of the Broadway hit, acquired by Samuel Goldwyn at enormous cost, would be adapted and directed by Joseph L. Mankiewicz and star Marlon Brando and Frank Sinatra. Brando in a musical sounds odd, and Sinatra was horribly miscast, but this was still a heavy-hitting event, one that might give Monroe the sort of Hollywood prestige she craved. It would also be an opportunity to act with Brando after the non-starting *Egyptian*. She was not Goldwyn's choice for Adelaide, however. The producer wanted Betty Grable, and when that didn't work out, he and Mankiewicz opted for Vivian Blaine, who'd created the role on Broadway. Monroe, despite her intensive lobbying, was never seriously considered; never mind that she might have put a refreshing spin on the role and that Blaine gives a demonstration of what can happen when an actor does a role hundreds of times onstage and then is asked to do it again for the movies, that is, play to the balcony, not the camera. Monroe's disappointment over losing *Guys and Dolls* was magnified by something Mankiewicz said to her when she asked him about playing Adelaide. If he had worked well with her on *All about Eve*, now he was plain insulting: "Put on some more clothes, Marilyn, and stop moving your ass so much." The worst part of it was that she knew this was how the Hollywood establishment viewed her.

Instead of continuing on as she had, Monroe engineered a full-scale war. Under an assumed name (Zelda Zonk, no less), she flew to New York and camped out in the suburban home of Greene and his wife Amy and infant son Josh. While she did not completely discontinue talks with Fox, she was determined to make major changes in pretty much every area of her life. Step one was the announcement, by Monroe and Greene, of Marilyn Monroe Productions. At a press conference, an entity billed as "The New Marilyn Monroe" spoke hopefully of being taken seriously and of possibly playing Grushenka in *The Brothers Karamazov*. Later, a reporter would ask her to spell "Grushenka," which was a fast indicator of how seriously she was being taken. Another indicator was the film currently being offered to her by Fox, a comedy titled *How to Be Very, Very Popular*, which she quickly and wisely rejected. Instead, she began working on her craft.

The term "acting school" does little to convey the prestige, gravity, intrigue, and controversy that by 1955 was enveloping the Actors Studio. Founded in 1947, it quickly became known as the place where a new breed of actors went to learn from the inside out, probing and sorting through their own experiences to bring heightened truth and meaning to a playwright's words. The studio's renown and mythology were inextricably connected with two people: Marlon Brando, as famous in his sphere as Monroe was in hers, and Lee Strasberg, a cofounder of the studio and, unquestionably, its central force. Between these two men resided all the popular conceptions of the studio and of its feared, sometimes derided doctrine, Method acting. Neither the Actors Studio nor Brando's movie career had been long in existence when there arose the parodies and jokes about mumbling, the holy rites of "preparing," self-absorbed actors losing themselves in a role, and neurotic self-examination through psychoanalysis. Such disrespect made the Method's admirers and adherents all the more fiercely devoted to Strasberg and the studio, whereas the detractors and traditionalists looked upon it all as pretentious navel-gazing.

The truth, as usual, lay somewhere in between. Taking some of the tenets of Konstantin Stanislavski, Strasberg had derived an intensely inward process of character creation through which an actor would draw on, or even form, personal experiences to better align with a character. The depth and profundity possible with such an approach were self-evident, as with Brando's performance in *On the Waterfront* and Kim Stanley's as an MM-type character in *The Goddess*. The downsides could come with work that seemed overly mannered and self-indulgent, and again, Brando is an avatar with his work in something like *The Fugitive Kind*. Worse, there might also be the possibility of the actor experiencing physical or emotional damage stemming from an overcommitment to complete or excessive immersion in a role, with a resulting loss of perspective.

For Monroe, whose work with Natasha Lytess had often been a sort of mechanical replay of Stanislavski, Strasberg's Method seemed refreshingly honest. Even in her most formulaic roles, she had labored hard to achieve conviction beyond that in the printed script. Nevertheless, that work could be undermined by Lytess's reliance on phony externals such as overdeveloped diction, as well as by her own lack of self-confidence and an excessive need for approval from the teacher. If much of the work she did with Lytess was worthy, the truth is that her own instincts might sometimes have served her better. She had indeed been coming to a Monroe Method, which is a major achievement considering what she was called upon to play in something like *There's No Business Like Show Business*. Once again, there is that brief scene she did with Ethel Merman, whose acting style was based wholly on externals. As Merman charges in with her usual brash style, Monroe, even with the excessive diction, is trying to personalize the situation and own such characterization as there is to be gleaned. It may have been her own version of the Method's "sense memory," yet she needed more tools and guidance— as well as better material.

Strasberg, after meeting and speaking with Monroe, believed that he could be her guide and savior. And Strasberg was not being insincere when he proclaimed his belief in her potential. There remains the issue, raised by some of Monroe's associates and biographers, of what else Strasberg saw in her besides her talent. Not on a personal level, although Strasberg and his wife, Paula, and their daughter, Susan, did become family figures for her. Rather, there was the promise of more fame and clout for the Actors Studio if Monroe would be its most celebrated female alumna—and also financial recompense. For most of MM's subsequent career, Strasberg exercised a good deal of control, which extended to his demanding large fees for himself and for his wife, who replaced Lytess as Monroe's on-the-set coach. It must be noted upfront that Paula Strasberg would never be spoken of with the hushed reverence that greeted her husband. Indeed, she would soon become the least-loved member of the Monroe entourage, an object of perennial scorn and derision—more so, even, than Lytess had been.

While some of his wife's credentials and qualifications may have been dubious, Strasberg himself was hardly a phony. The success of the Actors Studio, and of the great work it engendered, cannot be disputed. Neither can Strasberg's work as a director and, later in his life, as an actor. He came to film (excluding very minor early work) in his seventies, and his performance as gangster Hyman Roth in *The Godfather: Part II* is so staggeringly good as to serve as a complete vindication for everything and everyone he taught. Monroe approached him as an almost godlike figure, and it is clear that her study with him—he took her on as a very rare private pupil—reaped major rewards. For most of the time in her post-1955 films, there is a new seriousness in her performances and, generally, a more palpable connection with the material. It is equally true that these were accompanied by a whole cluster of downsides just out of camera range: greater manifestations of neurosis and insecurity, a growing reliance on pharmaceuticals and alcohol, more frequent illnesses, an increasing disconnection with cast and crew members, and moments of flagrantly bad temper.

All of this added up, ultimately, to a complex, profound, and increasingly uncontrolled web of emotional difficulties, which, if anything, was exacerbated, not ameliorated, by Strasberg's prescription of self-examination through psychoanalysis. In the early months of 1955, Monroe began a rigorous course of analysis through which she might better comprehend herself both professionally and personally. The result, more often than not, was as complete a reliance on her analysts as that which she would have on her acting coach during a film shoot. In the eyes of many observers, her program of self-study came to mean that both her film sets and her home environments turned increasingly into minefields of crisis and dysfunction. If such unraveling could never be attributed wholly to her study with Strasberg and her work at the Actors Studio—or, for that matter, her work in psychoanalysis—there are numerous connections that cannot be totally disregarded.

At around the same time as she was beginning her association with Strasberg and the Actors Studio, Monroe also did some work with a far different acting teacher. Constance Collier was nothing if not formidable, with a career that ranged from Shakespeare to Bob Hope. A beauty when young and a battleship dowager in her maturity, Collier had appeared in film as well as on the stage, most memorably in *Stage Door* and *Kitty*. Her richly embroidered grand-manner style was pretty much the antithesis of anything proffered at the Actors Studio, and she had already served as a coach to some notable, emphatically non-Method stars, including Vivien Leigh and Katharine Hepburn. Since Collier died in April 1955, her association with Monroe was only a brief one, although the fact that she been sought out indicates both MM's willingness to explore diverse paths and the utter seriousness of her quest for self-improvement.

That quest, or at least a version of it, made it into America's living rooms on April 8, 1955, when Edward R. Murrow interviewed Monroe on the highly rated and highly regarded CBS television series *Person to Person*. Persons, in this case, since Milton and Amy Greene were also part of the live fourteen-minute segment, which should have been an excellent opportunity for MM to make a case for her new independence and her new production company. Instead, she seemed sweet, vague, and rather helpless, completely lacking in the poise she'd shown in her earlier TV appearance with Jack Benny. "Why do they always look like unhappy rabbits?" Miss Caswell had asked in *All about Eve*, and so it was here as well. Monroe stumbled over easy questions, fumbled for words, and punctuated her sentences with sudden, forced smiles. What a world away from *The Seven Year Itch* or Korea. In between numerous star-in-the-headlights moments, Monroe did mention that her favorites of her films were *The Asphalt Jungle* and *The Seven Year Itch* and that she was especially grateful to the help she had received from John Huston, Billy Wilder, Natasha Lytess, and Michael Chekhov. Unfortunately, the main takeaway, for most observers, was that this appearance did not aid her cause.[1]

Off camera, Monroe was moving with a resolve that seemed considerably firmer than what she'd shown with Murrow. Along with observing and later participating in classes at the Actors Studio, she was studying privately with Strasberg, seeing an analyst as often as every weekday, and renewing her acquaintance with Arthur Miller. Soon she would be signing with new representatives who would negotiate with Fox on her behalf. It was clear that *The Seven Year Itch* would be an enormous success, which meant that the studio was under intense pressure to bring her back into the fold by (almost) whatever means necessary. Along with a substantial raise in salary, she was demanding approval of director, script, and cinematographer, as well as the right to make films with Marilyn Monroe Productions. It was, all in all, an exciting time, and her proactivity seemed to radiate a confidence that was less an actuality than an appealing facade. In addition to her ongoing feelings of insecurity, she was increasingly placed in the middle of a sort of tug of war between Greene and Strasberg. The more she began to study and socialize with Strasberg, the less she trusted Greene's motives, and the tension of the situation would be heightened by the ascendance in her orbit of Miller. It would seem that in her bid for independence and integrity, she was acquiring less of a sense of stability.

One major professional disappointment during this time had a very Actors Studio patina. *Baby Doll* was a long-in-gestation collaboration between the *Streetcar Named Desire*/*Cat on a Hot Tin Roof* team of playwright Tennessee Williams and director Elia Kazan. For Monroe to take the title role in this particular project seemed the realization of nearly all her professional ambitions.

---

[1] Amy Greene, unlike both MM and her own husband, appeared poised, capable, and so at ease before the camera that she sometimes seemed to be answering questions on behalf of her famous yet skittish houseguest. Afterward, some jokes were made about how Fox should ditch Monroe and sign Amy Greene instead.

There were some complex personal associations as well: Kazan was a former lover, Williams was a major rival to Arthur Miller, and neither Miller nor the Strasbergs were currently on good terms with Kazan, in part because of Kazan's acquiescence to the House Un-American Activities Committee. In any case, *Baby Doll* was a project that Monroe pursued even more avidly than she had *The Egyptian* and *Guys and Dolls*. As with both of those, there was also a Brando connection: he was Kazan's first choice to play Silva, the role ultimately taken by Eli Wallach.[2] Williams wanted Monroe as Baby Doll, while Kazan, who tended to assess Monroe's gifts from a pointedly lofty viewpoint, did not. As the script evolved, the character had grown younger than the original conception, and Kazan cited age as the reason he passed over MM in favor of Carroll Baker, who was five years younger than Monroe and had studied with Strasberg at the Actors Studio. *Baby Doll*, which earned Baker an Oscar nomination, remains a major what-if for Monroe, so scandalous a success that it can only be imagined how much greater the outcry might have been had she taken the role.

Finally, in the weeks following the *Baby Doll* affair, Monroe and her representatives came to terms with Twentieth Century-Fox, up to and including a salary increase and director approval. A list of sixteen directors was submitted to Fox on her behalf, ranging from veterans such as Alfred Hitchcock and John Ford to film newcomer Joshua Logan and to Lee Strasberg, who would never direct a feature film. Of her previous directors, only Huston, Mankiewicz, and Wilder were included. The film to bring her back to the screen was chosen—agreed upon, really—with a care far beyond that which had marked the *Pink Tights* and *How to Be Very, Very Popular* debacles of earlier times. William Inge's *Bus Stop* had been a fair-sized hit on Broadway, running for more than a year and drawing some rave reviews. The lead role, a hicksville nightclub singer desperate for respect, was played by Kim Stanley, an Actors Studio alumna whose performances were already being spoken of in hushed and awed tones. By taking the part of Cherie for the film version, Monroe, who saw Stanley in the play several times, was aiming high.

The other sign of her intent and ambition came with the announcement of the first Marilyn Monroe Production. Immediately after *Bus Stop* wrapped, there would follow a film adaptation of Terence Rattigan's *The Sleeping*

---

[2] Wallach, who later costarred with MM in *The Misfits*, once gave a succinct picture of one of the more extreme manifestations of the Actors Studio experience: "We were all steeped in the Method . . . and it was like we had discovered a new religion. No one else mattered. No one else had any skill at whatever they were doing because we had the answer to all great acting."

Prince. Subtitled "An Occasional Fairy Tale," it had been a successful London vehicle for Vivien Leigh and Laurence Olivier, who also directed. Olivier would be directing the film version as well, with MM stepping into the Leigh role. Although no one could ever mistake the play for a work of real substance, there was, again, a sheen of aspirational prestige, Monroe as the equal of an actor popularly felt to be without peer. It might all have been seen as a truly elevated endeavor had something curious not occurred when Monroe, alongside Olivier and Rattigan, spoke at a Manhattan press conference announcing the new film. As she talked about her ambitions and her work at the Actors Studio, a strap broke on her low-cut gown, immediately pulling the focus away from her august cohorts. Many felt, and perhaps not without cause, that the stunt had been engineered—the old Marilyn impinging on the new one.

Before leaving New York to shoot *Bus Stop*, Monroe was given a uniquely Actors Studio opportunity to prove herself and show the result of her work and study. Opposite the formidably gifted Maureen Stapleton, she performed a scene from Eugene O'Neill's *Anna Christie*—the same scene in which movie audiences, back in 1930, had learned that Greta Garbo was as convincing vocally as she was visually. The episode eventually became one of the mythic moments in Monroe's life: overcoming a terminal case of nerves, she delivered a performance so luminous that a tough Actors Studio audience burst into wild applause. Was it really that good, or had expectations been that low? While no one who wasn't there will ever know for sure, Kim Stanley was one of the many in attendance who was convinced:

> She was wonderful. We were taught never to clap at the Actors Studio, like we were in church and all that, but it was the first time I'd ever heard applause there. And some of us went to her privately and apologized [for not having believed in her ability]. . . . She was uncanny in the way she did it. There was nobody that didn't love her in that . . . anybody who had any largeness of spirit loved Marilyn. And she won us all.

The only demurrals came from some in the audience who noted that her voice was not loud enough. Otherwise, the triumph was complete, save possibly in her own mind.

On that high note, she made her way back to California. At a post-arrival press conference, dressed in conservative attire, she seemed more assured and sophisticated than she had in the past, with the unhappy rabbit of *Person to Person* apparently supplanted by a woman who seemed to be in charge of her destiny. The impression grew when she returned to Fox and exercised the prerogatives of her new contract. By this point, Zanuck had left his post as head of production, and his successor, Buddy Adler, was eager to placate his studio's leading asset. One way to do this was the selection of a director for *Bus Stop*. Joshua Logan, who had been on her "directors of choice" list, was not happy with the idea of working with her until Strasberg assured him that, yes, she was indeed a genuine talent. She proved the accuracy of this when she began to confer with Logan on every aspect of the character she was to play. Having developed a concept and a biography for Cherie, she rejected most of the planned costume designs in favor of some ratty specimens she found deep in the studio's wardrobe department. Wherever possible, she remained deeply involved in major production decisions, even as the selection of her costar began to make it seem more like *Hamlet* than *Bus Stop*. After some consideration given to casting Albert Salmi, who had played the role of Bo on the stage, MM began to favor Rock Hudson as the young cowboy in single-minded pursuit of Cherie. Then she became dogged by concern that he might overshadow her. Back and forth she went, until finally deciding that he might be acceptable. This might have been fine except for the fact that Hudson, wearied by her indecision, now said no. The eventual choice came late in the day: Don Murray, a Canadian-born New York stage actor, would here be making his first film.

Monroe's newfound authority also asserted itself with her steely elimination, from her film sets and her life, of Natasha Lytess. During MM's hiatus, Lytess had continued coaching other actors at Fox, but it was obvious to all (with the possible exception of Lytess herself) that her time with Monroe was over. Instead, there would be the presence of Paula Strasberg, serving as her husband's surrogate. Many thought of Paula as a fraud, an empty if affected conduit through which Lee could keep bending Monroe to his authority. In an intense two-person rite, coach would speak to actor while using metaphors that ranged from the inspired to the ridiculous, all aimed at guiding her famous pupil to "rev up" for a scene. The process, during which the black-clad Paula would hover over Monroe like a bird of prey, also involved MM frantically waving her hands and fingers as if to dry wet nail polish. While this was going on, and afterward, other actors, directors, and crew members would be excluded completely. The self-containment that had long marked Monroe's comportment on film sets became here even more hermetic, on and off camera. Eileen Heckart, who played Cherie's friend Vera, later said that actors in a scene with Monroe were basically on their own: "When you played opposite her in a scene she wouldn't look in your eyes. . . . There was nothing in her performance that you could take from or use, and I think the reason she didn't give as an actress is because she didn't know how."

Logan, having heard his fill of Lytess stories, decreed that Paula Strasberg would not be physically present on the *Bus Stop* set, so Monroe would collude with her coach prior to leaving her dressing room. None of this lessened the bouts of lateness and the need for multiple takes of a given scene. Indeed, Monroe's traditional, deep-seated insecurity became increasingly overlaid with the protocols her study had taught her was necessary to build a character. This nearly reached the crisis point during the Phoenix location shoot when Logan was preparing to film Cherie running to the bus station to escape Bo. The scene was being shot at "magic hour," that brief window of twilight when day looks like night. The minutes ticked by without a Cherie, until finally, Logan burst into her dressing room and found Monroe sitting before her mirror, deeply immersed in something or other. Grabbing her wrist tightly, Logan yanked her onto the set and called "Action!" The breathless distress visible in the scene is far less Cherie's than it is Marilyn's.

In spite of some problems and Monroe's illness later on in the production, the *Bus Stop* shoot went smoothly enough that the film was in theaters by the late summer of 1956. To most observers, it was a near-total vindication of everything Monroe had done in the past year and a half, and the critics were virtually unanimous in praising her. Most of them also made the point of extolling her work in *Bus Stop* at the expense of everything she'd already done. In the *New York Times*, Bosley Crowther praised her to the skies while noting, with daintily backhanded condescension, that in her earlier works, *The Seven Year Itch* included, "her magnetism was set forth by other qualities than her histrionic skill."[3] Very little of the praise, at any rate, could alleviate Monroe's bottomless reserves of insecurity and suspicion. Taking little delight in the abundant validation she received from the film's reviews and popular success, she opted instead for anger toward her director. In her unyielding perfectionism, she blamed Logan for the deletion of some moments she had felt to be her best. Months later, when the Academy Award nominations were announced, she cited Logan and Fox as the cause of her exclusion from a Best Actress nod, as if the greater truth were not that she was still being treated as

[3] He might, at the very least, have phrased it correctly. Or was he simply foreshadowing the present-day culture of instant online reviews crafted from misshapen grammar?

a carnival attraction more than a respectable actor. The fact that Don Murray, with his background in the theater, received a nomination when she did not was probably irksome to her, even as it tended to demonstrate the way much of the film community was disposed to regard her.[4]

Bus Stop, then, is neither the first nor the last Monroe film with a complex backstory, though it would be the final one she made that was not completely hobbled by, and beholden to, the personal crises that would subsume her professional identity. Fortunately, it is good enough to be viewed on its own merit, apart from all its historical connotations. Good, not great. Inge's pleasant play has a few richly drawn characters and enough of a viable storyline to have made for a worthy 1955 night of theater. There is, however, a reason it has not been revived as often as *Picnic* and *Come Back, Little Sheba*. It has a pat kind of predictability to it and, really, few surprises. Inge's work often has a touch of "little people have lives, too" archness, and it's so present here that it becomes text instead of merely subtext. Perhaps more pertinently, seven decades on, the whole nature of the "Bo kidnaps Cherie" storyline will not come across to most audiences as it once did and as Inge intended. Call it changing attitudes, heightened sensitivities, or even that wretched phrase political correctness. In any case, it's still the story of a young woman being forcibly abducted by a man who desires her and is oblivious to the notion of taking no for an answer. Yes, they both grow and change in the course of the action, but this does not mean that the journey to that destination will not make some queasy. If something like *The Seven Year Itch* has regressive attitudes as well, this is more serious and pointed.

In some ways, the film might be viewed a shade more charitably than the play, and this has to do with Hollywood's propensity for opening up and reassembling. George Axelrod, of *The Seven Year Itch*, reconfigured the scope of Inge's work well past its original parameters, so much so that the putative action of the play does not begin until the movie is nearly three-quarters over. Instead of just the diner, there's a virtual pageant of lead-in: Bo's ranch, two bus trips, Cherie's club, a parade and a rodeo and views

---

[4] MM's omission from the 1956 Oscar nominations is, for some and in retrospect, nearly as much of a head scratcher as that of Judy Garland losing to Grace Kelly two years earlier. (In both cases, studio politics and personal feelings were major factors.) The actual nominees for 1956 were a mixed bag. Ingrid Bergman (the ultimate winner, for *Anastasia*), Katharine Hepburn (*The Rainmaker*), and Deborah Kerr (*The King and I*) all had prestige and previous nominations. But Nancy Kelly in the now-camp-classic *The Bad Seed*?—stage pedigree, yes, and also the kind of embellished performance that gives the word "actressy" a bad connotation (gestures, many, many gestures). And Carroll Baker's nod for *Baby Doll*, while comprehensible, was surely an annoyance to Monroe, given her own history with that role.

of Phoenix. The effect of this opening up, at best, is to make some of the material seem a shade less calculated, if still theatrical. It also places Cherie and Monroe in a suitably cinematic context, as well as giving the audience a precious, terrible opportunity to see and hear Cherie at work. Well and good . . . and there remains an emperor here without many clothes whose initials are not M.M.

By 1955, when he directed his first "real" film—there had been an apprentice effort back in 1938—Joshua Logan was one of the most esteemed directors in the American theater. Hit after hit had his name on it—most famously, *South Pacific* and *Mister Roberts*—and, like Kazan, he was considered a true collaborator instead of merely a traffic cop. Small wonder that his move to film, with *Picnic*, was considered a momentous event. Lee Strasberg was among those seeing to it that Logan was placed on Monroe's approved directors list, and when *Bus Stop* was released, Logan did indeed win much of the credit for the effectiveness of her performance. There is no question that despite her later disillusionment, he had worked productively with her. Yet it's good to have a look at Logan's full body of film work, from *Picnic* to *Paint Your Wagon*. While most of the basic properties are viable, it's a pretty ponderous lot, with a few exceptions (*Bus Stop*, *Picnic*, parts of *Fanny* and *Sayonara*). If Logan could conceptualize a whole piece of theater, film could be another matter entirely. The intriguing moments and performances in the Logan filmography generally don't coalesce, and after *Bus Stop*, they get heavier and heavier. *Sayonara* is burdened by Brando's Southern-fried accent and lots of soap opera, *South Pacific* is a turgid iteration of the vibrant stage original, and *Camelot* has pretty visuals and very many problems. Then there's *Paint Your Wagon*.

In truth, while Logan does not do a poor job with *Bus Stop*, it plays out as a staging rather than a filming (or reimagining). Even with the changes and opening up, there remains that vague background hum of theatrical gears turning. Plus, again, there is the labored Inge folksiness, literally underscored by faux-country music. Between the direction and some of the writing (both Inge's and Axelrod's) and too much rodeo location footage, it all sometimes feels a little off. Not destructively so, but despite wholly committed performances by Monroe and Murray, it stops short of being a complete success. Call it, instead, an extraordinarily worthy try, as well as a document of Monroe's study at the Actors Studio.

From its very first frames, *Bus Stop* is intent on making a clear announcement that this is not just another Monroe film. Really, there could be no greater show of determination than the first sounds heard on the track after the Fox and CinemaScope fanfare: it's *accordion* music, with the Four Lads singing an updated folk ditty about giving your love a paper of pins if she'll marry you.[5] Between the song and the sight of Murray roping a steer, it's obvious that this is all going to be a major step away from accustomed Monroe territory. Not even the glossy wilderness of *River of No Return* can hold a candle to this or to Murray's bull-in-a-china-shop physicality. Monroe's entrance, some minutes later, is another signal. Wearily perched on a window ledge fanning herself with a newspaper, she is light years away from Lorelei or the Girl Upstairs. If the dingy kimono and slightly unkempt hair are fairly extreme, it's the skin color that really startles, with a pallor that is one shade away from dead white. It was Monroe and Greene who made the decision that Cherie worked and lived after dark and thus never saw daylight; Greene had wanted the color to be even whiter until MM's makeup man, Whitey Snyder, advised him that might be going too far. Finally, after taking in how she looks, we hear the voice, a dissonant Arkansas twang pitched well higher than the Girl or Rose Loomis or any voice previously heard from her. Thus, in the seconds it's taken for all of this to be revealed, there's been a complete demonstration of Monroe, the creative and enterprising actor.

That voice, with its jangle and dropped final g's and drifting emphases, is something of a microcosm of everything Monroe does in *Bus Stop* and had been working toward in her previous year-plus of work and study. It makes it clear how obsessively devoted she was to finding and feeling the truth of this character and conveying it to the audience by every possible means. Indeed, she was so dedicated to this goal that she evidently would speak only in Cherie's voice during the entire making of the film, not just when she was on camera. That, needless to say, is a very Actors Studio thing to do, and Monroe's thorough immersion in the internals and externals of this sad little waif is as brave as it is resourceful. Still, as is true of most of the film, there's something that seems just a hair off-kilter and excessively worked out. Some odd stresses in her speech patterns, for example, strike vagrant notes of actorish inauthenticity that ultimately make it clear that this is less a creation of a character than a sincere and very

---

[5] As "The Bus Stop Song," the Four Lads' recording made it onto the pop charts in September 1956, a fact that probably had more to do with Marilyn Monroe than with the Four Lads, accordions, or even papers of pins.

good performance of a role. (Doubtless, if given the time and wherewithal, Monroe would have been willing to go to Arkansas to study the people, the culture, and the speech.) Where she cannot be faulted is in her emotional candor. Clearly, she feels Cherie's pain and confusion and shows it quite movingly, and along with Murray, she makes the intimacy of the final scenes both touching and convincing. Wisely, Logan keeps the camera close to them as Cherie and Bo fumble their way to a tenable relationship, so close that a string of saliva can be seen coming from Monroe's mouth. The apparent "realness" of such moments is a contrast to an overall mood that can best be termed theatrical realism: the genuine exteriors, shot on location, can make for a jarring contrast with dialogue and situations that clearly have been schematically plotted out. Monroe's famous rendition of "That Old Black Magic"—reportedly sung live on the set—is amusing and oddly poignant, with its ridiculous gestures and lighting effects. (The clothespins on the light switches are a grand touch, possibly from Logan.) Still, would even a B-girl in a Phoenix clip joint make quite this bad a job of it? As with so much in the film, its internal truth has been compromised by overly worked-out externals. Some of it comes from Inge's patronizing sincerity, some from Logan's cinematic inadequacy, and some, perhaps, from Monroe's completely understandable need to show everyone what she'd learned and what she could do.

Many cite Cherie as MM's finest achievement, and the enthusiasm is certainly justifiable. She has worked so hard, and it's so different from anything she'd done previously. Even so—and this is a completely debatable conclusion—it may be that these facts on their own may not be enough. Many critics at the time felt that this was the first time she had been given a role with any substance. Conceivably true, even as it raises a question: Which is the firmer triumph, working with well-delineated material or creating something completely memorable out of the sheerest nothing, as she did in *The Seven Year Itch*? In both performances, she worked to fill out the details in her own way, with her own talent and experience and voice. Consequently, some will feel that all her preparation for Cherie—a character so far away from her accustomed norm—makes this the more valid achievement. For others, however, the Girl Upstairs may be a more convincing realization of Monroe's talents and gifts—less cerebral and detailed in its composition, to be sure, yet also more joyful and, in its own fantastic sphere, more candid. Not that Monroe's work as Cherie is anything other than deeply felt and beautifully done. It's just that in her next two films, she would be graced with better-fitting means to assemble all the pieces. Perhaps it's best to compare her work as Cherie to that of a talented pianist performing an intricate étude: ultimately, it may possibly be more satisfying for its skill and effort and intent than for how it comes across to the audience. And if Cherie is an étude, by the time of *Some Like It Hot*, Monroe will be conducting the whole damn concerto.

10

A Sense of Self

By most measures, not necessarily including her own, *Bus Stop* achieved what Monroe wanted and intended. The plan, then, was for her to redouble the stakes by going farther afield, literally as well as figuratively. And what better way to further burnish one's credentials than to go to England and appear as the partner of the World's Greatest Actor? And to make the victory even more absolute, in a film she herself was producing? This was all heady stuff, not least for the way she was deliberately bucking the formerly unassailable studio system, just as Burt Lancaster and others were doing. If the quality of the actor-as-producer films could be as variable as anything coming out of MGM or Paramount, they frequently carried an edge and individuality that seemed fresh and different. When Lancaster's company produced the sleeper hit *Marty* in 1955, the beginning sounds of a systemic shift became increasingly audible.

Given much of Monroe's experience with Fox, it's no wonder that she would be drawn to the possibility of producing films that she herself thought were worthy and permitted her to select the material and the personnel. With Milton Greene as her cohort and catalyst, she asserted her authority with the name of her company. Lancaster called his company Norma, after his wife, and Kirk Douglas had Bryna, after his mother. Monroe had Marilyn Monroe Productions, in which she would be majority stockholder. The boldness of all this, at this time, must be emphasized. Bette Davis had made a stab at production with her BD Productions' *A Stolen Life* in 1946, but apart from that, the production companies were pretty exclusively male territory. Thus was MM's announcement of her company met with skepticism and outright ridicule, as with the reporter asking her to spell "Grushenka." Yet she persisted, and Greene went into hock to make the company happen. Its first (and only) production would follow very shortly after Monroe completed *Bus Stop*.

The Sleeping Prince was one of the lighter works to come from the facile and easy-flowing pen of Terence Rattigan, Britain's most successful playwright of the early postwar period. Rattigan's works were typically conventional, well-made dramas, such as *The Browning Version*, *The Deep Blue Sea*, and *Separate*

Tables, which were dramatically valid and, in an unthreatening way, modestly insightful and provocative. *The Sleeping Prince* was far slighter than these, a comedy more amusing than funny, which was written to coincide with the coronation of Queen Elizabeth II. The slender nature of the diversion, with its "love, not war" message, was made to look notably more substantial because of some high-octane star power—Vivien Leigh at her most vivacious as a pert actress and Laurence Olivier as the dead-serious Regent of Carpathia. Olivier also directed, and the play—a break from the couple's current roster of Shakespeare and Shaw—ran for nine months in London's West End.

It was the opinion of both Rattigan himself and agent-producer Charles Feldman that *The Sleeping Prince* would make a fine film vehicle for Monroe, possibly alongside the Regent of Richard Burton. Rattigan wrote to Darryl Zanuck about it, and Feldman gave MM a copy of the script. Nothing happened, and Rattigan eventually began to negotiate a possible deal with John Huston. Then, after her disappointment over *Baby Doll*, Monroe turned her attention back to *The Sleeping Prince*. Whatever its slightness, it had an aura of theatrical respectability that tied in extremely well with her current mindset. In a relatively short period of time, a deal and a package had been assembled: *The Sleeping Prince*, starring Monroe and Olivier, would be filmed in England under Olivier's direction. Meanwhile, she had completely renegotiated her contract with Twentieth Century-Fox. She was already the most famous woman in show business. Now it seemed that she would be one of the most powerful. Monroe and Olivier were all smiles at their joint press conference to announce the new film. There had, however, already arisen some conflict. Not yet with Olivier—that would come later, in abundance—but among Monroe, Greene, and Lee Strasberg over the selection of Olivier as both costar and director. Greene, after discussing the matter with Rattigan and Olivier, had suggested to Monroe that Olivier could direct as well as costar. Monroe, as with all artistic matters at the time, consulted with Strasberg, who allowed that it was an interesting idea. Through a network of miscommunication, Monroe evidently took Strasberg's reply to mean yes, after which Greene went ahead with the deal. Later, after Strasberg clarified (or walked back) his position, Monroe came to believe that Greene had overstepped his authority, which hastened the already-started erosion of their relationship. In hesitating to give full approval, perhaps Strasberg was being a kind of Cassandra, anticipating the clash of styles and approaches and temperaments that would become the hallmark of this production. There was also the fact that all three of the films Olivier had already directed—*Henry V*, *Hamlet*, *Richard III*—were Shakespearean dramas. Even though he was already well acquainted with *The Sleeping Prince*, it was a major change for him in terms of cinema; having a camera prowl moodily through Kronborg Castle denotes an aesthetic worlds away from a two-hander set in a fussily decorated parlor in the Carpathian embassy. That particular unease lay some months away; for the time being, there was immense curiosity about how these two would pair together on the screen. No less an observer than Joshua Logan termed the Monroe-Olivier matchup as "the best combination since black and white." Certainly, from Monroe's standpoint, it had the potential to be the best possible move to make following the sea change of *Bus Stop*. There, she could prove herself as a gifted actor; here, in a bona fide Marilyn Monroe Production, she could display every professional facet. In collaboration with an actor of limitless prestige, she would be enhancing her status as a mature thespian at the same time as she was serving, all things considered, as her own auteur.

Between the wrap of *Bus Stop* and the start of *The Sleeping Prince*, there was much to keep Monroe occupied. Now considering the East Coast her home base, she returned to New York and busied herself with both the coming film and a new life. She married Arthur Miller on June 29, 1956 (civil ceremony) and July 1, 1956 (Jewish ceremony), and less than two weeks later, the couple flew to London. Insofar as the British press and the British public had both been demonstrating an enormous advance interest in all things Monroe, some disillusionment began to set in quite promptly. The "New Marilyn" was not the warm and inviting person of Korea and the subway grate; she was subdued and cool, perhaps in reflection of her new role as mistress of her destiny. Miller, meanwhile, was an especially aloof and uncommunicative consort, giving the impression that he was made of a notably forbidding variety of granite. After the briefest of honeymoons for both marriage and *The Sleeping Prince*, matters began to proceed in a difficult and sometimes dismaying fashion.

The shooting of *The Sleeping Prince*, later retitled *The Prince and the Showgirl*, has been documented in fascinatingly painful detail in two books, a television documentary, and a feature film. All four of these sprang from the recollections of Colin Clark. In 1956, Clark was a recent Royal Air Force veteran and Oxford graduate with good family connections. With a fierce desire to break into the film industry, he managed to wangle a humble position on the crew of *The Sleeping Prince* as third assistant director. Modest as it was, it enabled him to observe a sizable portion of the personal and professional stress that was as essential to the film as the words of Terence Rattigan. He also kept a journal, and the first of his books, *The Prince, the Showgirl, and Me*, is a chatty day-by-day rundown of everything he saw. The second book, *My Week with Marilyn*, is a more personal—and, it must be noted, not entirely convincing—reminiscence of his own time with MM, a relationship that, in this telling, could be said to qualify as a platonic fling. This is the one that made it onto movie screens as a 2011 film of the same name, with Michelle Williams and Eddie Redmayne as star and gofer. In both books, there was very little that seems to have missed Clark's eye, which makes it completely fitting that he later became a well-regarded producer of documentaries. Perhaps his observations—over and apart from what he wanted the public to believe almost happened between him and MM—were not completely objective, and at least one Monroe biographer has convincingly poked a few holes in some of his narrative. It should be added that, as with nearly every Briton working on the film, Clark had a somewhat superior view toward Monroe and some members of her American entourage. He liked and sympathized with Greene, had no use at all for Miller, and found Paula Strasberg's sycophancy almost mesmerizing. However, his criticism fell on the British participants as well, above all on Olivier, with whom he worked closely. Over and over again, he made it frighteningly clear that this star-producer and star-director pairing was a mismatch to put the film's Elsie and His Grand Ducal Highness to shame.

It was not simply through Clark's recollections that one particular fact is clear: this would be the first Monroe film in which crisis rated top billing.[1] Earlier, there had been the conflicts, the illnesses and latenesses, the takes repeated ad infinitum due to blown or unremembered lines. Here it soared to another realm. On *Bus Stop*, Logan was sufficiently prepared to handle most of MM's vagaries and dependencies, and to his credit, he sent a series of directives to Olivier in advance of the *Prince* shoot. (Among them, do not let Paula Strasberg on the set.) Whatever Olivier did to heed or respect Logan's words was not enough, and the situation would only worsen as shooting

---

[1] Beginning with this movie, there were only four completed films remaining in Monroe's career. In three of those, it could be said that a "what happened on the set" film could well be a more compelling work than what actually emerged on the screen. (And yes, three of them—*The Prince and the Showgirl*, *The Misfits*, and *Some Like It Hot*—did get documentaries.) *Some Like It Hot*, as we know, was able to soar magnificently above everything that had been a problem during its creation. As for *Let's Make Love*, perhaps it's too much of a black hole to justify close examination, although how could a behind-the-camera look not be more absorbing than what ended up getting released?

proceeded. The disconnection between these two all-but-mythical figures was no less than total. There was nothing in Monroe's approach that Olivier felt he could connect with, and the Method-derived warm-up exercise of vigorously shaking out her hands and fingers between each shot was a special irritant. It was as if his own brilliant intransigence blinded him to the necessity of accommodating someone working in a completely different fashion.

Monroe, for her part, had no difficulty intuiting his feelings and growing irritation, which made her turn more and more to Paula Strasberg. Despite Logan's warnings, Strasberg was a constant presence on the set, a barrier between Monroe and Olivier both figuratively and literally. The more pressure she felt, the more MM deferred to her coach; the more Olivier seethed, the less he was willing to comprehend how the situation might be improved. He was hardly alone among actors of his generation, British or no, in finding the Method-derived ways of the Actors Studio incompatible with his own technique and style. For Olivier, it would always remain so. There is a famous (and apparently factual) story about Olivier set some twenty years later, on the set of *The Marathon Man*. In order to appear sleep-deprived in his scene with Olivier, Dustin Hoffman stayed awake for something like three nights, to which Olivier reacted in a fashion that could only be termed predictable. "Dear boy," he drawled to Hoffman, "why don't you try acting?" And as if he were not provoked enough by Monroe's on-set conferences with Strasberg, there were a number of occasions in which shooting had to be temporarily halted as MM walked off the set, Strasberg in tow, to make a transatlantic phone call to Lee Strasberg to confer on something in the script that she felt required his clarity. The point of no return came when the specific direction Olivier gave her, before one scene, was "Be sexy." This precipitated an existential crisis of major proportion, after which Monroe would never regain the ability to trust him as her director.

The difficulties were hardly limited to a clash of method (or Method) and culture. By this time, Monroe was entering a spiral of substance dependence that would be with her for the remainder of her life. Her insomnia required sleeping pills, waking up necessitated ever stronger stimulants, and the quantities kept growing. So did her employment of champagne to wash down her meds. This toxic chemical brew was a main culprit on the many days when she came to the studio extremely late or, quite frequently, not at all. None of it was lessened by an emotional bombshell that occurred midway through filming, involving her discovery of a diary entry written by her husband. If it was distressing enough to read of his disillusionment with her, the capper came when (as she recounted) Miller mentioned his concurrence with Olivier that she was "a troublesome bitch." Immediately, she began to view Miller with some of the same distrust she felt toward Greene, who she felt was taking Olivier's side in their disagreements. Suspicion, conflict, insecurity, paranoia—they all make for an ill-fitting foundation while one is attempting to bring sparkle to a wordy light comedy. Matters and shooting proceeded in an extremely wobbly fashion until, finally, reinforcements came in the form of a visit from her New York–based psychoanalyst. Perhaps this was part of what sustained her until the production tottered to its conclusion.

The Prince and the Showgirl—with its prosaic post-shoot retitling intended to bring Monroe more fully into the equation—was not the transformative work she'd hoped for. She herself took note of this fact after she screened the final version of the film, some weeks prior to its premiere, and discovered to her great displeasure that it had been reedited from the earlier cut she had approved. Her cable to Jack L. Warner regarding the changes shows her at her most thoughtful and observant:

> It is not the same picture you saw last time, and I am afraid that as it stands it will not be as successful as the version all of us agreed was so fine. Especially in the first third . . . the pacing has been slowed and one comic point after another has been flattened out by substituting inferior takes with flatter performances. . . . We have [shot enough] film to make a great movie, if only it will be as in the earlier version. I hope you will make every effort to save our picture.

Little or none of that effort was exercised, unfortunately, and the film was a financial disappointment upon its release in June 1957. The reviews—especially of Monroe's work—were all over the map, and neither her newfound respect as an actor nor her role as producer won consensus approval. A number of critics did applaud her work, calling it her finest to date, and eventually, there would be commendation from several European film organizations. The naysayers, for their part, were harsher than ever. It would be one thing to call out the film for the singular way in which it managed to be both ponderous and insubstantial. It was worse to call Monroe out for her temerity. Often in the past, her reviews were tinged with insult; here her ambition seemed to provoke ridicule. *Time* magazine, which earlier had applauded her work in *Bus Stop*, made attacks that it would be difficult to not take personally:

The Prince and the Showgirl lifts Marilyn Monroe to the probable ceiling of her serious career as a comedienne. It also leaves her ankle-high to such giants of the theater as her fellow performers, Producer-Director Laurence Olivier (her co-star) and cloud-capped Dame Sybil Thorndike. . . . Such a bagatelle of a plot demands—and gets from Dame Sybil and Sir Laurence— high acting to fetch high comedy. From Marilyn it gets a spasmodic effort to conquer the awesome heights. Her most persuasive line is just plain "Gosh!"—but it is never clear whether she is overwhelmed by the dictates of the script or the awesome dramatic company she is keeping. Parading and posing with an even more voluptuous silhouette than most 1911 showgirls had, Marilyn is alternately spirited and lethargic. Especially in her tussling with Olivier, she seems more directed by him than acting with him—as if by wiggling his off-camera ear he gives her the cue to giggle.[2]

The critical indecision regarding *The Prince and the Showgirl* was, in a particular fashion, not at all inappropriate. This is a very difficult film to pin down, in some ways as problematic an entry in the Monroe canon as *The Misfits*. In both cases, it would be easy to ascribe the problems to the calamities and clashes attending their creation. Nevertheless, in *Prince*, there are even more fundamental reasons for this than the total incompatibility of Monroe's and Olivier's respective approaches to acting. (And also their personalities.) One lies in Olivier's fealty to the printed word. If many critics were unhappy with the slashing cuts he had made in his film of *Hamlet*, they need not have worried about his treatment of Rattigan. A running time just under two hours is far too long on film for this slender a premise, which means that moments of grand sparkle are in constant juxtaposition with talkiness and tedium. As with *Bus Stop*, a one-set play has been opened up considerably, yet the basic confined action, as framed with much dialogue and a good deal of repetition, has been allowed to remain—and to plod. There was, in fact, little in Olivier's résumé to indicate that he would ever have had the light Ernst Lubitsch–like touch needed for this kind of charade, with its mythical kingdoms and easily quelled battles that Rattigan limns all too tediously.[3] In individual scenes and

[2] Then in her sixth decade as a working actor of immense achievement and acclaim, Dame Sybil Thorndike had a far higher opinion of MM's work than did the *Time* critic. During one of Monroe's many absences, Thorndike told Olivier, "We need her desperately. She's the only one of us who really knows how to act in front of a camera." Unfailingly gracious even under the most trying circumstances, she remained MM's leading British advocate through the entire shoot.

[3] Onstage in London, evidently, some of the play's duller aspects had been disguised by the chemistry between Leigh and Olivier and by Leigh's trademark ability to make something sparkling out of very little. The situation was less propitious later, on Broadway, where it played after the film was

moments, it can seem plausible and even irresistible; as a whole, it rapidly accumulates talk and detail in a way that proves tedious and even alienating. There may have been some awareness of this early on, since it was thought at one point that the proceedings would be enlivened by giving Monroe a couple of musical numbers. This plan, according to Clark, was nixed by the eternally dour Miller. One missed opportunity would have made for something delectable: Elsie teaching the young king to foxtrot, which is discussed without being shown. In the end, Monroe was left with only a brief and quite delightful dance, which arises logically out of the action, and a short song delivered to Olivier, which doesn't. Musically, this song ("I Found a Dream") is a far cry from "Lazy" or "River of No Return," and her post-synched rendition, done with her trademark fast vibrato, is extremely fetching.[4]

So, in this cacophony of British and American styles of acting and deportment, this bonbon that seems to weigh many pounds, what exactly is there to be salvaged? A great deal, as it happens. Famously, this is the film to watch for anyone curious to know how beautiful Monroe could look on the screen. Between the ministrations of Greene, who helped conceive her look for the film, and the artistry of master cinematographer Jack Cardiff, she is from beginning to end absolutely stunning. The garish lipstick of earlier films and the unearthly whiteface of *Bus Stop* are here replaced by a soft and subtle interplay of creamy pastel shades lit and shot with painstaking delicacy. MM's love affair with the camera is here at a peak that recalls the words of one of her greatest photographers, Richard Avedon: "She was more comfortable in front of the camera than away from it."[5] Her rapport with Cardiff was one of the few smooth aspects of the production, and many of her close-ups are as dazzling as his work on *Black Narcissus* and *The Red Shoes*. His only miscalculation, if that's the word, comes near the end of the coronation sequence,

made but before it opened. This time, the director-star was Michael Redgrave, alongside Barbara Bel Geddes. (As with the movie, the character was remade into an American.) In spite of a good deal of care and an elaborate production, it was judged a ponderous trifle and was off the boards in less than two months.

[4] *The Sleeping Prince* did, in the end, become a musical, albeit an unsuccessful one that never ran in London. *The Girl Who Came to Supper*, with music and lyrics by Noël Coward, opened on Broadway in 1963, with Jose Ferrer playing the prince to Florence Henderson's showgirl, here called Mary (as in the play). Her big moment was a show-stopping capsule version of Mary's musical, *The Coconut Girl*. Would that MM had had a similar opportunity.

[5] Once again, Clark furnishes some background that seems convincing. When Monroe first came to Pinewood Studios to shoot hair, costume, and makeup tests, Olivier and his associates were horrified at the way she looked—washed-out, blotchy, unkempt. Coming onto the set made-up and costumed, she appeared somewhat better yet still a good way from the expected MM incandescence. Then they ran the film. A miracle had occurred.

when he shoots MM through so many filters that it's akin to watching later Doris Day or, worse, Lucille Ball in *Mame*. One striking difference from the close-ups in most of MM's other movies comes with the amount of time she spends with her mouth closed. The parted lips were a Monroe trademark, and her face had a different look when they were shut—a little more thoughtful and serious, perhaps more determined.

It isn't just that she looks great, either. Of all the characters she played, Elsie Marina was probably the most adept in terms of brain power, with a native intelligence that corresponded well with Monroe's own. She has some of the cunning of Lorelei Lee without the venality, the wisdom of the Girl Upstairs with less of the mock-innocence, and even a little of the calculation of Rose Loomis without the murderous impulse. As she had done with Cherie, Monroe supplies a voice markedly different from that famous whisper; this time, it's a Yankee soprano with tinges of both pluck and whimsy. The familiar giggle is well in evidence, and a few times, even the overenunciated consonants can be heard. Appearances, in this case, can be inordinately deceiving, since none of her anguished insecurity shows on the screen; the performance seems completely confident from start to end. She has no problem at all with Rattigan's sometimes excessive verbiage, and though the tempo of her delivery is generally faster than usual, it's also been carefully modulated, charting Elsie's humor, her growing attraction to the Prince Regent, and, especially, her increasing sense of her own dignity. Her vocal tones seem especially fresh in juxtaposition to Olivier's carefully ponderous pseudo-Hungarian accents, which are part character delineation and part stunt. For all its skill and moments of real charm, Olivier's performance shows a good deal of the construction that went into it. However worthy and accomplished the effort, the craft shows, just as parts of MM's *Bus Stop* performance imply how much work it took for her to stray outside her accustomed realm. The truth is that, as good as she was in *Bus Stop*, she's better here. Elsie, with her healthy self-respect, seems to connect with Monroe in ways that the borderline-pitiful Cherie did not. "Seems" is the operative word, of course, and perhaps it was Monroe's hope that in playing a character with such a firm sense of herself, some kind of osmosis might occur. At any rate, the vivacious naturalism of her performance here shows a further refinement of her skill—and, truly, her art.

Given her physical and emotional state during the filming, it's a tribute to her professionalism (a word not always used to describe her) that the strain shows as little as it does. The main giveaway comes with several scenes that seem to be overly edited, making a mosaic of moments that shouldn't necessitate assemblage of this sort. This was done far less as an aesthetic choice than as an expedient needed to grab whatever of Monroe's performance would be usable and then assemble the pieces in the editing room. As was becoming more and more frequent, consistency was not a sure thing with her. On some days, she produced long and excellent takes filled with dialogue and business; other times, you took what you could get, sometimes in tiny pieces. Her directors on *Let's Make Love* and *The Misfits* would need to resort to the same device, less smoothly and effectively than here. The only downside of it all is that the stodginess and tedium that the film often displays make it a less rewarding viewing experience than she warrants. Even so, and "ankle-high" *Time* be damned, her work requires absolutely no need to be graded on a curve.

By no measure had the clash between Monroe and Olivier been less than fraught and unpleasant. Each was a self-contained entity, and neither had the ability or inclination to extend an olive branch in the name of compromise, peace, or art. They were so divorced from each other by the end of the shoot that it can only be imagined how that subsequent photo session went months later, the one with the romantically stimulating shots of them together.[6] As everyone has known since this movie was first announced, these are two different kinds of performer we're dealing with here. At best, a clash of differing approaches can benefit the action, as it did so indelibly with Vivien Leigh's Blanche DuBois and Marlon Brando's Stanley Kowalski. Needless to say, Rattigan's work was no *Streetcar*, and opinions will always vary wildly on how well Monroe and Olivier mesh together, though it should be noted that Olivier himself, in his autobiography, confessed that MM's was the better performance. She herself considered the entire experience a letdown of Olympic proportions and would never again attempt to be her own producer. At least she was able to muster some degree of pride over the achievement when awards came from Italy and France. Those, in the end, would be a truer gauge of her achievement than the sniping from *Time* and other publications. Just as Elsie Marina demonstrates her intelligence and

---

[6] Warner Bros., which released the film, had decided that audiences might be enticed with ad art that made the movie look a good deal steamier than it was. So in Milton Greene's New York studio, Monroe and Olivier donned costumes not in the film (a sequined gown and a smoking jacket) and acted all hot and bothered for Greene's camera. Since Greene was on his way out of MM's orbit by that time, the whole experience must not have been fun. Those pictures may even have created something of a backlash when Bosley Crowther ended his *New York Times* review by griping that the movie wasn't as sexy as the posters.

insight, so does Monroe overcome all the obstacles—the problems with her own health and well-being, her director, the script, her enablers, and everything else. In spite of it all, she proved just about everything she had set out to prove. A better film would have been nice, too, but watch it anyway. You can see her soar.

11

Wait for Sugar

A film as triumphantly realized as *Some Like It Hot* could never have just one simple factor accounting for its brilliance—or, for that matter, for its success and its permanence. However splendid the writing and direction, however perfect the cast, there isn't an individual component that can be held responsible for that wondrous final result. This, in fact, is the key to its endurance: seldom have the elements of a film meshed together so master-fully. Years earlier, Marilyn Monroe had been part of a similarly well-formed film, although in *All about Eve*, her participation was less a cause than an effect. In *Some Like It Hot*, her finest film and her finest performance, she is an essential part of that central axis, along with Billy Wilder, cowriter I. A. L. Diamond, Jack Lemmon, and Tony Curtis. (Joe E. Brown is next up.) Nor is it simply a case of her being given a good script and direction, since she was an instrumental force in its creation. The rocky road through which this occurred—due primarily to difficulties connected with Monroe herself—is quite well known. Yet in this marvel of comedic filmmaking, there is ample greatness to justify all that trouble. Enough, even, to raise a question: would it have turned out nearly so well if it had been easier to make?

Monroe had been away from film for a year and a half when Wilder contacted her regarding *Some Like It Hot*. In 1958, this long an absence by a front-rank movie star was, if not unprecedented, certainly unconventional. After *The Prince and the Showgirl*, with its attendant difficulties, Monroe and Arthur Miller had returned to New York, dividing their time between a country place and a Manhattan apartment. He battled with the House Un-American Activities Committee and began a screenplay called *The Misfits*. She commenced work with a new psychoanalyst, continued study with Lee Strasberg, and, sadly, struggled through an unsuccessful pregnancy. If Hollywood seemed far away, she constantly received screenplays and offers, especially from Twentieth Century-Fox. Anxious for her to start the second of her four contracted films, her home studio was particularly high on something that now (perhaps even then) seems a ghastly idea; the Marlene Dietrich role in a remake of *The Blue Angel*. This fortunately did not come to pass, though she feigned interest in it for a while.[1] Even as a return to work was not the highest item on Monroe's agenda, she was receptive to ideas from those she respected. Billy Wilder was one such figure. Their work together on *The Seven Year Itch* had been productive and, all things considered, harmonious. This time, her reaction upon reading the outline Wilder sent her was decidedly mixed.

While it's fairly well known that there was a 1951 German predecessor to *Some Like It Hot*, it's less remembered that the whole thing had started with a French film made in 1935. Both of these were called, in English translation, *Fanfare of Love* (the German was in the plural), and, like many European productions, neither had been considered important enough to rate a release in the United States. Each mined the time-honored comedic possibilities of unwilling necessity, in this case the financial need that compels two men to dress as women and join an all-female orchestra. Many elements of farce were in place—the protocols of drag, the juggling of identities, role reversal, somewhat awkward romance, and much running around. In both France and Germany, it all worked well enough in a light and nonthreatening way; female impersonation has, after all, had its place in comedy since around the Pleistocene era. Many men can look pretty funny dressed as women, which contributes to the fantasy aspect of the premise: Can't the people around these two unappealing specimens see that they're not for real? Thus, the suspension of disbelief that's a necessary part of most comedy becomes even more pressing here.

For Wilder and Diamond, the drag was less of a problem than the underlying cause. In a European film, two men deciding to dress as women in order to obtain work was not particularly bothersome. In America, Wilder and Diamond observed, there needed to be more. In a film shot in the United States in 1958, men dressing as women might make for a shaky proposition, which meant that a sense of urgency was needed over and beyond employment and a paycheck. For this, Wilder and Diamond imparted a genius notion: they tossed in the St. Valentine's Day Massacre. Joe and Jerry are speakeasy musicians who find themselves in the wrong garage at the wrong time and are sufficiently recognizable to the gang members that they have

---

[1] Fox, then in a period when really lousy notions were becoming commonplace, eventually went ahead with the project, with May Britt in the role intended for MM. The result would not be termed the Worst Movie Remake of All Time, since there's *way* too much competition. Surely, however, it can stand as a contender for a runner-up prize, Most Unnecessary (possibly an honor shared with what happened with *Psycho*).

to resort to drastic measures. With this, pretending to be a woman becomes a matter of life and death. Plus, with this particular setting, Wilder and Diamond were able to give the story a more complex and nuanced texture. Atop the farce of gender switch, masquerade, and sexual ambiguity, there is also satire of gangsters and Prohibition, as well as the movies that depicted them. To underscore this, the cast would be filled out with a number of actors who had actually been part of cinema back then—Brown, George Raft, Pat O'Brien, and, as the unfortunate Toothpick Charlie, George E. Stone. The screenplay adds to this ambience by references to all sorts of period phenomena, from a pre-Tarzan Johnny Weissmuller to Hupmobile and the Graf Zeppelin. Given the straight-line nature of most American film comedy in 1958, this was an elaborate setup, rich and dense enough to accommodate nearly everything from Keystone Kops slapstick to pointed sexual innuendo—straight, gay, and everything in between. Indeed, wild sexual comedy was more present here than in any film (or at least American film) since the heydays of Ernst Lubitsch and Preston Sturges.

The believability was the part that tripped up Monroe when Wilder first sent her the plot synopsis, graced with the working title *Not Tonight, Josephine!* In her ongoing quest for truth in acting, she found that her character's inability to spot the disguise seemed irredeemably phony. After all, wouldn't "Marilyn Monroe" (she would frequently discuss her on-screen self in the third person) be able to spot a bogus woman when she saw one? Whatever an MM character's naivete or innocence, she, of all people, would hardly be a pushover where gender was concerned. It took some effort by Wilder, Miller, and Strasberg to convince her that this was a sound comedy premise, and it was Strasberg who provided her with her a solution to her dilemma. This young woman, he told her, has not been treated well by men and has not had close friendships with other women. And then here come these two nice (if unlovely) women who want to be her friends. No wonder she's willing to accept them at face value. With this, it finally clicked for Monroe, and so did the hefty salary-plus-percentage deal she was offered.

Even as she agreed to do the film, she was aware that her character was less initiator than reactor, a glittering part of the film's fringe rather than a core constituent. This also could have been said, in one way or another, about her last five films, even *The Prince and the Showgirl*. Sugar, the role she would play here, was nearly as subsidiary to the main action as the women had been in the French and German originals. This, surely, is why Wilder's initial casting thought had been Mitzi Gaynor, an engaging song-and-dance talent but not necessarily a dominant performer.[2] By offering the part to Monroe instead, Wilder knew that her "flesh impact," as he called it, would make the role appear more significant than it actually was. Perhaps he was also able to foresee that she would be taking the matter into her own hands.

Fully aware that she ran the risk of being overshadowed by a pair of female impersonators, Monroe proceeded to do everything she could to give herself, and Sugar, as much primacy as possible. Upon discovering that the film would not be shot in color, she objected forcefully—which, given how she'd looked in Technicolor in her last film, was understandable. Wilder, for his part, knew that black-and-white was the way to go. It fit the tabloid/period setting, recalled those earlier movies, and, perhaps most important, fostered the central premise. Tests showed that Curtis and Lemmon would look far more convincing, and far less freakish, in monochrome, and some color stills survive to bear this out. Monroe agreed and turned her attention to her musical numbers. Although her songs required little in the way of choreography, she requested the help of Jack Cole, who would stand just off camera demonstrating her Charleston and shimmy as she performed "Runnin' Wild." She also determined that her costumes were going to catch more eyes than anything worn by her costars. Accordingly, she prevailed on designer Orry-Kelly to come up with two dresses that would pull the focus away from an elephant stampede. Far more revealing than anything Kelly had done at Warner Bros. for Kay Francis or Bette Davis, the dresses were in silver for one, black for the other, and a great deal of Monroe skin for both. The silver gown, in which she sings "I Wanna Be Loved by You" and seduces Curtis on the yacht, seems nearly topless, with Monroe's breasts covered only by thin chiffon and a few sequins. It necessitated very careful lighting, especially during the song, and remains startling even today. It also showed that her figure had filled out some from previous films, a fact several critics ungallantly noted.[3]

---

[2] Another casting notion that went nowhere, fortunately, was Frank Sinatra. Wilder reportedly nixed him after Sinatra failed to show up for a scheduled meeting. Just try to picture him dressed as a woman.

[3] Among the snipers was, again, *Time*, whose rather pathetic assessment of MM's performance was confined to noting that she'd been "trimmer, slimmer, and sexier in earlier pictures." The story goes that as Monroe was being fitted for her costumes, Orry-Kelly observed that Curtis had a shapelier rear end than MM, to which she retorted by facing him to proclaim, "Yes, but he doesn't have *these!*" Perhaps it was a sort of revenge that gave the film's costume credit only as "Miss Monroe's Gowns," although Kelly had costumed Curtis and Lemmon as well, and in a style more true to the period than what MM wore. Orry-Kelly's Oscar for Best Costume Design (Black and White) was the only win among *Some Like It Hot*'s six nominations, which did not include a Best Picture nod (really).

Before and during filming, Monroe worked steadily to give Sugar more depth, significance, and humor. In her prompt book for the film, she jotted down dozens of tiny notes to herself about how best to convey what Sugar might be thinking. "<u>What</u> am I doing, not <u>how</u>," she wrote on the inside cover. When Sugar meets "Shell Oil" on the beach: "Lets herself go . . . really relaxed." "Sensory—Night" is her reminder/cue when Sugar takes a nocturnal boat ride. Sugar enters the yacht salon with the advisory "Trust it. Enjoy it. Be brave." (Possibly, MM was directing these tips to herself as much as to Sugar.) Whenever possible, she sought to make more out of the character than was written in the script. Originally, Sugar was to enter the film only as one of the band members, with the camera singling her out. This, clearly, would not be enough, so on her first day of shooting, she spoke to Wilder about it. He quickly came up with a classic moment: Sugar tootling along until the train shoots a blast of steam at her derrière. Not only a winning comedic accent, it was also a slyly affectionate nod to the subway scene in *The Seven Year Itch*.

Much of the earlier portion of filming was the location work at Coronado Island, near San Diego. Monroe, who had newly discovered that she was pregnant again, made it through even some of the longer and more complicated beach scenes with relative ease, and it was Wilder's contention that Paula Strasberg's steadfast, black-draped presence on the set posed surprisingly little hindrance. Back at the studio, matters took a different turn, and the many horror stories told about Monroe during *Some Like It Hot* were neither fabricated nor, evidently, exaggerated. From his earlier work with her, Wilder was familiar with the lateness, the blown lines, the multiple takes. Nothing, however, prepared him for what happened here. Dozens upon dozens of times, she was unable to knock on a door and say, "It's me, Sugar," and it proved to be all but impossible for her to say the line "Where's that bourbon?" (In the film, she says it with her back turned, which indicates that it had to be post-synched.) For take after take, it was necessary for Curtis and Lemmon to stand there in painful high heels while she repeatedly fumbled through her lines. Both men's comedic flair, shown so vividly throughout the film, came at a high price: they quickly realized that they had to be at their best during every single take, because the final selection would be based on MM, not them. On one famous occasion, someone noted while watching the dailies, that Curtis seemed to enjoy kissing her. "It's like kissing Hitler," he spat, though much later, he claimed he hadn't *really* said that. Apparently, he had, though, and if it wasn't a remotely defensible remark, his anger was, on some level, comprehensible. Curtis, at least, had the clout to speak up, unlike the poor assistant director sent to fetch Monroe to the set after everyone had been waiting for hours. With Paula Strasberg most likely in attendance, she was holed up in her dressing room intently reading (what else?) Thomas Paine's *The Rights of Man*. Upon getting the request to join the company, she responded to the gentleman with an obscene, anatomically impossible directive.

Why so much difficulty, even more in some ways than that which had hampered *The Prince and the Showgirl*? Some came with what might be termed a general unraveling, fairly obvious to many of her associates, which could make her behavior careen from helplessness to wrath, with stops at all points in between. There was also her ongoing uncertainty about the material, which was not diminished by Paula Strasberg's well-paid inability, at times, to coax her into a functioning professional mindset. Monroe's concern about her pregnancy was also a factor—which, paradoxically, did not seem to hinder her ingestion of pills and alcohol. (Vermouth, reportedly, was her libation of choice on the set, and this was likely not simply a way to "live" Sugar Kane's drinking problem.) Plus, as with Laurence Olivier, there was her awareness that her director was losing his patience and his respect for her. By the end of shooting, Wilder was making witty, barbed statements to the press about how awful it had been. After one especially pointed remark, Miller wrote to Wilder to demand an apology, asserting that his wife was "the salt of the earth." Wilder responded by noting that "the salt of the earth told an assistant director to go fuck himself."[4]

At the end of it all, there was a film that had gone far over schedule and an impressive half-million dollars (more than 20 percent) over budget. For Monroe, the misery of the experience was multiplied after she returned to New York and suffered a miscarriage. Wilder, for his part, knew quickly that all the suffering and frustration attending the film's production had, paradoxically enough, produced a comic masterpiece. For some reason, the very first preview was a laughless disaster—which may be the only recorded instance of a *Some Like It Hot* audience not completely losing it. From the second preview onward, over six-plus decades, the reaction has been consistent: this is not only one of the cleverest and best-crafted comedies ever made but also

---

[4] Not too long afterward, Wilder extracted an amusing revenge by putting a Monroe-parody character in *The Apartment*. Still, there's no people like show people, and sacred monsters roam the earth via self-determined paths. Thus, a while before MM's death, she and Wilder were on good enough terms to be discussing the possibility of her starring in *Irma la Douce*. (He also conceived *Kiss Me, Stupid* with her in mind.) And, speaking of *The Apartment*, imagine how good Monroe could have been in the role played so memorably by Shirley MacLaine.

one of the funniest. The reviews said as much, the financial returns did the same, and, with the possible exceptions of *La Cage aux folles* and *Tootsie*, drag has never again been so funny and so worth it, on the screen and possibly off it as well.

Exactly what is it, then, that makes *Some Like It Hot* so good? Much, naturally, has to do with Wilder, who was able to bracket the decade of the 1950s with two timeless masterpieces, *Sunset Boulevard* and this. Wilder's sync with "Iz" Diamond was unerring, if sometimes harrowing, and their ability to transform and elevate amusing, trivial source material was little short of miraculous. The one-liners fly by steadily, and some extra resonance is applied with such recurring script motifs as Sheboygan and type O blood. There was also Wilder's singular gift as a director: he did not overshoot. For such a large and complex production, there was surprisingly little footage for the editor, Arthur P. Schmidt, to assemble. Essentially, Wilder had already laid out the blocking and done the editing in the camera—a cost-saving boon given the astronomical amounts of film stock being used up for MM's multiple takes. Such an approach also meant that the pacing—lightning-quick at some moments, easier in others—was basically built-in. Witness, for example, that final chase, beginning with the murder of Spats Columbo and ending with two couples in a speedboat and a classic last line. Most of it is done at a furious tempo—including the hilarious shot of Monroe racing along on a bicycle—yet in the midst of the frenzy, Wilder gives her plenty of time to sing a sad "I'm Thru with Love." Most famously, there is the single best example of cross-cutting since the heyday of D. W. Griffith: Monroe and Curtis horizontal on the yacht, counterpointed by a very vertical Lemmon and Brown in what is surely the most devastating tango ever performed.

However excruciating their relationship, Wilder and Monroe were made for each other. *The Seven Year Itch* had already demonstrated how unerringly she responded to his direction, while he knew exactly how best to present her. Each had an impeccable sense of comedic timing, with her innocence and his cynicism mixing together as well as, say, gin and tonic. (Or even a Manhattan made in a hot-water bottle.) For all his annoyance with her, his frustration and anger when she would look past him for approval from Paula Strasberg, he knew that she could do many things better than anyone else. While he was shocked at how much she had come apart in the four years since *The Seven Year Itch*—the outbursts of temper were a new and especially unwelcome development—he could also observe how much she had grown as an actor. This he could respect, and the wonder of her performance in *Some Like It Hot* is how deftly it balances the best qualities of her earlier work with what she developed following her decampment to New York. An intersection, perhaps, of the Girl Upstairs with Elsie Marina, adding touches of Cherie and Lorelei Lee. If Sugar has some of the same hovering-above-terra-firma quality as the myopic Pola, she is as firmly aware of certain hard realities as Cherie was about most things, except her own talent. She may be subsidiary to Joe and Jerry on paper, yet she is fleshed out (sorry) with an unusual amount of backstory. This, especially, is where we can see the dividends being paid by Monroe's study at the Actors Studio.

In most far-out comedies, the audience knows comparatively little about the lead characters. They exist in the now, and whatever got them to that point is incidental or secondary. A Charlie Chaplin or a Groucho Marx had a preestablished persona and then was given the opportunity to react to the current situation, such as it might be. In *Some Like It Hot*, Joe and Jerry spearhead the action by deciding to dress as women, travel to Florida, and find two incredibly dissimilar kinds of romance. That's what they do and why we're drawn to them. What got them there is a mystery that Wilder and Diamond do not solve. They've been musicians working different gigs, Joe plays the ponies and sleeps around, and Jerry follows along. That's it, without even last names. Sugar, on the other hand, gives us her whole life—her last name (Kowalczyk, for which MM wrote the pronunciation in her prompt book), her hometown (Sandusky, Ohio), even her parents' occupations. We didn't have quite this much biography on Cherie. Sugar's obsession with saxophone players brings her a steady stream of bad boyfriends, which is one reason she drinks, and her physical appeal ensures that many women are suspicious of her. She's flighty, yes, but despite her protestations, she's not dumb. Nor does she display the exhaustive naivete Cherie has about show business. She's as optimistic and sweet-natured as the Girl Upstairs, and if she's a little less clued-in than Elsie, she generally manages to have a least one foot on the ground. Yes, she's deceived by all the disguises she encounters, less because of ignorance or passivity than because of kindness and trust. Monroe covers all this territory with skill, charm, and even more detail than in her previous two performances. Her physical presence is more assured, her facial expressions rich and varied, and her transitions from slapstick to sophisticated completely effortless. By creating such a full character, she manages to make the film, even with her delayed entrance, as much about her as it is about those two musicians.

Monroe's song numbers warrant special attention, not least for being so nuanced and detailed. Eons earlier, in *River of No Return*, the sleek professionalism of her songs came as so jarring a contrast to the stilted amateurishness of her acting that it was almost like watching two separate performers. Here she outdoes even *Gentlemen Prefer Blondes* in the smooth interrelation of spoken and sung words. Following one early try (*Emperor Waltz*), Wilder stayed away from musical filmmaking, which is why *Irma la Douce* had all its songs removed when it moved from stage to screen. Yet, for an ostensibly non-musical piece, *Some Like It Hot* contains a large amount of music. Adolph Deutsch's musical score is almost entirely made up of period pop standards, including a jazz-hot version of "Sugar Blues" as an MM leitmotif, "Stairway to the Stars" for the big love scene, and "La cumparsita" during that epic tango. Monroe sings three times, four if we count a title song that was recorded but not used in the film. Her style and technique had both changed since *There's No Business Like Show Business*. Her voice pitched in a slightly higher range, she uses more of that famous whisper and relies more on a quick vibrato on sustained high notes, as in "I must have *yoooouuu* or no one" in "I'm Thru with Love." Brief as it is, her "Runnin' Wild" is indelible, with possibly the best moves Cole ever gave her and a wink so infectious that it has become a much-used GIF. For "I Wanna Be Loved by You," the doll-like chirp of the song's creator, Helen Kane, has been replaced by MM breathiness, which makes the song more real—she truly *wants* to be loved. This is no small achievement for a number most notable for its repeated use of the deathless non-phrase "boop-boop a doop." The recording (supervised by Matty Malneck, with some dandy orchestrations) is excellent, but the visual element, with that cautiously lit dress, makes it a knockout. Watch especially how Monroe's facial expressions provide a visual equivalent of orchestral details, as when she gives a slight shrug to reflect the tiny "pow" from the percussion after that first "boop-boop a doop." She brings Sugar's offstage life into the mix with several anxious looks into the audience as she searches for "Junior" and caps it all off with another shrug to punctuate that final "boop." Lastly, "I'm Thru with Love" becomes totally about Sugar's broken heart. It's a tattered, hokey old song, cowritten by Malneck himself, and after you've experienced Alfalfa shrieking through it in that *Our Gang* short, you may never be able to keep a straight face when you hear it. Somehow, and it may be an act of alchemy, Monroe makes it real and poignant. "*Why* did you lead me to think you could care?" she accuses, adding a sardonic chuckle before "with deep emotion, devotion to you." She never felt a song as genuinely on the screen as she does here. It's no wonder that her name on the cover of the soundtrack album is appended with the announcement, in smaller letters, "SINGS!"[5]

Accounts vary about what Monroe herself thought of the completed film and her work in it. The great reviews, and the financial recompense from that 10 percent share of the profits, may have mattered less than her own opinion of the way Wilder had presented her. At least one Monroe biographer has recounted her dismayed reaction when she saw the completed film: "I don't want to be funny. . . . Everybody's going to laugh at me. And not because of my acting. I looked like a fat pig." In addition to her ongoing uncertainty about the script and her feelings about Wilder—not to mention about Curtis's "Hitler" remark—she possibly associated the whole experience with the pregnancy that had, once again, ended so unhappily. There was also a lingering feeling that this was not the kind of work she should now be doing. *Bus Stop* was a comedy-drama by a respected playwright, while *The Prince and the Showgirl*, for all its downsides, had Olivier and a British pedigree. *Some Like It Hot* had drag and slapstick and comic gangsters. Her ongoing drive for respect and respectability blinded her to the fact that this script was the cleverest and best-crafted material she'd had since *All about Eve*. (The scene in *Anna Christie* not excepted.) Her underestimation, then, was total—neither the script, nor the direction, nor her own work was sufficient. The saddest part of this is how much she failed to acknowledge her own accomplishment in transforming and elevating a possibly sketchy role into something sublime. Her own insecurities, monumental as they were, had seen to it that she was unable, or unwilling, to give herself anywhere near the credit she deserved.

Fortunately, an overwhelming number of reviews said otherwise. *Time* was a churlish exception, including the asinine observation, in a follow-up capsule review, that "The primitive Monroe, before Miller and Method, seemed funnier, lusher, smarter." Pauline Kael, too, skirted this reductive mindset with her "both charming and embarrassing" line. Others were far more accurate in their assessments, although the repeated mention of the

---

[5] Monroe's zingy performance of the title song (music by Malneck, lyrics by Diamond) may have originally been intended to be played under the opening credits. In the end, the credits were scored with a medley of "Sugar Blues" and "Runnin' Wild," and MM's recording was released only on a 45-rpm "extended-play" disc. In this cut, more than any other, she can be heard really leaning in on that fast vibrato of hers, to the point where some find it intrusive. Speaking of that soundtrack album, on the United Artists label, was it recorded with tin cans and a string? The sound quality, unlike that in the movie itself, is terrible, far inferior to that of records actually made in 1929.

"dumb blonde" persona must have annoyed her mightily, even in reviews that praised her comedic skill. Archer Winston's review in the *New York Post*, while perhaps edging toward a patronizing attitude, made a rather provocative observation: "To get down to cases, Marilyn does herself proud, giving a performance of such intrinsic quality that you begin to believe she's only being herself and it is herself who fits into that distant period and this picture so well." What higher accolade could one give an actor striving to convey a role's inner truth? *Intrinsic.* By working from the inside outward, Winston is saying, Monroe has realized not only the character but her time, place, era, and ethos. Perhaps this is a debatable opinion, given the fact that she seems (and looks) far more 1958 than 1929; still, it's a commendation of a high order, a signal that the work and study and anguish, post-Miller and post-Method, had produced something extraordinary. Even with all the skilled people in front of and behind the camera doing brilliant things, it might all otherwise have been simply an uproarious stunt, an audacious tweaking of gender roles, even an unwitting harbinger of gay liberation. With Monroe, and the unexpected emotional resonance she bestowed, it became something significantly more. In all likelihood, *Some Like It Hot* will go on forever and, no surprise, continue to place at or near the top in those infernal "Funniest Movie of All Time" polls. Never doubt, then, not for a single moment, that Monroe's achievement is at the very center of both its success and its longevity. Anyone who doesn't comprehend this is simply not paying attention. Of course, nobody's perfect.

12

Off Broadway

The Seven Year Itch

was produced because it had been a successful play and had an ideal role for Marilyn Monroe.

Bus Stop

was produced to demonstrate and celebrate Marilyn Monroe's growth as an actor.

The Prince and the Showgirl

was produced to show that Marilyn Monroe could perform as an equal alongside the most acclaimed actor of the time.

Some Like It Hot

was produced because Billy Wilder had a wonderful idea for a comedy which he and Marilyn Monroe were then able to realize perfectly.

Let's Make Love

was produced because Twentieth Century-Fox had nothing better for Marilyn Monroe to do and, presumably, because nature abhors a vacuum.

A film—really, any created work—that has no defensible reason for its existence is a dispiriting thing indeed. Among the many sins committed by *Let's Make Love*, this may be the worst. An overpriced, underachieving carcass of a movie, it can stand as a symbol of everything that was wrong with the American film industry as the 1950s turned into the 1960s. Essentially, the old ways of filmmaking were dying because of an inability to adapt to wildly changing times. *Some Like It Hot*, smash hit that it was, had been produced away from the big-studio system, as would be MM's next planned film, *The*

Misfits. Tastes were evolving, and so were business practices, and a studio like Twentieth Century-Fox seemed to counter this by looking backward instead of forward. Increasingly hobbled by poor management, Fox was demonstrating an increasing inability to discern the kinds of films the public wanted to see. As a series of ineffectual leaders succeeded Darryl Zanuck, the studio rapidly became awash in red ink. There was the major hit of *Peyton Place* in 1957, a few middling successes, and much disaster. Even the critically lauded film of *The Diary of Anne Frank* was a box-office failure. One good indicator of how things were going came with that asinine notion of putting Monroe into a *Blue Angel* remake. (That had been financially beneficial for her, if not Fox, since her attorneys saw to it that she was paid in spite of not being in it or ever truly intending to be.) Then, after the smash of *Some Like It Hot*, Fox scrambled to put her in something that could cash in. Anything.

Having passed on the option to produce *The Misfits*, Fox had two disparate, and not altogether unpromising, properties for her. First up was *Can-Can*, which Fox had first offered her around the time she was considering *Some Like It Hot*. On Broadway in 1953, it had been a major hit, with Cole Porter's songs, Michael Kidd's choreography, and a star-making turn by Gwen Verdon. Although Fox sent out hopeful announcements that Monroe would star in *Can-Can* alongside Maurice Chevalier, she eventually turned it down.[1] Next, and more to her taste, was Elia Kazan's *Time and Tide*, which eventually saw the light of day as *Wild River*. An unglamorous dramatic story, Kazan as director, and Montgomery Clift as costar were all inducements, until, this time, it was Kazan who said no to Fox. As he had done with *Baby Doll*, Kazan offered that MM was too old for the role, for which he had already decided on Lee Remick. So Fox made a third try, this time with a marked drop-off in inspiration. It was titled *The Billionaire* and eventually became *Let's Make Love*.

One of the many egregious aspects of *Let's Make Love* is its dishonesty: it was a remake that pretended it wasn't. As such, it was a product of a wearisome moviemaking trope that was big at the time and continues up to now: Why come up with something new when we can remake something that was a hit the first time? An old story, in this line of thinking, can be decked out with newer stars and details and promises about it being made more "current." This was an especially hot notion in 1959 with MGM's blockbuster sound

---

[1] It's not easy picturing MM as turn-of-the-century and French; it was even less easy to do so with the star duo who made it into the film. Alongside Chevalier and Louis Jourdan, fresh from *Gigi*, Frank Sinatra and Shirley MacLaine seem even more out of place than Monroe would have been.

version of *Ben-Hur*. Fox, which had already tried to inveigle Monroe into that nightmare *Blue Angel*, was just then preparing to go all the way back to Theda Bara to outdo *Ben-Hur* and an even costlier MGM remake, *Mutiny on the Bounty*. Its new version of *Cleopatra* rapidly proved to be the most expensive and mismanaged production made up to that time and came close to shutting down the studio.

Even apart from *Cleopatra*, as if anything could be apart from *Cleopatra*, Twentieth Century-Fox had that history of retooling and remaking its former successes, so much so that it was part of the company's ethos and heritage. And, being no stranger to the workings of her studio, Monroe knew that when she came to do *How to Marry a Millionaire*, she would be appearing in a reworking of at least four previous films. At least in that case, the details were freshened up with something approximating wit and style. Unfortunately, those commodities were becoming increasingly rare; witness *Pink Tights*, for which Fox had gone back to the Betty Grable well for story ideas, and *There's No Business Like Show Business*, so hackneyed that it played like a remake even thought it wasn't one. As for *Let's Make Love*, the studio claimed that it was an original script by the prolific screenwriter and playwright Norman Krasna. Krasna had a long string of successes (plus some flops) and an easy, facile way with comedic situations. One recent credit of his, *White Christmas*, had been a marathon hit, although Krasna's script, extensively rewritten by others, was probably its least distinguished aspect. He was, in any case, a name, albeit one whose best work was behind him. This was readily apparent in his script for *The Billionaire*.

What no one deigned to mention at the time was that *The Billionaire*'s script was a reworking, with the genders switched, of a long-ago Fox hit. *On the Avenue*, released in 1937, starred Dick Powell as Gary Blake, writer and star of a Broadway revue called (what else?) *On the Avenue*. One of his show's sketches makes wicked fun of the excesses of the much-publicized and uber-wealthy heiress Mimi Caraway (Madeleine Carroll), her father, and her fiancé. After she sees the parody, Mimi demands that Blake remove it from the show—which results in conflict, interference from Blake's jealous girlfriend (Alice Faye), and, eventually, Blake and Mimi setting aside class and conflicts in favor of true love. If this plot wasn't the most devastating frame on which to hang a fine bunch of Irving Berlin songs, it had enough edge to put it a cut above the scripts of all those other *Broadway Melody* and *Big Broadcast* backstage musicals being made at the time. There was, indeed, a bit of novelty at its core: instead of portraying an heiress being libeled by a newspaper story, this one considered herself defamed by onstage ridicule. No one likes being made fun of, especially by people you don't know, and the ultra-rich can be especially touchy about such things. What the film shows of the offending sketch, with numerous digs at wretched excess and Faye going over the top as a hoity spoiled Carroll, is sharp enough to make Mimi's anger comprehensible.

While *On the Avenue* had been a success, it was, more than twenty years later, moderately easy to pretend that it had never happened and act as if this *Billionaire* script was something new and (all other things being equal) fresh. Producer Jerry Wald initially announced a splashy production, with many stars taking cameo appearances, though the more pressing issue came with casting the lead. A rich man would now be the sinned-against party, and Krasna was envisioning someone far away from a musical-comedy idiom. The gimmick would then come with the billionaire's decision to join the show in order to cozy up to its leading woman, thus charting a hopefully amusing path from no-talent stick to would-be song-and-dance man. First, Krasna had thoughts of casting the likes of Gary Cooper or Jimmy Stewart, and then he moved on to the more realistic choice of Gregory Peck, who accepted the role.

Enter Monroe, through all-but-shady means. With *Can-Can* and *Wild River* having come to naught, some Fox genius thought of the woman's part in *The Billionaire*. Wald was already in talks with George Cukor to direct it, and Cukor was on MM's "approved directors" list. If he signed on, she would be contractually obligated to appear in it, like it or not. So, voilà, it was done. Monroe, who had no particular interest in doing it, made the predictable request that Jack Cole stage the musical numbers. (He had already worked with Cukor on *Les Girls*.) At the same time, she was paying more attention to the coming production of *The Misfits* and also trying to wangle the lead in *Breakfast at Tiffany's*. Finally, she read the script of *The Billionaire* and immediately demanded a major round of rewrites to improve her role. This job went to a well-paid and (at his insistence) uncredited Arthur Miller. Not then, or ever, noted for his comedic gifts, Miller later asserted that the material he was given to work with was "not worth the paper it was typed on." Around this time, there was also a change in title to the far more provocative *Let's Make Love*. Peck read Miller's rewrite, saw how much his role had been reduced in favor of Monroe's, and quit. As a parting shot, he offered a comment to the effect that pushing someone's grandma down the stairs was funnier than this script.

In 1959, major stars like Peck did not ordinarily leave productions this far along in preparation, let alone take the magnanimous step of returning the advance the studio had paid him. Having thus been caught short, the Fox casting department immediately started making calls, which soon took on a tone of desperation. Cary Grant said no, and so did Charlton Heston, who later wrote that he had been put off by the reports of Monroe's lateness and conduct. Rock Hudson, Yul Brynner, William Holden, Kirk Douglas, and even Tony Curtis were among the other ideas. None worked out. As with *Cleopatra* after Elizabeth Taylor's near-death experience, this could have been the time when a sane producer pulled the plug on what clearly seemed to be a benighted enterprise. Instead, the search for a billionaire went on. Perhaps one should never follow a tip from an agent, yet this is what Arthur Miller did, leading to a casting idea that could truly be termed, if one cared to be polite, offbeat: Yves Montand.

Italian-born but purely French, an ex-protégé and lover of Edith Piaf, Montand had garnered a *formidable* (use the French pronunciation) reputation as a singer, a serious actor, and a sex symbol. Miller and MM became familiar with Montand and his star-wife, Simone Signoret, when they appeared in the Paris production of Miller's play *The Crucible* and then in the film version (both retitled *Les sorcières de Salem*). At the time Miller mentioned him for *Let's Make Love*, Montand was in the United States with his one-man show, which had played a limited run on Broadway to immense acclaim. Fox, running out of ideas, said yes and signed him almost immediately. There were two inordinately piquant aspects to this casting choice. Once was that Montand, unlike Peck and other candidates for the role, actually *was* a musical performer, thus throwing out of whack the entire fish-out-of-water point of the script. The other: he spoke virtually no English at all. His wife, then at her own career peak with the film *Room at the Top*, served as his chief translator. Since his rival in the film (essentially, the Faye role) was being played by British entertainer Frankie Vaughan, this archetypally American project suddenly began to seem somewhat international.

In spite of a casting process haphazard nearly to the point of farce, *Let's Make Love* was hardly a second-rung enterprise. Along with a sizable budget and accomplished technical personnel, there was Cukor, whose body of work encompassed a long list of worthy and classic titles, from *Dinner at Eight* and *David Copperfield* to *The Women*, *The Philadelphia Story*, and Judy Garland's *A Star Is Born* remake. He was the best-known "woman's director" in the business and did indeed have a special touch with actresses, besides that being code for saying that he was gay. His career was not, at this point, at one of its high points. *Les Girls* and *Heller in Pink Tights* had fared disappointingly, and his most recent job had been especially desultory: finishing up the waxen *Song without End* after the original director opted to die instead. Perhaps that experience dampened Cukor's enthusiasm for filmmaking; *Let's Make Love* trudges along over a long 118 minutes with no discernible narrative drive, alleviated only by a bleak kind of sparkle and a sometimes credible theatrical ambience. Not that anyone else would or could have done much better.

Having roused herself into fabricating a small amount of initial enthusiasm for *Let's Make Love*, MM began rehearsals in a fashion that was capricious and inconsistent even for her. Sometimes, as Vaughan remembered, she would be so connected and spot-on that "Everybody [else] smartened up, as if her presence was the light that fell on everyone." At other times, she was numbingly late if she showed up at all. Normally, working with Cole showed her at her most professional and hard-working. Not so here, at least on a regular basis. Although the dancers enjoyed working with her, even the volubly profane Cole was rendered nearly speechless on the numerous occasions when she failed to show up. Silence, in some estimations, may have been preferable to the time he told her off, in quite obscene terms, in front of Montand and the crew.[2]

Things got even worse late in preproduction, when Monroe sat down with Cukor, Wald, and head of production Buddy Adler to view the hair, makeup, and wardrobe tests. What a shock it must have been for these men to have moved heaven and earth to get her to do a film and then see her looking terrible. By general opinion, Monroe's included, the tests were so disastrous as to make the announcement that her long love affair with the camera was finally over. Neither her makeup nor her hair was flattering, and the costumes seemed to accentuate her weight gain rather than conceal it. As he began to recover from this unpleasant surprise, Adler directed Wald and Cukor to run *The Seven Year Itch* and *Some Like It Hot* to see how MM *should* be presented. For her, the situation was worse: she fled the screening room after the tests ran and refused to come back to the studio for several days. Somehow, after

[2] Normally, even as he had no illusions about her limitations as a dancer, Cole was almost as close to Monroe as her devoted "crew"—the makeup, hair, and wardrobe people who worked with her in film after film, understood her, and knew how kind she could be toward those she considered friends. As the *Let's Make Love* nightmare ground to its close, she sent Cole a $1,500 check, along with a sweet note of apology. "I really was awful," she wrote. "Please go someplace nice for a couple of weeks and pretend that it never happened." Then, a couple of days later, came another check, this time for $500, with the message, "Stay another three days." Cole loved her for that.

all this, the production finally got started, none too smoothly. With unerring timeliness, something then happened that, wonder of wonders, was not MM-related: in reaction to a pair of strikes by the Screen Actors Guild and the Writers Guild, the production was shut down for more than a month. Even apart from that extra jinx, Monroe was constantly aware, often to a debilitating extent, that this one was a dead duck. Cukor, for his part, was generally patient with her, at least in public, although it was observed that during the uncountable hours spent waiting for her, he would sometimes tear off pieces of the script, stick them in his mouth, and chew nervously on them. Usually, when she did show up, he could pretend to ignore the fact that after every take, she looked past him to Paula Strasberg for approval. Later on, he would offer a pungent characterization of her work at the Actors Studio: "A lot of shit-ass studying."

All the problems in filming *The Prince and the Showgirl* and *Some Like It Hot* eventually found considerable redemption in the final result. Monroe looked glorious and acted superbly in one, and in the other, she was a radiant cornerstone of one of the greatest comedies ever made. None of that happened with *Let's Make Love*, a film that asks the question "*This* is the best they could give her?" It does, in fairness, contain some good moments, at least enough to tempt us with how much better it all could have been. The essential premise, as taken from *On the Avenue*, is reasonably sound, and adding the "millionaire pretending to be poor" angle is not necessarily bad, either. Monroe had already done well with a similar/reverse trope in *Some Like It Hot*, and Doris Day had done a variant ("wolf pretending he's gay") in the recent *Pillow Talk*. Unfortunately, that was where the inspiration halted, as far as the script was concerned. MM's role, an off-Broadway actress named Amanda Dell, has virtually no backstory apart from the fact that she's going to night school to get her high school diploma and she's devoted to her father, a minister. Little else comes through. Sure, Amanda is nice and trusting, but her path through the story is less of a progression than an accumulation of moments that seem random and slapdash. As Miller knew when he was futilely working on rewrites, the script didn't offer Monroe any real character, and neither Cukor nor Paula Strasberg could help her remedy that situation. Amanda clearly has enough gumption and professional expertise to rate a lead role in this musical revue, and MM performs those parts with confidence and sparkle. Offstage, she seems so passive, even apathetic, that it's disorienting. And what's her relationship with the full-of-himself alcoholic Tony Danton (Vaughan)? Whatever it is, that part of the plot is so underwritten that it's incomprehensible. Nor, in the sweet way Monroe interacts with both Montand and Vaughan, does she get the opportunity to give off any real erotic charge.

In the homestretch, it's actually quite moving to see how hard she works to give the character some depth, most evidently with Amanda's pained reaction to the billionaire's manipulation. Yet it's far less Amanda than Monroe we care about here, trying as hard as she does to add some substance where none is present. She holds the screen but does not seize it in her usual fashion, and as endearing as her warmth is, she often seems less vital than maternal. Plus, as those awful tests had demonstrated, she doesn't look her best. If some of it comes with the enhanced curves, a little more weight does not entirely account for the pasty appearance. She is almost as pale as in *Bus Stop*, this time looking so washed-out that there isn't the customary play of light and shadow on her face. Some interesting attempts to vary her hairstyle don't always work, and the dark red lipstick is harsh and distracting. All this is compounded by the DeLuxe Color process Fox was using at the time, which (at least in the prints seen today) is a wan and flat comedown from the lush Technicolor of *Niagara* or *The Prince and the Showgirl*. And speaking of *Niagara*, there are her costumes to contend with. Dorothy Jeakins had done right by her with designs for the despicable Rose Loomis, but here she does few favors to either Amanda or Monroe. Reportedly, MM found such fault with the Jeakins design for "Specialization" that she substituted the fancy number she'd worn to the premiere of *Some Like It Hot*. The worst, possibly, is the gown she wears in the title number, an unhappy pleated thing that looks like a cross between a maternity dress and a knickknack shelf. Rose Loomis would have never worn it, alive or dead.

Fortunately, there are those good moments, the musical numbers in which MM truly comes alive. Finally, as virtually nowhere else in the movie, she is an active force, initiating instead of simply reacting. As he had done during *Some Like It Hot*, Cole stood alongside the camera and danced along with her so she could copy every move—due less to her lack of training than to the paralyzing insecurity that Cole knew was now engulfing her. There are the familiar gestures and busyness to take the place of fancy footwork, and they really do make her seem professional and secure, perhaps more than ever before. The songs, by Sammy Cahn and James Van Heusen, are serviceable enough to give the impression that they actually could have come from a snappy 1959 off-Broadway revue, or at least a Hollywood version of one. "Specialization," the satirical number that gets the billionaire's attention, is passably clever. With Elvis Presley, Maria Callas, and Van Cliburn all getting affectionate digs, along with "Jean-Marc Clement" (Montand)—even as, and unlike in *On the Avenue*, the kidding draws more ire than it warrants.[3] In this number, as in "Incurably Romantic" and the title song, Monroe is magnetic even when she's only listening while Vaughan or Montand is singing. Her reactions and facial expressions are spot-on, and when she does sing, her assurance as a vocalist is as great as it would ever be. In these portions, at least, she's engaged enough to be entirely convincing as a gifted and hard-working New York performer.

"My Heart Belongs to Daddy" is the only thing most people recall about *Let's Make Love*, along with the fact that Monroe and Montand took the movie's title quite literally off camera. Again, as with "Diamonds Are a Girl's Best Friend" and some of their other work together, Cole was able to come up with an optimal way to showcase her. It's a busy number, with its chorus boys and calisthenics and pieces of business, and it's all about her. As presented here, it's supposed to be a rehearsal, though it's fair to wonder how different it would have been in the final performance. Once more, Monroe doesn't do sustained dancing as much as she acts through movement, her knowing expressions in complete sync with the mock-innocence of Cole Porter's song. With its saucy new "Lolita" verse and scat-singing interludes, there is, again, the feeling that this could actually be part of a smart revue. No, Monroe doesn't look as scintillating here as she had in *Gentlemen Prefer Blondes*, seven years (and much on- and off-screen drama) earlier. What matters more is the fact that she's grown as a performer and, at least here, can park those desperate apprehensions on the other side of the camera and come through as a true pro. She even gets to parody the excessive enunciation of earlier years: in each iteration of "Dad-dy," the consonants are slyly savored. This was the MM whom Cole adored—theirs is truly one of the happier collaborations in musical film history—and one of the few felicities of the *Let's Make Love* script is that Jean-Marc Clement falls in love, or at least lust, with Amanda as he watches this performance.

---

[3] During all the Sisyphean writing and reworking of the script, the billionaire character's name changed frequently. First it was Mark Clemens, then Mark Bruester, then (after Montand came in) Charles Clement, Jean-Pierre Clement, and finally Jean-Marc Clement. Someone dropped the ball at some point, since in "Specialization," Vaughan sings it as "Mark Clemens." He does it with a French accent, but it's still not the character's name. And look to the very last bars of "Specialization" for one of those tiny but grand MM moments that run through nearly all her films. In this case, it's her naughty, boastful "I specialize," after which she grabs Vaughan so voraciously that it appears she's going to have him for lunch.

Montand, Montand, *pourquoi* Montand? It may have been an intriguing, even provocative idea to attempt such think-outside-the-box casting, and ultimately it doesn't work. There are a few moments where he can connect as a light comedian, and the rest of the time, he seems either blank or lost. Evidently, his facility with English improved as production went along—that month-plus hiatus may have been a boon—but he isn't always comprehensible and doesn't appear particularly comfortable with the language or, for that matter, the circumstances. In his black-and-white European movies, he smoldered; to watch him in *The Wages of Fear* (*Le salaire de la peur*) or *Les sorcières de Salem* is to see a magnetic and involved performer at work, and there are enough clips of his musical performances to show his mastery in that area as well. Here he's pallid and hesitant, even recessive, and, like Monroe, he doesn't photograph all that well. His much-discussed chemistry with MM—a nail in the coffin of her marriage but not his—must be taken on faith, at least on-screen. We know from the beginning that she'll end up with him, and it isn't particularly stimulating to watch how they reach that point. As with so much else in *Let's Make Love*, there isn't much to care about. Nor is Montand especially comfortable acting alongside the ever-dependable Tony Randall. Surely Randall knew that he was being wasted in this nothing role, yet he soldiers on valiantly.

Frankie Vaughan was one of those pop singers whose massive popularity in his own country was essentially untranslatable abroad. Having already starred in several British films, he was imported to the United States for this and for a long-forgotten Fox throwaway mistitled *The Right Approach*. His character in *Let's Make Love* is even less well defined than those of Monroe and Montand, although he manages to pair well enough with her in their numbers together. If he's on surer footing than Montand—speaking English certainly helps—there's no getting around the all-encompassing air of lounge-act smarminess. It's pretty easy to discern why he was a hot commodity in the world of 1950s British pop, with his swagger and vocal confidence and with that big, wide vibrato (think Anthony Newley) that contrasts interestingly with MM's faster, higher one. It's just as plain to see why he never acted again after that one last film. He does, it must be said, strike a few more on-camera sparks with MM, in a couple of the numbers, than Montand does. Speaking of smarmy, there is also the presence of Milton Berle, who, in fairness, is often quite funny here, with more energy and a higher percentage of amusing lines than anyone else in the film. (Bing Crosby and Gene Kelly have far less to do in their guest spots.) The extent of Berle's participation, and surely one measure of the film's quality, came with the headline emblazoned over the *New York Times* review: "MILTON BERLE STEALS SHOW IN 'LET'S MAKE LOVE.'"

In that review, *Times* critic Bosley Crowther was ungallant enough to term Monroe "rather untidy." This was a painful assessment if not altogether an inaccurate one, despite some critics who were more predisposed toward charity. They were more charitable, apparently, than the public, which added to the eternal bad luck of this production by largely staying away. And in still another piece of misfortune regarding *Let's Make Love*, the premiere planned for it went up in smoke. It was to have been held in Reno, Nevada, where Monroe was shooting *The Misfits*, but rampaging fires caused a massive power failure at next to the last minute. The event was canceled and not rescheduled. It should be noted that the choice of a Reno venue was made only because Monroe would be in attendance and, it can be further mentioned, did nothing to lessen her awareness that the movie was a dud. By that time, *Let's Make Love* mattered far less to her than the massive and ongoing struggle to get through *The Misfits*. That, naturally, is a tale in itself.

13

The Desert

"It shouts and sings with life . . . explodes with love!"

Truth in advertising is a curiously tenuous thing, and *The Misfits* does at least shout at one point. Otherwise, the tag line that appeared on most of the posters was as hopeful as it was misleading. *The Misfits* is unquestionably the most ambitious film Marilyn Monroe ever made. It is also self-conscious to a numbing extreme, incessantly uneven, curiously affecting, and quite annoying. In the minds and hearts of some of its creators, especially its producer, it did have aspirations to be the life- and love-affirming pageant that its publicists tried to hawk. Even so, and regardless of the effect being hoped for, the question must be asked: In all the history of film, is there a movie that casts a sadder shadow than this one? In terms of what is there on the screen, the actual film itself, of course, there have been works of greater melancholy. Plus, it must be said that it does end on a note, however equivocal or arbitrary, of warmth and hope. Off the screen, and in terms of its creation and execution, this one likely is unparalleled. Few films, no matter how worthy their intentions, have been called upon to carry as much unhappy baggage as this one.

The most obvious aspect of the whole *Misfits* saga is that it was the last released film made by Monroe and the last by Clark Gable. That part everyone knows, and added to it is the poignant overlying truth that these two icons of Hollywood glory were playing their last act in a project about people enmeshed in a dying way of life. (Meanwhile, the studio system that had created them both was on its own route to extinction.) Many are also familiar with at least some of the drama attending its creation—Gable overworking himself toward a fatal heart attack, Monroe's struggle with illness and her dependence on pills, the dissolution of her marriage to Arthur Miller, the tragic figure that was Montgomery Clift, the brutal shoot in the Nevada desert, the letdown felt by many who saw the finished work. Plus, from first to last, there was the strange, downbeat, and possibly foolhardy nature of the entire project. Over more than six decades, the arguments have continued. Some have sought to redeem it as a (possibly flawed) work of art, while others dismiss it as a scrambled mass of pretensions. All this overlay gives *The Misfits* a monumental, tragic quality which, strictly as a work of cinema, it could not earn.

Some of the blighted air about *The Misfits* likely comes from the fact that it was, from first to last, a product of Monroe's hopeful and ultimately unhappy union with Miller. He had first conceived the story while waiting out his Nevada residency in order to divorce his first wife, Mary Slattery, so he could marry Monroe. As he wandered around the city of Reno, Miller was struck by the number of cowboys he saw. Some of them worked actively in rodeos, and many others were rootless wanderers, reminders and remainders of a time and culture that were dying or dead. Out of his observations, Miller crafted a short story, "The Misfits," that ran in *Esquire* in October 1957. A deceptively simple mood piece, it tracked three rootless cowboys on a search for wild mustangs—the inbred and feral creatures that helped give the story its title. The horses are seen as good for little other than making dog food, and naturally, parallels are drawn between the captives and the captors. In the course of their hunt, the cowboys discuss a woman they know named Roslyn. Colorful yet bleak, less a narrative than a vignette, the story stayed with Miller sufficiently for him to want to keep going and turn it into something more. One way to effect this was to build up the character of Roslyn, and Miller's intentions here seem to have been worthy. With Monroe heartbroken over the sudden end of a recent pregnancy, Miller determined that this role would be his gift—a "valentine," she would call it—to her and that Roslyn would be a heightened variant of the real Marilyn. The script, which stumbled through many drafts, was the only sustained work he did during their marriage. Eventually, he sent it to John Huston, and it was telling that Monroe had not facilitated that connection between her husband and her first important director. It appears that she was already beginning to have reservations.

Monroe's hesitance over the script was an early sign of the trouble that would plague this production to its miserable end. Instead of the polished film screenplays she was accustomed to, Miller's work read to her as didactic and obscure, an uneven and frequently incoherent rumination that seemed wholly unsuitable for film. There were more personal objections as well. Her awareness that the role of Roslyn was not only for her but also about her was not an especially pleasant thing given her own fragile state at the time. As originally conceived, Roslyn was a radiant and almost otherworldly figure, so idealized as to be virtually unplayable. The love of nature and animals and underdogs, the sense of not quite being in an earthly dimension, even prowess with a child's paddle ball, were all things he had observed in Monroe. Then, as Miller continued to write and revise, the marriage grew increasingly frayed, and the role took on more of the less happy aspects of her personality. The insecurity, the mood swings and disconnectedness, the troubled relationship with her mother, were all there, and as Monroe recognized them, she grew increasingly hostile toward *The Misfits* and toward Miller. She could also see that, like the script as a whole, the role was a collage of pieces that did not coalesce. Nevertheless, she was so connected to the project that despite all those misgivings, she determined to make Roslyn her defining statement as a mature actor. Her doubts remained and increased, as did her reliance on increasingly heavy doses of prescription medication.

After Huston read the script, he cabled Miller to pronounce it a masterpiece, which in no way meant that he was not aware of its problems. Before the filming and all the way through to the end of the shoot, he was constantly directing Miller to keep changing, revising, rewriting. This could only feed into Monroe's anguish in having to constantly learn new lines, as well as her suspicions that this supposedly great screenplay was, in reality, extremely flawed. What, exactly, was it saying? Was it a sweeping examination of the state of America or of humanity, or was it a far more intimate slice-of-life piece about some people who, as the title implied, didn't belong? Since Roslyn/Marilyn was the closest thing to a central axis, was she an all-encompassing earth mother or, in reality, something of a mess? Even as a mood piece, it didn't seem to scan, with one scene coming after another in an often arbitrary fashion, some completely striking moments followed by others that didn't land or correspond. Roslyn, for instance, tells Gay that she's not attracted to him, and in the next scene, it's clear that they're shacked up together. "It's almost kind of an honor sitting next to you," Gay tells her, which is touching until it begins to seem quite absurd. Constantly, often at length, the characters explain themselves, instead of showing who they are through action and interaction. Even less effectively, they are being commented on by others, a major giveaway that this script was the product of someone with a theatrical, not cinematic, sensibility. Who are these people? They're not given much backstory. Roslyn is a sensitive dancer coming out of a bad marriage, Gay is a rootless old cowboy, Perce is a rodeo rider with mother issues, Guido has avoided coming to terms with his wife's death. The most rooted of them all—if still an underdefined character—is Isabel, the jolly and philosophical landlady played with characteristic warmth by Thelma Ritter. When Isabel abruptly drops out of the narrative midway through, the remainder becomes more of a grim slog.

For all the earthiness of his characters and situations, it was clear to some who read it that Miller's writing had a ponderous self-importance that was as alienating as it was conspicuous. For many, the sheer and stark truth was that the script was plain incomprehensible. This was indicated to Huston after he sent the script to Robert Mitchum in the hope that he would consent to play Gay. Sending Huston a quick no in reply, Mitchum offered the explanation that he would not be comfortable acting in something he could not understand. Next up was Gable, who said pretty much the same thing. Later on, he changed his mind, his newfound comprehension no doubt aided by some major incentive: he would be receiving one of the largest salaries ever offered to an actor up to that time.

Like its screenwriter, the producer of *The Misfits*, Frank Taylor, was not a movie person. Instead, he was a respected book editor, his work in that capacity including Arthur Miller's only novel, *Focus*.[1] The two men had become close friends, and Taylor's enthusiasm for the script was such that Miller asked him to serve as producer. Initially reluctant, Taylor soon became the project's leading cheerleader, so much so that he made an exuberant and sweeping proclamation before shooting started:

> This is an attempt at the ultimate motion picture. This is not only the first original screenplay by a major American writer but the best screenplay I have ever read, and we have the best director, John Huston, for it. And if anything happened to one of our players, I don't know what we'd do. Each of them, Marilyn, Clark, Monty Clift, Eli Wallach, Thelma Ritter, *is* the person they play.

That "ultimate" moniker was a fair indicator that prestige would hover over the project like buzzards over roadkill. A major director (albeit one who had not had a real success in quite some time), an original screenplay by a great

---

[1] He had, however, taken a flyer into the film world about a decade earlier and produced *Mystery Street*, which was shot at MGM at the same time as *The Asphalt Jungle*. It was a decent film but not a great experience for Taylor, who returned to publishing with the intention of never going near movies again.

American playwright, two of the brightest stars imaginable plus the brilliant Clift—this was as high-powered a package as any in movie history. Miller began to envision the completed film as a major roadshow attraction à la *Ben-Hur*, playing in limited showings at higher prices. While Huston talked him out of that notion, it remained clear that this would not be a standard Hollywood product, one whose ambitions were lofted in the direction of an Ingmar Bergman or Federico Fellini. Like *Some Like It Hot*, it was an independent production and would be shot in black-and-white, in this case to indicate the seriousness of its intentions.

It was mostly shot essentially where it would have happened. Miller himself selected many of the shooting sites in and around Reno, having recalled seeing them while waiting for his divorce. Although the production was initially set to roll in the fall of 1959, its start date was postponed due to the grim reality that was Monroe's commitment to Fox and *Let's Make Love*. It was moved up to March 3, 1960, when the climate in "The Biggest Little City in the World" would still be judged hospitable. Then came the delays on *Let's Make Love*, with both strikes and MM-related difficulties, and now it would be necessary for *The Misfits* to get started in July, in the middle of a fierce Reno summer. Such an environment would exhaust anyone not already accustomed to it, let alone a fragile performer just coming off a long film shoot, with the further complications of chemical dependency, a failed romance, and a crumbling marriage.

Everyone knew going into it that this would not be an ordinary movie shoot. The point was made clearer with Huston's decision that it be filmed in sequence, which he said would aid the actors in charting their characters' progression. The first scene was shot first, and the poignant final moments with Monroe and Gable came at the end. This choice added to both the budget and the difficulty of logistics, while at the same time playing into the notion of this being a film above and beyond other works.[2] To further demonstrate its importance, there would be the steady presence of photographers from the elite Magnum organization, as well as a young writer, James Goode, who later published a record of his observations. Nearly all of the company spoke frequently and at length with Goode; Monroe, at first said to be too immersed in the creative process to speak about it, eventually discussed her approach to her craft and her work with Huston. Goode's account, *The Story*

---

[2] This was rarer at the time than it might seem. *Some Like It Hot* had also been filmed roughly in sequence—though its nice beach locations made for an easier time of it than that Nevada hellscape.

of The Misfits, is notable not only for its detailed, almost day-by-day record of the shoot but also for a demeanor and tone so calm and temperate that not even the hellish temperatures rate much of a mention. The drama of later reports about making *The Misfits* is largely absent here, possibly because Goode was shielded from some of the more difficult moments and partly because of the professional courtesy shown to him by most of the participants. As Goode listened and took notes, Huston, Taylor, Gable, Monroe, Clift, and Wallach all extolled the quality of the script—its depth, the roundedness of the characters, the insight, and the profundity. Surely, too, they believed it, at least part of the time.[3]

The difficulties, as shooting got under way, were too present for Goode not to occasionally pick up on them, as when one crew member said to him, "Don't form any opinions of movie making from this. This is how not to make a movie." Another asked, with rhetorical acid, "Did you ever see anything so pitiful?" At least some of this was in direct reaction to Monroe, with her lateness, indisposition, insecurity, and ever-growing dependence on both pharmaceuticals and her acting coach. Even Gable, who generally demonstrated forbearance and a courtly professionalism around MM, was heard to tell a reporter, pointedly, that Jean Harlow was always on time. Then he grinned and added, "In those days when stars were late, they were fired." The impatience and annoyance many felt toward Monroe were commonly rerouted in the direction of Paula Strasberg, whose presence drew more animosity than ever before. As it turned out, the collusion between coach and actor would be, for many, the most corrosive aspect of the entire shoot. Eternally clad in voluminous robes of funereal hues, with a pointed hat that put most people in mind of a witch, Strasberg was quickly given the nickname "Black Bart." At first, this was not said maliciously; as delays continued and increased, fewer crew members were inclined to tolerate her constant head-to-head conferences with Monroe and, most irksome of all, the fashion in which she seemed to take the role of director away from Huston and put it upon her own shoulders. Over and apart from the large salary she was being paid, per MM's contract with United Artists, "Black Bart" viewed herself as one of the linchpins of the entire project. "I feel," she told Goode, "that I have

---

[3] Thelma Ritter was initially hesitant about speaking to Goode and, noting that her job was creating an illusion whereas his was destroying one, said of her character only that "She's uncomplicatedly complicated." She also offered her view of method acting: "I'm not running it down, but as an actor it's not natural for you to express yourself and ignore the audience." And regarding her current project, "I don't remember a picture that depends quite so much on oddity. If anyone were average, it wouldn't work." You can almost hear how this would sound as expressed in that unforgettable voice.

contributed to every frame of *The Misfits*. If it doesn't work out, that's something I must share with her." In her defense, it could be offered that in some major ways, she was helping to keep Monroe held together, if sometimes tenuously. In an earlier conversation with Goode, Strasberg compared her preparation work with MM to that done by Pablo Picasso or Arturo Toscanini, adding, "This is the first time she can stretch her talents. This is the bare beginning of what she can do. . . . The actor is the only artist who, when he dies, the creation dies with him." That statement is, to say the least, debatable: the creative process does indeed die, as does the actor's tortuous evolutionary path, but the work, in cinema, remains.

Having embarked on *The Misfits* immediately after wrapping up *Let's Make Love*, Monroe was on shaky physical and mental ground from the very start. On that previous film, she had struggled with an underwritten character with few identifiable traits. Here the proposition was completely reversed: a role overladen with meaning, intention, and verbiage, which seemed to play out as a broken funhouse-mirror reflection of her off-screen self. Nothing seemed to help her along. Fully cognizant of her non-relationship with punctuality, Huston had her start times scheduled for a later hour than would normally be the case, but if anything, this only made things worse. In her quest for a decent night's sleep, she took larger and larger doses of barbiturates, which then led to doses of amphetamines to help her get started in the daytime. Her makeup man, Whitey Snyder, often found himself applying her face while she was still in bed and not completely conscious.[4] Some days found her unable to come to the set at all, while at other times it was clear that, as Roslyn said of her husband in the script, she was there without really being there. If on occasion this fuzzy quality could add to the character's dreaminess, more often it was plainly unfocused. There's one shot in the film where she seems completely gone. Although she has no dialogue—Roslyn is simply sitting in the car as Gay talks to Perce—the haze of her disorientation is unmistakable. Monroe's marriage, meanwhile, was trudging toward its grim conclusion. A shockingly candid photo, taken at the Millers' Reno hotel before they stopped sharing a room, could be a frame from a Bergman

---

[4] *The Misfits* is perhaps the only one of her starring films in which a still-beautiful Monroe resembles something approaching a real person and not a glow-in-the-dark apparition. While some critics made slighting comments about extra weight, the real issue seems to lie in the frankly honest way her appearance reflects the true state of her physical and emotional well-being. Occasionally, it seems it's only the wig and makeup keeping her from breaking into pieces.

film: the two of them stand a few feet and many worlds apart, each hermetically lost in thought and isolation.

The illness and indisposition continued until, after more than a month of shooting, production was temporarily shut down. Monroe spent a week in a Los Angeles hospital to rest and recuperate. Presented to the public as a case of "exhaustion," which was not a completely untrue statement, it was largely an attempt to downsize the heavy doses of medication. Here, and later on, her issues were seen as the overriding problem besetting *The Misfits*. Yet in the estimation of some participants, there were other factors that mattered as much or more. Many of them stemmed, both personally and professionally, from Huston. Did his disillusionment with Miller's script exacerbate Huston's gambling problem, or was it perhaps the other way around? Even Goode found it necessary to report on the many times Huston would leave the film set and, almost immediately, get settled in the casino for an all-night session. Then, with no sleep at all, he would go back to work. By all accounts, his losses totaled well into five figures, possibly higher, and as with any gambling addict, he had to reach past his own grasp to cover the debt. In this case, it was the cash funding the production, which he dipped into so liberally that the collapse of the project became a looming possibility. Finally, to replace what he had taken out of the kitty, Huston returned to California to obtain an advance on his next film, *Freud*.[5] Monroe went to the hospital at the same time, and some connected with the production felt that she had been used as a scapegoat for Huston's difficulties. "We had the Errol Flynn of directors," MM stand-in Evelyn Moriarty recalled, elaborating that the gambling and carousing also included an extensive amount of paid companionship. The truth, most likely, encompasses both star and director. Monroe was in bad physical and emotional shape, and Huston's financial condition and compulsions were in a comparable state. Both required at least temporary repair in order to finish the film, and one was publicized while the other stayed relatively under the radar.

Another issue that became clearer in hindsight was Gable's health. Alongside Monroe and Clift, both already known to be train wrecks, Gable appeared, for a fifty-nine-year-old man, to be in good shape. He had a happy

---

[5] *Freud* is, in the Huston canon, every bit as much a curiosity as *The Misfits*. While Montgomery Clift's personal difficulties were not an issue during the *Misfits* shoot, *Freud* was another matter entirely, with major conflicts between star and director. Huston had asked MM to appear in *Freud*, but she was disinclined to do so. The role went to Susannah York, and we are left to wonder how Monroe might have done playing a troubled patient of Sigmund Freud. Would her own extensive history of psychoanalysis have been a help or a hindrance?

marriage, his wife was pregnant with his first (legitimate) child, and on the set, he seemed the soul of hearty equanimity. The role of Gay Langland was, for him, a challenge and a departure, and his wholehearted commitment under trying circumstances earned everyone's respect. Later accounts would overstate his impatience with the MM-related delays and include an overly dramatic claim that he did most of his own stunt work in the mustang sequence as a way to deal with his frustration. The truth was that his vigorous air was something of a facade. He had been drinking and smoking heavily for years, and there had already been numerous indicators of heart problems. As for his alleged impatience with the many production delays, it might be noted that his contract stated that his overtime pay would kick in, when the film ran over schedule, at an abundant $48,000 per week. He was, moreover, already contemplating retirement. None of this means that the massive heart attack he suffered one day after finishing work on the film could be viewed as anything other than a huge shock. At first, it appeared that he might recover— and then, eleven days after the first attack, a second one ended his life.

Posthumously released films, from Jean Harlow in *Saratoga* to Heath Ledger in *The Dark Knight*, are by their nature sobering affairs, and it becomes more affecting still if there appear to be any portents. In *Saratoga*, Harlow announces that "There's nothing the matter with me," even as it's clear she's ill. In *The Misfits*, it was promptly noticed that Gable speaks several lines about death, up to and including "We all gotta go sometime, reason or no reason." His death became so essential a part of the film that audiences could only view it in terms of his mortality. Then, a year and a half after it opened, Monroe was gone as well. That their deaths became the ultimate significance of *The Misfits* is a measure of just how much can attach itself to a beloved public figure—the esteem, the envy, the vicarious living through them, the different forms identification can take, and finally the personalization of loss. These, ultimately, would subsume whatever else this "ultimate motion picture" was trying to be or to achieve.

It was Gable's death, and a hope to cash in on it, that led to *The Misfits* being premiered earlier than originally planned, early in 1961. Since there had also been the very public announcement of the end of the Monroe-Miller marriage, the question immediately comes up: Would it have been possible in this climate to give the film anything like an objective evaluation? Perhaps the reviews reflected this, since they seemed to cover the entire spectrum of opinion. Some acceded to producer Taylor's hopes and proclaimed it a major work, with the cast called out for praise, Gable most of all. A few found it necessary to balance commendation for MM's sensitivity against some disappointment with her appearance, and a significant number took the "emperor's new clothes" approach to question what it all meant. "There is a lot of absorbing detail in it, but it doesn't add up to a point," said an unusually accurate Bosley Crowther in the *New York Times*. An even more direct statement came in *Esquire*: "Good-by, Clark Gable, and I wish your last line hadn't been written by Arthur Miller." The disappointment was echoed in the financial returns. The delays and difficulties had shot the cost well over the original budget, and the grosses were not judged a sufficient compensation.

So, with this amount of backstory, what exactly can be observed in this film that constantly veers between the comprehensible and the enigmatic, the tiresome and the touching? Start, perhaps, at the beginning, which is to say with Arthur Miller. What he had observed in Reno had obviously affected him, and so had, far more so, what he had seen in the woman he married. While combining these observations might seem a sound notion, the final result is more dialectical than dramatic. The cowboys are living anachronisms doomed for extinction as much as those poor horses, and Miller, at least originally, would have it that Roslyn is their lifeline. As his feelings about Monroe began to stray off that idealized path, it became harder to tell, and not always happily, where Roslyn left off and Marilyn (and Norma Jeane) began. In his equivocal view of Roslyn as a valiant and generous soul, Miller keeps instructing the other characters to pay tribute to her life-affirming qualities: "You have the gift for life, Roslyn," and "When you smile, it's like the sun coming out." Some sun. Even as these praises are directed toward her, Monroe often seems lost, insulated, and so amorphous that all the talk about her "gift of life" can seem nonsensical.

In fairness, she does seem at times to be deep inside the character, or at least *a* character, clearly feeling some of Roslyn's emotions quite deeply. At other points, it's as if she took too literally Roslyn's statement, "I always like to feel I'm on my own." Someone whom others see as a force of nature should seem generous, not isolated, and have the ability to connect with those around her. Monroe often does not, certainly not in the way she had connected with Jane Russell or David Wayne or Tom Ewell. Instead, she gives the impression that either she's concentrating too hard on her technique or whatever metaphor Paula Strasberg has given her, or else she's just not up to it. Ritter relates to her in their scenes together with easy affection, but Monroe doesn't always seem able to give even that seasoned pro much to play off. (This recalls what Eileen Heckart said about working with her in *Bus*

Stop.) There are also those moments, intended to pay tribute to her lyricism, that seem more off-kilter than anything else; Roslyn's drunken solo "nature dance," for instance, is less lyrical than borderline embarrassing. There's also that peculiar moment when she keeps running up and down the makeshift steps Gay's just put in. Gable, not Gay, seems to be the bemused one in that scene, and no wonder. At points, she seems so overtaken by tremulousness that it's unclear how much of this is an actor's choice and how much is an unhappy woman's distress. Eons before this, she was able to distance herself from the troubled Nell in *Don't Bother to Knock* and deliver an intermittently effective performance. Even in *Let's Make Love*, she managed a degree of discipline that brought moments of meaning into a role that, by and large, did not exist. In *The Misfits*, it frequently seems to be a display of exposed nerves and trembling insecurity. Hers.

Clift's entrance into the film halfway through—just before Ritter leaves it— seems to bring out some of the discipline that enables Monroe to summon her craft and resources. In the long "Pietà" scene with Perce, she clearly relates to Clift as both the talented actor he is and, probably, the damaged soul. Perhaps some of their rapport was an actorly empathy, a mutual understanding of, or curiosity about, how to approach interesting, flawed writing. Everyone applauded when Monroe and Clift accomplished the scene without undue difficulty, although it's worth noting that the scene appears pieced together in a back-and-forth fashion when two-shots would have made it more meaningful. In any case, Monroe was justifiably proud of the professionalism she showed here. Then, in the short scene that came immediately afterward, Huston had difficulty getting her to reply to Gable's call with the words "Here we are." Archetypal latter-day MM.

Huston's direction makes it clear, at least intermittently, that he could work in as inconsistent a fashion as Monroe and (on other projects) Clift. While his work is never less than that of an accomplished pro, it's clear that Huston is sometimes as stumped by the script as Robert Mitchum was. As with that script, there are passages of assured direction alongside others that seem mere head scratchers. It's quite obvious, too, that the mustang episode forming the film's final third clearly captured his imagination in a way that the earlier portions did not. (The same holds true for composer Alex North, whose music finally acquires some of his wonted edge in those later scenes.) Perhaps in the pursuit, capture, and liberation of the wild horses, Huston was able to find a generic connection—now it's a western!—that he couldn't find earlier on. He was less comfortable with the ending, which is why he was in constant discussion, and sometimes disagreement, with Miller, Taylor, and others about just how the movie might conclude. Originally, the ending seemed to indicate some hope for Roslyn and Gay together. Then the second-guessing began. Should everyone separate instead? Should Roslyn leave Gay and instead be "awarded" to Perce? Should Guido's motivations be explained further? Miller wrote several versions of the ending covering several options, and as he did so, Monroe grew increasingly upset. In the end, it was Gable who put his foot down, noting that his contract gave him script approval, and his preference was for Roslyn going off with Gay. So it stayed as it was, which was not necessarily an indicator of Huston maintaining a firm hand on the material. Sure, some kind of vagueness would be valid in a look at rootless people, but this wasn't *Last Year at Marienbad*.

At points during the course of the film, Huston appears to have even less of a grasp on Roslyn than Monroe does. Sometimes he resorts to simple crudeness, as when the camera ogles her bouncing bottom as she rides a horse. (The famous paddle-ball scene comes close to this as well.) Then there's the business with the mustangs. Especially considering the circumstances, Monroe shows a bracing physicality through much of this sequence, in part because she had been at least somewhat restored following her time in the hospital. Also, the anguish she shows is more comprehensible now than when the movie was new and animal rights were virtually a nonissue. Nevertheless, it appears once again that Huston had to piece her moments together as best he could, including a couple of shots where the camera is so out of focus that one can wonder why they were included. The famous moment when she starts screaming—"Murderers!"—isn't as primal or cathartic as it needs to be. Huston shot it as both a medium and a long shot and opted for the latter, which he said was akin to a cry from the wilderness. It looks striking—this tiny figure completely losing it on the barren Nevada flats—yet by using the long shot, Huston was making an odd choice for what might have been a showcase moment, "Marilyn's Big Mad Scene!" For many viewers, it simply seems awkward. Her voice is certainly powerful, partly because it's the only time audiences ever get to hear MM like this, but her bending and twisting body language doesn't appear to coordinate with the sounds she makes. Did Huston do it this way because he didn't know what else to make of her suffering, or did he think this truly was the most valid way to present her? Either way, it isn't the only "big scene" in *The Misfits* that careens off the road. Gable has a go-for-broke moment when Gay drunkenly calls to his children, and instead of reining him in, Huston lets him go over the top. As with MM shouting about the horses, we admire the actor's bravery and openness but may cringe at the result.

With all her own reservations about it, MM hoped that public and critical response to *The Misfits* would move her a step forward as a serious performer. That validation was not to be. In spite of some critical approval, everyone knew about how the shoot had gone and how the Monroe-Miller marriage ended right after the film did. Some also passed along the ugly and baseless tales that linked her own behavior with Gable's death. To put it bluntly, none of this gave much credence to the notion that hiring her was worth all the trouble. Above all, there was the movie itself—hopeful yet despairing, polished yet inchoate, a European art film with Old Hollywood trimmings, neither one thing nor another, less a career marker than an oddly compelling asterisk. Perhaps this is why, at the time and later, some offer it up as a sort of masterpiece. No, it is not, and even if it had been, its greater distinction might still have come with everything that occurred off the screen.

The Misfits is excessive at the same time that it is insufficient, and in many ways. But at the very least, it finds its way to a proper ending. After all the arguments about the last scene, it seems that Gable was right. So, too, was the argued-over decision to have it conclude without explicitly stating "The End." That may well have been done to indicate its ambition, its reach toward some American new wave not beholden to Old Hollywood ways. In any case, anything along that line is quickly buried under the immense weight of stunning iconography. As Roslyn and Gay ride to some kind of future, Huston gives us one last two-shot of the two marvelous faces. Gable speaks his closing line—"It'll take us right home"—and Monroe sighs. If they both look more tired and worn than ever before, there hovers over them a palpable sense of peace. Finality, too, since everyone knows that we're seeing them, really, for the last time. Then Huston cuts to a shot of stars in the sky, followed by a fade to black as North's music winds down dreamily. That's it. An end title, under these circumstances, would have been redundant.

14

Full Stop

After the back-to-back distress of *Let's Make Love* and *The Misfits*, it was hardly surprising that Monroe would retreat, as much as possible, into a private life. Settling into the New York apartment she had previously shared with Miller, she ended her marriage, resumed her study with Lee Strasberg, and continued in psychoanalysis. By February 1961, she was in such a dire condition that her doctor had her institutionalized; when this proved to have the reverse of the intended effect, she was moved to a conventional hospital. Following her release, she began to pick up, professionally speaking, where she had left off. There was still Twentieth Century-Fox to contend with, and although the studio had begun its preoccupation with the epically misbegotten *Cleopatra*, it had not forgotten that she owed them at least one more film.

George Axelrod had already done well by MM with *The Seven Year Itch* and the screenplay of *Bus Stop*; less happily for her, he had also satirized her in his play *Will Success Spoil Rock Hunter?* Though his newest play, *Goodbye Charlie*, had not been as successful as these, Fox decided that Monroe would star in the film version, in the role Lauren Bacall had created on Broadway. It was essentially a one-joke comedy, and Monroe was not especially taken with the idea of playing a crass screenwriter who is shot and then reincarnated as a beautiful young woman. George Cukor, originally slated to direct, became unavailable, and the project finally fell apart when, at Monroe's behest, Fox approached Strasberg to direct and he asked for too much money. The play itself was hardly on the level of *The Seven Year Itch*, let alone Axelrod's incisive screenplay for *The Manchurian Candidate*, and the film version that Fox eventually made (Debbie Reynolds directed by Vincente Minnelli) was a thoroughgoing dud. With all that, it remains one of the more intriguing entries in MM's what-if canon. Had the role interested her, she might have brought to it a beguiling palette of comedic colors. Truly, she would have done more for it than it would have done for her.

Another prospect that did engage her, quite thoroughly, revolved around one of Broadway's most imperishable legends: Jeanne Eagels as Sadie

Thompson in *Rain*. The 1922 play, adapted from W. Somerset Maugham's story "Miss Thompson" by John Colton and Clemence Randolph, had been filmed three times with mixed results. Gloria Swanson had triumphed in a late-silent version called *Sadie Thompson*, Joan Crawford tried (hard) and failed (honorably) in 1932, and, as *Miss Sadie Thompson*, Rita Hayworth fared moderately well in 1953 in Technicolor and 3D. While there had been a flop Broadway musical version, any number of parodies, and scores of female impersonators doing their take on tropical-hooker-deluxe Sadie, Eagels always remained the template. Naturally, the legend was burnished by the fact that Eagels had lived hectically and died young from an overdose, yet those who had seen her perform, Strasberg among them, could attest to her brilliance.[1] Noting Monroe's similarities to Eagels—especially in the complex mix of fragility and sturdiness—Strasberg painted irresistible pictures of a new MM Sadie. It would no longer be a hackneyed joke in this new conception, he told her, and was precisely the kind of thing she should be doing, rather than junk like *Goodbye Charlie*. Before too long, Monroe and her representatives were discussing a televised adaptation of *Rain* with NBC. Fredric March (formerly a candidate for the aborted *Blue Angel* remake) and Florence Eldridge were in talks to play Reverend and Mrs. Davidson, and Rod Serling was approached to write the adaptation. Monroe, naturally, was the be-all of the production, and she knew who she wanted to direct. Strasberg, who had placed her on a pinnacle alongside Eagels and Eleanora Duse, understood her like no other director and would be the only one who she felt could guide her along this exciting new path. This, it should go without saying, was the downfall of the project. Strasberg had not directed for television (nor would he ever), and NBC would not entrust an important production to someone with no experience with the medium. The notion of a compromise, with Strasberg as artistic supervisor, was something the network would not consider. What major director, after all, would consent to such a forfeiture of his own concept and vision? Adamant about Strasberg's participation, Monroe and her mentor dug in until finally it all died.

How would Monroe have done as Sadie Thompson? By 1961, *Rain* was considered a tired relic, and because of the serious and

---

[1] Eagels is one of those mythical performers who fortunately left behind tangible evidence in a few films. The best known is the early-talkie first version of *The Letter*. She is completely riveting, both for the intensity of her performance—that last scene is a killer—and for the fact that with her jittery demeanor and skeletal arms, she's clearly headed for an early grave. Yes, there are parallels between this and MM in *The Misfits*, since in spots it can be hard to tell which parts are the performance and which are sad real life.

comedic knock-offs, plus all those drag performers, there were definite camp overtones. Nevertheless, Strasberg, with his memories, authority, and powers of persuasion, had convinced her that this would move her dramatic advancement well beyond the equivocal success of *The Misfits*. With great enthusiasm, she corresponded with Maugham about playing Sadie and expressed her ongoing commitment to Strasberg's take on the role. Surely there was some personal identification at work in this, as she hinted when she spoke about Sadie to a reporter: "She was a girl who knew how to be gay, even when she was sad. And that's important—you know?" Perhaps with the help of updated dialogue in a Serling script, she might have given it some resuscitation, and Sadie certainly had more definition and consistency than Roslyn. From raucous party girl to contrite penitent, then to sad cynic, there might have been opportunities for something substantial, at least if she were in the condition to take on such a challenge. NBC, for its part, could only be enticed by the notion of Monroe in a legendary role in a prestigious offering. There were, then, possibilities, and MM would have been a definite improvement on Kim Novak, who was not up to the snippets of *Rain* she performed while playing Eagels in a fictionalized 1957 biopic. Unfortunately, the intransigence over Strasberg could have been predicted by anyone familiar with the situation, which also encompassed Monroe's unyielding reliance on Paula Strasberg as his conduit and representative. The notion of him directing *Goodbye Charlie* was essentially nonsensical, but *Rain* was far more important and a far greater loss. Ultimately, for Monroe, Strasberg mattered more than Sadie.

Around the time *Rain* fell apart, Monroe withdrew once more for medical reasons. This time, it was gallbladder surgery, then back to California and negotiating with Fox. The studio's terrible financial shape, at that time, was not completely attributable to the queen of the Nile. In addition to *Cleopatra*, with its insane cost overruns, Fox was being hobbled by weak leadership and terrible artistic and financial choices. *Let's Make Love* was only the tip of an iceberg that also included such ill-wrought monstrosities as *Satan Never Sleeps*, *Hemingway's Adventures of a Young Man*, and *Snow White and the Three Stooges*. The upshot for 1961 would be a net loss far greater than any the studio had previously posted. As *Cleopatra* continued to hemorrhage cash, Fox sought a quick fix at home, and beyond its scant and uninspiring roster of contract actors, it still had that 1956 deal with MM. After the demise of *Goodbye Charlie*, the studio made a proposition with at least the potential to be an improvement on that and its other losers. It was the latest entry in

Fox's ongoing fetish for remakes, although the novelty of this one was that it had originally been produced elsewhere. The 1940 comedy *My Favorite Wife* had been a hit for RKO, the studio where MM had made *Clash by Night* and which shut down production in 1957. The premise of *My Favorite Wife* was the timeworn story about a spouse who disappears, then returns years later to find that the former partner has remarried. It was Alfred, Lord Tennyson's *Enoch Arden* (filmed multiple times) and Maugham's *Home and Beauty* (filmed twice) and *Tomorrow Is Forever* and others. The novelty here was the gender switch: Ellen (not Enoch) Arden goes missing after a shipwreck in the Pacific, then returns home just as she's being declared dead and her husband, Nick, is remarrying. If the premise came off as somewhat strained, there was sufficient amusement to be had, mainly due to the smart cowriting and direction of Garson Kanin and, especially, the chemistry of its two stars. Three years earlier, Irene Dunne and Cary Grant had made a priceless team in *The Awful Truth*, and *My Favorite Wife* was a happy enough follow-up, as well as a box-office hit. Now, more than two decades later, the powers at Fox began to conceive of a remake.

At a time when Fox was preoccupied with *Cleopatra*, a smart remake of a proven success was not altogether a bad idea. Certainly, it held more promise than a concurrent Fox retread, the unnecessary and unsuccessful third version of *State Fair*. (Not to mention the *Blue Angel* bullet that MM had already dodged.) It was also well in line with the current film trend for comedic romps with early-'60s sexual overtones. To one degree or another, these were all in reaction to the hit Doris Day and Rock Hudson had in 1959 in *Pillow Talk*, a success they repeated in 1961 with *Lover Come Back*. Fox had already tried something similar with *The Marriage-Go-Round*, in which Susan Hayward's comedy technique might diplomatically be termed emphatic. For Monroe, with her comedic bona fides, a piece such as this might serve well, at least if she and it were handled properly. It would also give Fox a way to use up her contractual obligation while paying her only a modest fee. While her last two films had not been commercial successes, she still had the name and the magic. Perhaps, too, the Fox executives were able to convince themselves that the difficulties of making *The Misfits*, real and rumored, would not be a factor here. When *Goodbye Charlie* was put to bed as far as MM was concerned, a retooled *My Favorite Wife* came to the fore. At first, it was renamed *Do It Again*, recalling the George Gershwin song MM had recorded years before. Then it became the title of another song, this one conveniently owned by Fox: *Something's Got to Give*.

While at least part of her was eager to return to work, there was no way that Monroe was going to approach this new film with any great joy. First and last, she hated the fact that Fox was taking advantage of an outdated contract. Star salaries, including her own for *Some Like It Hot*, had skyrocketed since she signed that deal with the studio, and it galled her that she would be paid a small fraction of what Fox was giving Elizabeth Taylor to portray Cleopatra. There was also the fact that, for her, this seemed like a regression. Under the tutelage of the Strasbergs, she was continuing to seek validation as a dramatic performer in challenging roles. While *The Misfits* had been only a questionable success for her, it indicated, at least in theory, the direction she was hoping for. So did *Rain*, despite how it played out. *Something's Got to Give*, in contrast, did not appear to offer her much more than *Let's Make Love* had. Even in the realm of "adult" comedy, this story, with its long list of antecedents, hardly portended anything especially fresh or stimulating. With these downsides, there were still some incentives lurking in *Something's Got to Give*. First was the nature of the role. Except for her brief outing in *We're Not Married*, she had never played a mother, and having two on-screen children was an appealing notion given her real-life disappointment in that area. And instead of her usual role as some sort of entertainer, she would be playing a working woman. Ellen was a professional photographer whose assignment in the Pacific led to her disappearance, and whatever the character's farcical travails, there was a sense of maturity and responsibility unlike in previous roles. Plus, with her recent weight loss, she could look devastating on camera once again. While the Fox lot was then a far quieter place than in previous years—*Cleopatra* was soaking up most of the cash and effort in Rome—she would be in familiar surroundings without having to cope with the hellish location work of *The Misfits*. The director would be from her approved list, she would be allowed input on the script, and again, it would be a way to finally be done with the damned Fox contract. With the encouragement of her new L.A.-based psychiatrist, Ralph Greenson, she cautiously agreed to move ahead.

At the first and last, there were difficulties with the script, and this was an area in which the studio severely underestimated how perceptive and exacting Monroe could be. Through hard work and curiosity and a good deal of reading and study, and even before her work with Strasberg, she had become a shrewd judge of what would and would not work for her and the "Marilyn" character she had developed. Indeed, the dire experience of *Let's Make Love* was predicated in large part on the fact that she knew it wasn't giving her decent opportunities, up to and including the revisions written by her husband. There had also been the incessant rewrites of the *Misfits* screenplay, which she felt had sabotaged her role and her well-being. As the new script for *Something's Got to Give* passed through several drafts before reaching her, she became ever more wary. The version she was finally sent, credited to comedy writer Arnold Schulman, failed to meet even lowered expectations. This, she saw immediately, was far closer in merit to *Let's Make Love* than to *Some Like It Hot*. While reading the script, she took a pencil and began to file her objections. Referring to her on-screen persona in the third person, as she often did, she printed "not a story for MM" on the title page. "It's for a man and just any two girls except the first 45 pages," she wrote, adding the kiss-of-death comments "Not funny" and, after the final scene, "NO NO NO."[2] Things got a little better when Fox assigned the next round of rewrites to Nunnally Johnson, who had already done well by "the MM character" in *How to Marry a Millionaire*. In discussing *Something's Got to Give* with Johnson, she led off by asking him, "Have you been trapped into this too?" After extensive work on his part, she declared herself pleased with the script, even as she scrawled an ominous message on its title page: "We've got a dog here— so we've got to look for impacts in a different way." On page 12 of Johnson's script, she also sought to distance herself (however ungrammatically) from the original Ellen Arden: "Ellen is no longer Irene Dune [*sic*]—and the only people on earth I get on well with is men so lets [*sic*] have some fun with this opening scene."

Monroe's objections were hardly the only problem. David Brown of Fox's story department had been responsible for the initial idea and was originally scheduled to produce *Something's Got to Give*. When he abruptly left the production, it was announced that he and Fox had parted company over disagreements about the script and the basic concept. While this was partly accurate, other forces seemed to be at play as well. Brown's successor was Henry Weinstein, who had one film (*Tender Is the Night*) to his credit and was hired in part upon the recommendation of his friend—and MM's psychiatrist—Dr. Greenson. The implication here, perhaps even the operative notion, was that Greenson's connection to the production, through its producer and especially its star, would ensure that things would move along

---

[2] Another observation she wrote on the title page is, to modern eyes, somewhat less helpful: "At one point in the story two women like each other but hate the man—all the fags are going to love it." Even with her gay friends and associates, MM was still, and in a number of ways, a product of her time.

at a satisfactory pace. Monroe's relationship with Greenson and his family was already transcending the conventional boundaries of doctor-patient relationships, and here he was clearly injecting himself into her professional life.

As Johnson and others continued to plug away on the script, the production took shape. George Cukor was on the MM list of acceptable directors, and despite the failure of *Let's Make Love*, Fox hired him once again. Cukor, who had little investment in the film save as a well-paying job, decided that the script should not deviate too far away from that of *My Favorite Wife*. That, in his opinion, had worked well the first time, and sticking with it now ensured that there would be less need to rethink things. Perhaps his greatest investment in the project came with its setting, specifically the main set on which the film would take place. For reasons of both expedience and stylishness, art director Gene Allen, a close friend of the director, decided to make the Arden house a close copy of Cukor's own residence.[3] The casting process was a little less clear-cut. For the role of the disputed husband, Fox's preference was James Garner, who had also been up for the stillborn *Goodbye Charlie*. Then, when it felt that Garner was asking for too much money, the studio moved on (with typical logic) to someone demanding far more. If Dean Martin's name carried more clout than Garner's at the box office, few of his recent films, some of them suggestive farces, had been major successes. Monroe knew him well and looked forward to working with him, while at the same time being aware that Fox would be paying him multiple times what it was paying her. The third lead, the frustrated second wife, was taken by Cyd Charisse, who was then searching for roles other than those requiring her to dance. Tom Tryon would play the hunk who shared Ellen's five years on a desert island, Steve Allen would be Charisse's psychiatrist, and Phil Silvers was cast as a wiseacre insurance man. Another MM friend, Wally Cox, was cast as the dweeby shoe salesman Ellen tries to pass off as said hunk.

Something's Got to Give, as everyone eventually learned, was a near-masterpiece of mishandling, and there was a good deal of blame to go around. First, there were the Fox executives who convinced themselves, and were convinced by her psychiatrist, that Monroe could get through the filming without major interruption. When this proved not to be the case,

---

[3] Allen later said that the very short time he was given to come up with a set led him to simply reproduce Cukor's Beverly Hills home, which was distinctive as well as elegant. It would be not only Cukor's house being copied but also his backyard and swimming pool. The latter would figure very prominently as the *Something's Got to Give* saga continued.

they would proceed to excoriate her in as public a fashion as possible. As the delays began, she was held to be a prime example of a willful and uncooperative star. If *Cleopatra* was too big and complex for them to pull the plug, the powers at Fox determined that *Something's Got to Give* would be far easier to control. Surely, if there was little they could do about Taylor in Rome, they could hang tough with Monroe in California.

A number of accounts have also called out Cukor for his role in the disaster, and not unreasonably. Less than three years earlier, Cukor and Monroe had begun *Let's Make Love* as a happy team. She admired his sterling work with actors, and he knew the magic she could produce on the screen. Then, as time passed, both became disillusioned. If her absences and memory lapses tried his patience, the larger factor was her complete reliance on Paula Strasberg. He was already aware that *Let's Make Love* would not be one of his better films, and the MM-Paula equation could only add to his unhappiness. Then, later, he was compelled to put his feelings to one side because he owed Fox another picture. First it was to be *Goodbye Charlie*, and then it became *Something's Got to Give*, neither of which held much interest for him.[4] Since his name remained on that ironclad list of directors Monroe had drawn up back in 1956, the two of them were tied together no matter how much either might have preferred otherwise. An early sign of his hostility came when she shot the tests for her clothes, hair, and makeup. These were, in everyone's opinion, utterly spectacular, and a director normally would have been present when she shot them. Cukor was not.

As she headed toward *Something's Got to Give*, Monroe was presenting a dazzling facade. Having recently purchased her first house in order to put down roots, she seemed to many more assured and self-possessed than she had been in a long time. This masked problems with her physical health, including recurring bouts of bronchitis and sinusitis, and her emotional health, which was governed by bipolar fluctuations and chemical dependencies. There were personal dependencies as well, since she was granting Greenson, the Strasbergs, and members of the Kennedy family disproportionate importance in her life. Meanwhile, her reliance on medications and alcohol

---

[4] He was also, at the same time, engaged in the production of another film whose star made him even more unhappy. Although he was pleased to be directing an adaptation of Romain Gary's novel *Lady L* at MGM, he did not exactly bond with the Lady herself, Gina Lollobrigida. That's putting it way too mildly: their hostility toward each other was so monumental that it caused the film to be shut down completely. While Cukor claimed illness, everyone knew that George vs. Gina had been the real cause.

continued unabated. Champagne was now her drink of choice, and there seemed to be an inexhaustible pipeline to such drugs as Demerol and chloral hydrate. An early warning came on the day after she had filmed those sensational tests, when she failed to show up at the studio for a meeting with producer Weinstein. After a series of unanswered phone calls, Weinstein rushed over to her home to find her so overmedicated that she was barely coherent. When he sent Fox executives a memo advising that the production should be postponed, he was given a reply that said, essentially, she always does this and always manages to get through to the end.

When production on *Something's Got to Give* began on schedule on April 23, 1962, Monroe was not present. Having taken a quick trip to New York to confer with the Strasbergs, she had contracted a cold from Lee Strasberg. She was finally well enough to come to the set a week later, when Cukor shot reaction shots of Ellen seeing her children for the first time since her "resurrection." The following day, she fainted in her dressing room and was sent home. Days of absence followed, during which Cukor shot scenes with Martin, Charisse, and other cast members. Monroe returned, finally feeling somewhat better, on May 14, completing the scene with Ellen encountering her two children and the family dog. Monroe had seen to it that the dog was named Tippy in honor of her own childhood pet. This Tippy, a cocker spaniel named Jeff, was less than responsive in his scenes with Monroe, which necessitated nearly as many takes as her worst moments during *Some Like It Hot*. The children, for their part, also required a number of takes, and with both the dog and the kids, Monroe remained friendly and professional. Cukor, for his part, seemed often to be working with a short fuse, letting his impatience show, barking at the children, and insisting on more takes of scenes that had already been done adequately.

In the midst of all this, there was the president's birthday. Shelves of books have been written about Monroe's association with both President John F. Kennedy and his brother, Attorney General Robert Kennedy. Much of what has been written and discussed—real, invented, speculative, prurient, hysterical—fortunately lies well outside the scope of these pages. Yet, regardless of how it was manifested, her relationship with the president did impact her work significantly during the shoot of *Something's Got to Give*. Before filming began, the studio had granted her permission to fly to New York to perform at President Kennedy's birthday gala on May 19. Powering past her apprehension over performing live, she was fully prepared to make a polished job of it and worked closely with designer Jean Louis on a gown that would be, to say the least, impactful.[5] By May 11, with her absences from the set totaling nearly three weeks, Fox rescinded its earlier edict and forbade her departure. Monroe responded by finally making it to the set, performing well for more than three days, then flying to New York for the gala. Before she went onstage at Madison Square Garden, she received a notice from Fox that she was in violation of her contract.

History can collide with innuendo in any number of peculiar ways, and it is quite an irony that Monroe's rendition of "Happy Birthday, Mr. President" may be the best known of all her recorded performances. If some people, then and later, have professed to find MM's "Happy Birthday" an exhibitionistic embarrassment, a wider perspective shows how much she was in command of the situation. Amid a roster of luminaries ranging from Jack Benny to Maria Callas to Ella Fitzgerald to Bobby Darin, Monroe was the one who stole the show. Everything had been minutely coordinated—her dress and hair and musical arrangement, even her supposedly late arrival onstage. While most simply recall the heavy-breathing insinuation of "Happy Birthday," she also managed a professional rendition of "Thanks for the Memory," with special presidential lyrics. Then, as an immense cake was wheeled out, she led the audience in another chorus of "Happy Birthday" while elatedly jumping up and down, in spike heels and tight skirt, to the music, while managing somehow to come across as both an untouchable siren and the most engaging pal imaginable. On the opposite coast, the mood was far more grim, with some outside her intimate circle viewing her trip as a willful act of starry self-indulgence.

Upon her return, Monroe continued to work, despite often feeling the effects of a bronchial infection that was not helped by the hot lights and the proximity of the swimming pool. Later, when Martin attempted to work while having a cold, she refused to do scenes with him until he felt better. Then, on May 23, came the nude swim. At the time, and especially after her subsequent firing, it was said that her nudity was an impulsive and unsanctioned act, an out-of-control diva flouting convention and possibly even decency, when she began the scene wearing a skin-colored strapless bikini

---

[5] The "Happy Birthday" gown, described by MM as "skin and beads," eventually became, with the *Seven Year Itch* subway dress and perhaps one or two others, one of the hallmarks of her legend. Jean Louis had just designed her wardrobe for *Something's Got to Give* and, before that, for *The Misfits*. He had also done her clothes for *Ladies of the Chorus*, fourteen years and what seemed many lifetimes earlier. Speaking of lifetimes, six decades after MM's appearance, the dress turned up again in New York City at the 2022 Met Gala ball. Wearing it this time was Kim Kardashian, whose celebrity— let alone achievement—lay in quite different precincts from Monroe's. Putting it mildly.

intended to simulate nudity, then midway through gleefully took it off. None
of it was as spontaneous as alleged, although Fox was certainly willing to have
it play into later accusations of unprofessional behavior. Monroe and Cukor,
both aware of the publicity such a stunt would bring, had apparently planned
it carefully, and she was especially eager to wrest the public's attention away
from Elizabeth Taylor, Richard Burton, and *Cleopatra*. While photographer
Lawrence Schiller and others shot numerous rolls of film, Monroe-as-Ellen
cavorted in the heated water. Cukor, for his part, was careful to position the
cameras so as to avoid undue exposure. It was not the first time Monroe
had been naked on camera—she had done so in *Niagara*, *Bus Stop*, and *The
Misfits*—yet there was something about it that seemed especially audacious
and, for some observers, perhaps self-defeating.

Monroe filmed the last scenes of her career on June 1, which also happened
to be her thirty-sixth birthday. Illness then forced her to stay home, and
by June 6, her studio had decided to terminate her contract. One incident
followed fast upon another: Fox's decision that her psychiatrist could no
longer guarantee her presence and health; Cukor criticizing her intemper-
ately in an interview with columnist Hedda Hopper; the quick engagement
of Lee Remick to replace her; Martin's insistence that he would work with
Monroe only; suits and countersuits and ugly headlines. With her effortless gift for self-promotion, Monroe responded to it all by doing a series of
high-profile photo sessions and by granting an honest, in-depth interview
to *Life* magazine. Weeks later, it seemed that it was all coming back together,
with the Nunnally Johnson script reinstated, Jean Negulesco directing, and
shooting scheduled for sometime in the fall. Then she was gone.

Something's Got to Give was finally released, late in 1963, under a different
title. It was now *Move Over, Darling*, and featured the same set of Cukor's
house, a redone script, a different director, and a completely new cast including an Ellen who was at that time just about equal to Monroe in popularity. There were few roles that Monroe could have shared with Doris
Day—*The Prince and the* reworked *Showgirl*, maybe?—and, partly per Day's
insistence, there was notably less innuendo than in the original script. Apart
from the premise, scenery, and character names, the main reference to the
Monroe version seemed to be Day's hair, blown out and teased in a slightly
toned-down replay of the MM coiffure. The Arden children were now two
girls instead of a boy and a girl, and in place of a nude swimming scene,
there was obvious slapstick, especially in a sequence that had a distraught
Day taking her top-down convertible through an automated car wash. James

Garner made it in this time as leading man, and Polly Bergen was the second wife, with Chuck Connors now playing the hunk, Don Knotts as the nerdy shoe clerk, and Thelma Ritter in the reinstated role of Ellen's mother-in-law. Despite Day's popularity and some unusually strenuous goings-on, there was no way that this production could have been viewed apart from everything that had come before. Naturally, Fox had declined to announce that it was a retread of a production cut short by tragedy, which did nothing to deter critics, in unusually mixed reviews, from mentioning Monroe, the nude swim, and the events of May through August 1962. None of this prevented *Move Over, Darling* from being Fox's first major financial success of its cash-strapped post-*Cleopatra* era.

Monroe's death sent *Something's Got to Give*, the first one, into a hazy realm of speculation and legend for thirty or so years. (For some, it remains there.) Not unexpectedly, it would be subject to nearly as much conjecture and controversy as such other subjects as her association with the Kennedy family and the exact nature of her death. This could only be exacerbated by the fact that for many years, only an insignificant amount of footage was seen of the film, whose negative had reportedly disappeared quite mysteriously from the studio vault. All this led to a popular notion that little or no usable footage of Monroe had been shot, which, of course, backed up Fox's ongoing contention that she, with her many days of illness and absence, was responsible for shutting down the film. Later, when more of the film emerged from the Fox vault, the proposition changed somewhat. More than a third of the movie had been filmed, a fair amount of it with Monroe, and it was clear that a number of factors had led to the collapse of the production.

It might be nice to note that the surviving footage, after it resurfaced and was assembled, could give a complete, possibly even satisfying impression of what the film would have been. It does not, although "impression" may be the right term for the disconnected procession of scenes that exist. The most finished moments are those involving Martin, Charisse, and Allen, filmed in all those days Cukor had been compelled to shoot around MM. Martin gives off the same smooth, laid-back-and-not-appearing-to-care vibe that he'd had in many of his films, and Allen, working with an underwritten role, seems a bit lost. Charisse, who could sometimes be a beautiful blank on the screen, is making more of an effort and manages to garner some laughs in her interaction with a stuffy judge (John McGiver).

Monroe's scenes are harder to assess. She had not been so beautiful on-screen since *The Prince and the Showgirl*, with maturity and weight loss delicately sculpting fresh and elegant planes onto her face. Even with big bouffant hair, she appears timeless and fresh, moving with grace and assurance, interacting warmly with the two children, and even finding some delight working with that problematic spaniel. For nearly the first time onscreen, she affords an opportunity to hear her real voice, a somewhat harsher sound than the applied MM breathiness, which she resorts to only rarely. This gives her something of a different character, as does the amusing faux-guttural Greta Garbo imitation she does when Ellen impersonates a bogus Swedish nursemaid named Ingrid Tic.[6] During the carefully photographed nude swim, she appears especially joyful, with that famous giggle always near. In isolated moments, then, she is fine—but even given the raggedness that comes from the nature of the raw footage, she appears to go in and out of focus constantly. Sometimes her timing can be a bit erratic, and she seems distracted, as if she had trouble with her lines or her concentration. "Sorry, George, but we can do it," she reassures Cukor at one point after having trouble with her dialogue. If it might be unreasonable to expect consistency, she sometimes seems unable to sustain a mood from one line to the next. As in *The Misfits*, her tremulousness and fragility are at moments so palpable that it can be difficult to tell if they are an actor's choice or a personal difficulty. If, as can be seen in take after take, she tries and tries, the overall impression is one of disconnection, even fragmentation. Under these circumstances, it is difficult to see how she could have gotten all the way to the end of the shoot in that fate-filled summer of 1962.

Before *Move Over, Darling* opened at the end of 1963, the public had been allowed a small glimpse of *Something's Got to Give*. Rock Hudson, twice a prospective Monroe costar (*Bus Stop* and *Let's Make Love*) served as onscreen host and narrator for Fox's *Marilyn*, ostensibly a documentary tribute to the studio's most sensational employee. There was a fair amount of self-serving, plus the predictable clips—"Diamonds Are a Girl's Best Friend" and "Heat Wave" and the skirt blowing—with no mention of *Let's Make Love* or the films she did at other studios. In many opinions, the main reason to see *Marilyn* lay in a few moments near the end devoted to *Something's Got to Give*. It cannot be said that Fox was generous with the clips from the film itself, which were devoted mainly to the swimming scene and the briefest

---

[6] She coached her Swedish accent with actress Edith Evanson, who would later recall something Monroe said to her: "Isn't it a terrible thing about life that there always must be something we have to live up to?"

of exchanges between MM and Wally Cox. There was, however, a generous helping of shots from those same hair/makeup/wardrobe tests that had caused so much excitement at the studio. As an ethereally gorgeous Monroe posed and reacted, laughed and strutted and blew wisps of platinum hair out of her eyes, Fox's cash-in compilation acquired an unintended dimension. By letting her be seen so beautiful and assured, so seemingly happy right before her life ended, it showed, more than would ever be possible through words, much of what had been lost.

15

Legacies

Few were surprised at the extent of shock and grief after her death. It seemed that the entire world was shaken by the news and the loss, and no one doubted that she would continue to be remembered and appreciated. With her level of, call it fame, celebrity, stardom, notoriety, or glory, it was a given that she would go on. Of course she would. But who in the world could have envisioned that her legend would continue to grow so much, so long after her achievements were done?

Normally, the biggest movie stars receive some degree of legend and enshrinement after their death: Clark Gable had it, and Gary Cooper and Bette Davis and Paul Newman and Elizabeth Taylor, all of them having had rich and full careers. Humphrey Bogart was initially in that category as well, until the passage of time brought him a degree of veneration more intensive than when he was alive. Joan Crawford was a special case, with the backstory (such as it may have been) overtaking and sometimes burying the career. Greta Garbo was such a legend in her lifetime that her death only altered a tiny bit of the context. There were also the cases of Jean Harlow and James Dean, both gone at a shockingly early age. In Dean's case, the neuroticism of a "death cult" reverence was as unique as it was unhealthy, only rivaled later by the likes of Jim Morrison and, especially, Elvis Presley. With Monroe's death, an event that seemed inevitable to some became, to a far greater number, a case of "We should have saved her." And even "I *could* have saved her." She was so immediate and vivid that people felt that they knew her and thus might have played a role in her rescue. Suspended in time as she was, she became a more reachable and endearing heroine after she was gone.

Several factors contributed prominently to Monroe's postmortem stardom. One came with television and the nearly constant broadcast of all her films. NBC's *Saturday Night at the Movies* had started this when it launched with *How to Marry a Millionaire*, and from then on, on network and locally, latterly on cable and then streaming, the Monroe film canon became a surefire way to grab audiences. With her work so available, she was able to maintain her fame and her spell in a startlingly active and present way that seemed to render her death all the more tragic and yet, in a sense, irrelevant. The small screen and even black-and-white did not diminish her glow, nor did the way her six CinemaScope films were shown with about half of their image missing in action. Then, in the wake of the telecast movies, came the books, beginning (more or less) with a sensitive biography in 1969 called *Norma Jean*. It was the first respectable book to broach the Kennedy business, albeit in a cloaked fashion that had author Fred Lawrence Guiles referring to the president simply as "the Easterner." Norman Mailer had no such compunction, and his 1973 best-selling *Marilyn* was filled with magnificent pictures and self-indulgent prose, along with ruminative speculations about Kennedy and much else. With this book's enormous success, it became clear that Monroe's sensation, real and rumored, would not only be ongoing but could increase. With that ethos in place, the floodgates opened so wide that it seemed that anyone who ever met her, or claimed to, was willing to share a book-long account of the relationship to a well-paying publisher. Friends, employees, ex-husbands (Joe DiMaggio excepted) all had their say. These ranged from the affectionate to the eyebrow-raising, and few or none of them were more troubling than Arthur Miller's play *After the Fall*, which was quite difficult to see as something other than a self-justifying and unnervingly public airing of matters that likely should have remained private. The photographers, too, with whom Monroe had collaborated so rewardingly, jumped on the bandwagon with lavishly printed demonstrations of their work embellished by reminiscences that might, in some cases, have either amused or annoyed her. In many cases, truly, the pictures would have been enough.

There were also, increasingly as the years went along, the vultures. The fact that someone so vividly famous had died in a way clouded by some uncertainty—her death was ruled "probable suicide," with no note— guaranteed that all manner of innuendo and mud could be flung. Far too many books and programs were the fly-by-night products of those who claimed to possess private or sinister information about her and those who allegedly destroyed her. The name "Kennedy" was neon-imprinted in nearly all of these, with "Mafia" usually taking second place. Lifetimes before the absurd likes of QAnon or Pizzagate or any of the other latter-day hoaxes, Monroe's death was used as a staging area for garish conspiracy theories involving who might have murdered her, done a cover-up, gotten away with it, and kept going, possibly even to Dallas. And get this: some of these even found a "who knew?" connection between MM and UFOs, Roswell, and Area

51. The books and documentaries—and, later, miniseries—kept coming, and as they did, more speculation ratcheted up about how she lived and, especially, how she died.[1] While some of these so-called exposés were the work of self-described "experts" or "witnesses" who quite likely were neither of those things, the most relentless purveyor of these fictions went even farther. The man claimed not only to have been a confidant, from her earliest Hollywood days to the very end, but even a hitherto unrecorded ex-husband (between, for the record, Jim Dougherty and DiMaggio). For years and years, he and a few cronies would be invited onto talk shows to spin their Marilyn Babylon tales, speak nonsensically about the most nefarious plots, and in some cases libel the dead. The fact that no one in her life was familiar with this man or his troll cohorts did not deter networks or presenters from engaging them for interviews and appearances. To their everlasting discredit, even some of the more respectable biographers took to citing these as authentic sources, blithely disregarding the fact that reflected glory is sometimes no glory at all.[2]

Fortunately, amid the literally hundreds of books written about Monroe, there were many that sought to engage in fact over rumor and substance over sensation. In the most laudable cases, her biographers engaged in genuine research and investigation in an attempt to discover "real" truth, as it were, instead of simply something shocking. It goes without saying that in many of the psychological portraits drawn of her, Monroe could seem a doomed figure, in the words of one writer "a woman in crisis." The most astute writers could discuss such things dispassionately while at the same time not failing to talk about her considerable wit, her strength, the exceptional zest she had for life, and the unique objectivity she sometimes had about her accomplishments and potential. And again, shelves of glossy volumes

---

[1] For the record, there does seem to have been some sloppy work investigating the circumstances of Monroe's death, and it has been plausibly offered that some aspects of it may have been laundered or altered to remove mentions of members of the Kennedy family. Nevertheless, the circumstances overwhelmingly suggest that Monroe died deliberately by her own hand, though some who knew her have said that the overdose was the accidental result of incautious pill taking. Neither is out of the question, since there had been incidents of both of these a number of times prior to August 4, 1962. The record shows, in any case, that her emotional state was in constant flux during her final weeks, careening between manic highs and the lowest lows. Perhaps (and that's a really big word) the most valid assessment was given in a 2001 documentary by her last physician, Hyman Engelberg: a sudden reaction or thought plunged her (as had happened before) into a deep depression, and she took a large number of the pills that were always by her bedside. Then, as she began to slip into unconsciousness, she thought better of it and attempted to reach people by phone. "So," Engelberg concluded, "while it was intentional at the time, I do believe she changed her mind." Again, *perhaps*.

[2] Nor, incredibly enough, were sane professionals put off by the fact that the one other significant achievement of this purported "second husband" was as auteur of a 1971 movie called *Bigfoot*. Sometimes the truth is there in plain sight.

reminded everyone that perhaps her most enduring love affair was the one she had with the camera. In those, at least, there could be the intimations of how hard she worked to create and refine her image. Nor was it a surprise that many writers, Gloria Steinem included, would find her a notably rich subject for examination from a feminist point of view. If the occasional claims of "martyrdom" could be a bit much, few could deny her exploitation, time and again, by oppressive and demeaning forces. There was, for writers of every kind, too much there to overlook: the triumph and defeat, the eternal search for validation, that final immortality that seemed without parallel. As vivid and specific as she had been in life, she could now be something of a tabula rasa, upon which countless writers[3] might impose their notions.

Monroe also found a particular sort of endurance through the sincere flattery of imitation. During her lifetime, she was far too engraved onto public consciousness not to rate a host of wanna-bes and also-rans. Invariably, they would be blond and curvaceous, and most often they were molded to come as close, superficially, to MM as possible. Above all, there was Jayne Mansfield, whose desire to emulate Monroe was so intensive as to be poignant and often enough grotesque. Even Twentieth Century-Fox bought into the Mansfield act, employing her for a while as a sort of guardrail threat to keep MM in line. Mansfield, who was utterly besotted with fame and stardom in a way that went far beyond Monroe's most extreme ambitions, functioned at her best as a demented, and often amusing, parody of a sex symbol. Ultimately, it all collapsed in a sea of self-delusion and, as with Monroe, early death—albeit this time in so hideously grisly a fashion that no one could claim any manner of conspiracy. Nor was Mansfield the only faux-Marilyn to die relatively young. Among the others were Joi Lansing, Cleo Moore, Peggie Castle, the gifted comedian Barbara Nichols, and "British Bombshell" Diana Dors. In Lansing's case and possibly others, the cause of death was a particularly difficult sex-symbol tragedy: cancer that resulted from unintended effects caused by breast enhancement. Conversely, one of the earliest "MM-groomed" figures proved singularly durable. In spite of some truly rotten films and a number of odd career choices, Mamie Van Doren (born Joan Lucille Olander) was able to chart a remarkable journey from 1950s tabloid press to twenty-first-century social media, including a steady stream of Facebook selfies. Who would have imagined that an Eisenhower-era pinup queen could continue so vitally, and in much the same fashion, into her nineties?

---

[3] The reader's present company included, most definitely.

Supposed heirs to the Monroe throne have come along many different routes—movies, popular music, modeling, online media, and, most especially, television, with its constant stream of the aspiring, the hopeful, and the damaged. (Surely, in her own sad way, Anna Nicole Smith was a kind of Monroe/Mansfield retread.) The more specific echoes of MM have come with an endless procession of movies for TV and cable, some respectfully biographic, others overtly fictionalized. There have been plays and operas and much else, and doubtless, as new forms of media communication continue to be devised, Monroe will be part of them. In that special late-twentieth-century arena of music videos, there was Madonna, whose knack for self-promotion could put both Monroe and Mansfield into the shade. In 1985, she made an especially vivid claim to the MM crown with her "Material Girl" video and its overt recycling of "Diamonds Are a Girl's Best Friend." Obviously, she made a success out of it, since some people are still surprised today that it wasn't Madonna who first had the concept of the hot-pink dress and red background and tuxedoed chorus. Monroe, had she known of this, would probably have let out one of those loud, infectious laughs of hers, while Jack Cole would likely be muttering something unprintable.

While she later moved away from too-deliberate echoes of Monroe, Madonna did help to polish the myth for those too young to have experienced MM during her lifetime. Unfortunately, the myth has been propagated to be far more about "Happy Birthday, Mr. President" than, say, the timeless elan of *Some Like It Hot*, since the fame and the tragedy have so frequently outstripped the actual achievements that were always her prime motivating force. This is a special pity, since her accomplishments remain tangible while so much else is evanescent and speculative. Fortunately, her legacy is more accessible than ever before. "I now live in my work," she stated in her final interview, and recorded and streaming media have seen to it that this work is readily available. Most conspicuously, her "home studio," in its latter-day incarnation as 20th Century Studios Home Entertainment, continues with continually repackaged cash-cow releases of her films, including the ones not worth seeing the first time.[4] Beyond that, there is the fact that the simple mention of her name, associating her with anything at all, seems to guarantee

---

[4] How many minutes is she in the dire *Let's Make It Legal*? Less than five? Yet it's her image alone, not that of Claudette Colbert or anyone else, that graces the DVD cover. We can wonder why Fox doesn't just go the whole complete-the-circle route and plaster her image all over a release of *Scudda Hoo! Scudda Hay!* After all, like just about everything else she made or did, it acquires its main importance through her.

interest and a profit. Her image and aura have been used to sell pretty much everything, whether it has any true connection with her whatsoever. There is, in one example among countless, a rather tasty vintage called Marilyn Merlot; never mind that red wine was not her drink of choice. Until a dismantling ordered by a 2012 court ruling, the use of her image was controlled by her estate, as administered by Lee Strasberg's second wife and the Actors Studio. That connection, at least, seems to adhere to some of her wishes.

A more rarefied merchandising continues to move steadily upward with the auctioning, and reauctioning, of items from her films and personal life. It is as if anything she ever touched had a transmittable magic, and without exception, the results from these sales have been astronomical. The most extreme case in point is the white dress, designed by Travilla, that MM wore in *The Seven Year Itch*, most memorably in the scene that had her standing over the subway grate. For many in 1954, that scene and that dress appeared to define her image and did so again fifty-seven years later at an auction of movie costumes. When a bidder paid more than $5 million, the dress became the highest-priced single garment in history. Most likely, the figure would be much higher today, though probably not in the same league as Andy Warhol's silkscreen "Shot Sage Blue Marilyn," which fetched a heart-stopping $195 million in May 2022. Would anyone care to speculate on how much lower the bidding would have been had it been a portrait of someone else?

All these—the books and films and documentaries and all the packaging and selling and imitation and cashing in—are indicators of the power Monroe still wields. There is no one indicator that explains why she has endured to an extent that would seem preposterous were it anyone else. Many others in her profession have also lasted, almost without exception as occupiers of a niche called "movie star." Monroe's realm is far less delineated. Too much has been ascribed to her, applied to her, theorized about her, for this to be the conventional adulation given a famous person, not even one who created a grand sensation and then died young. It also remains sadly true that her legacy retains a great deal of the condescension that plagued her during her life, and it may be that the power of her mythology will forever obscure the extent of her achievement. If this is not the greatest of the tragedies that adhere to her, it is still as unjust as it is unfortunate. However numerous and profound her issues and conflicts, she worked toward high professional goals with skill and dedication and, more than frequently, great success. Sometimes, not often enough, she was given—or gave herself—sufficient recognition for what she did. Far more often, she was not, and this, too, remains part of her tragedy.

How good it is, then, that posterity can paint a brighter and more accurate portrait of her gifts. She studied intently, she worked damned hard, and in a real sense, she accomplished something that was quite often miraculously transcendent. If the era in which she thrived can seem so remote as to be irretrievable, her work has enabled her to remain more bright and current than anyone could have imagined. She has endured, and in all probability will continue to do so, in a stirringly present tense.

Epilogue

Exactly one month before she died, Marilyn Monroe made an unusually pointed and touching request to the last journalist who interviewed her. "Please," she implored, "don't make me look like a joke." Even though she burst into one of those laughs of hers right afterward, she had been serious when she said it. No one, after all, knew better than she did how the sensation she was always causing could slight and overshadow her achievements. Well before her death, she had moved beyond the point where her craft and her life could be easily differentiated. Perhaps, since she could be quite perceptive about professional matters, she foresaw that this would continue long after she was gone. The more she realized this fact, the more she sought approval for what she achieved, not for the excitement she seemed to constantly be creating. Unfortunately, she had been extremely thorough in creating "Marilyn Monroe," a manufactured persona that went well beyond simply performing a role for an audience. How sad that this image was able to overtake so much of what she could do.

In her lifetime and forever after, it can be hard to move past everything that has attached itself to her. She is now, and will remain, a composite of many things. It is not simply about the movies she made or the roles she wanted to play. Nor is it about the way she looked and that unfailing ability she had (or has?) to project sexuality and innocence at the same time. Neither is it that Cinderella story of hers, starting off in such sad circumstances, becoming the most famous woman in the world, and marrying men whose fame and achievement rivaled her own. Nor is it about her struggle to be respected in her life and her profession or about the people, famous or unknown, she encountered along the way. Each of those might have been enough, but she encompassed them all. At times, her status as a living legend was amusing to her, and far more often, it was frightening and debilitating, both in itself and in the price it exacted.

It will always be fair to wonder and consider just how large a role her work has played in her phenomenon. There is, after all, so much to confront about her life, including sorting out the real from the speculated or made up.

Fortunately, on film and on the ways film is now manifested, her work is a more constant presence now even than in her heyday. We are permitted, over and over, to watch, evaluate, enjoy, criticize, appreciate. Look at her, then, as objectively as possible, divorced from gossip, speculative theories, and exhaustively imposed agendas. With those necessary guidelines in place, she is permitted to exist in a state of constant vibrancy. She is endlessly exciting, continually generous, and inventive to a fault. Her talent is neither ambiguous nor disputable. It's *there*. From the earliest, even with the woefully overdone diction, she was presenting and creating and evolving. Sometimes with her, the tiniest moments can carry a startling amount of weight, and there are also the times when she tries too hard and overreaches. She knew this herself, which is why she kept striving for better performances in better material. She never coasted or phoned it in, which is one reason it's so sad to see her giving trivia so much more time and thought than it deserves. Fortunately, she and her best roles could meet in a space of complete connection, whether in a New York brownstone or a western diner, an ocean liner, a foreign embassy, or a Florida resort. These and the other portraits in her gallery remain clear and fresh and present. In spite of everything she did and experienced, they will always be the most authentic part of who Marilyn Monroe was and who she remains. They are, ultimately, her truth. What a blessing that they are our truth as well.

Citations

The sources cited are listed in the bibliography.

Introduction

"Both charming and embarrassing": Kael 1968, 348.

Chronology

Among the many sources consulted for this chronology, two were especially thorough and helpful: Carl Rollyson's excellent book *Marilyn Monroe Day by Day* (Rollyson 2014a) and the extremely detailed website Cursumperficio.net.

Chapter 1

"She was the hardest worker": Emmeline Snively, quoted in Zolotow 1960, 44–45.

"Jean Monroe": MM, quoted in Zolotow 1960, 52.

"Has been designated": George Wasson (Fox legal department), memos of December 6 and December 9, 1946. December 6 memo reproduced on cursumperficio.net. December 9 memo reproduced on julienslive.com.

"She hadn't had": Rand Brooks, quoted in Buskin 2001, 33.

"Nifty warbling": *Daily Variety*, December 3, 1948, 3.

Chapter 2

"The Johnston Office" (n. 1): MM, quoted in Martin 1956.

Paul Valentine (n. 2): conversation with the author, Hollywood, September 4, 1994.

"You will have to work on diction": Natasha Lytess, quoted in Zolotow 1960, 64.

Jeffrey Lynn and *Home Town Story*: quoted in Buskin 2001, 68–71.

"Glued-on innocence": Joseph L. Mankiewicz, quoted in Carey and Mankiewicz 1974, 75.

"She had a strange delivery": Celeste Holm, quote in Buskin 2001, 61.

Chapter 3

"The only person": Joseph L. Mankiewicz, quoted in Carey and Mankiewicz 1974, 75.

"An abominable waste": Mailer 1973, 89.

"Something was going on": David Wayne, quoted in Buskin 2001, 79.

"When Marilyn walked": June Haver, quoted in Hoyt 1965, 84.

"She was riding" (n. 5): Macdonald Carey, quoted in Buskin 2001, 87.

Chapter 4

"It's this way": Barbara Stanwyck, quoted in Zolotow 1960, 114.

"It wasn't that": Jean Peters, quoted in Buskin 2001, 90.

"You have built up": Darryl Zanuck, memo to MM, quoted in Leaming 1998, 39.

"Unable to take refuge": Natasha Lytess, unpublished memoir, quoted in Taraborrelli 2009, 135.

"Monroe's amateurish manner": Manny Farber, *The Nation*, February 27, 1953.

"It was one of those very rare times": Anne Bancroft, quoted in Guiles 1984, 205.

Goulding instructing her to breathe: McCann 1987, 43.

Koster: "She [MM] was just marvelous." Quoted in Davis 2005, 16.

Chapter 5

Hathaway's crush: John Kobal interviewed Hathaway and later speculated, "I got the feeling—it's really no more than a hunch—that he'd been in love with her. He just stopped more often [when discussing her] and thought about it." Kobal 1985, 612.

"[A] rather mysterious girl": Gavin Lambert on *Niagara*, in *Evening Standard Great Britain* 1953.

"Some of her best scenes": Charles Brackett, quoted in Zolotow 1960, 146.

Chapter 6

"Kissing your hand": Loos 1925, 100.

Approval of *Blondes* costumes: MPAA file on *Gentlemen Prefer Blondes*, Margaret Herrick Library, Beverly Hills, CA.

"I never thought" (n. 2): Howard Hawks, quoted in McCarthy 1997, 507.

"The ladies basically walked": Gwen Verdon, quoted in McCarthy 1997, 508.

Needlepoint: Jane Russell, speaking at the Film Society of Lincoln Center tribute to Jack Cole, February 4, 1994. (The author was in attendance.)

"Honey, I've had mine": Betty Grable, quoted in Spoto, 1993, 241.

Chapter 7

"Z cowboy movie": MM, quoted in Zolotow 1960, 186.

"Maybe we could suggest" (n. 2): Darryl F. Zanuck memo, December 1, 1953, quoted in Buskin 2001, 164.

"It's just not in the same league": interview quoted in Morgan 2007, 180.

Mitzi Gaynor would later recall: 2014 Q&A with Stephen Farber, quoted in www.Iseeadarktheater.com

"That was how Zanuck wanted it" (n. 6): Miles White, conversation with the author, June 7, 1996.

Chapter 8

"She was wonderful": Tom Ewell, quoted in Buskin 2001, 184.

Chapter 9

"Put on some more clothes": Joseph L. Mankiewicz, quoted in Leaming 1998, 125.

"We were all steeped" (n. 2): Eli Wallach, archival interview for Turner Classic Movies, 2002.

"She was wonderful": Kim Stanley, interviewed in Kobal 1985, 699.

"When you played opposite her": Eileen Heckart, quoted in Buskin 2001, 200.

"Her magnetism": Bosley Crowther, *New York Times*, September 1, 1956.

Chapter 10

""The best combination": Joshua Logan, quoted in Summers 1985, 162.

"It is not the same picture": MM, cable to Jack L. Warner, April 22, 1957, quoted in Spoto 1993, 388.

Time magazine: *Time*, June 24, 1957.

"We need her desperately" (n. 2): Dame Sybil Thorndike, quoted in Guiles 1969, 218.

"She was more comfortable": Richard Avedon, quoted in Guiles 1969, 131.

Chapter 11

"Trimmer, slimmer" (n. 3): *Time*, March 23, 1959.

Prompt book quotes: a facsimile of the complete book is included in Castle 2001.

"The salt of the earth": Riese and Hitchens 1987, 552.

"I don't want to be funny": Leaming 1998, 322.

"The primitive Monroe": *Time*, April 13, 1959.

"Both charming and embarrassing": Kael 1968, 348.

"To get down to cases": *New York Post*, March 30, 1959.

Chapter 12

"Not worth the paper": Miller 1987, 466.

"Everybody [else] smartened up": Frankie Vaughan, quoted in Hutchinson 1982, 74.

"I really was awful" (n. 2): MM, quoted in Spoto 1993, 421.

"A lot of shit-ass studying": George Cukor, quoted in Lambert 1972, 174.

"Rather untidy": *New York Times*, September 8, 1960.

Chapter 13

"This is an attempt": Frank Taylor, quoted in Goode 1963, 17.

"Don't form any opinions": Goode 1963, 123.

"She's uncomplicatedly complicated" (n. 3): Thelma Ritter, quoted in Goode 1963, 86–87.

"In those days": Clark Gable, quoted in Goode 1963, 105.

"I feel that I have contributed": Paula Strasberg, quoted in Goode 1963, 259.

"This is the first time": Paula Strasberg, quoted in Goode 1963, 194.

"We had the Errol Flynn": Evelyn Moriarty, quoted in Buskin 2001, 236.

"There is a lot of absorbing detail": Bosley Crowther, *New York Times*, February 2, 1961.

"Good-by, Clark Gable": Dwight MacDonald, *Esquire*, October 1, 1961.

Chapter 14

"She was a girl": Unpublished *Ladies Home Journal* interview, quoted in Guiles 1984, 404.

"Not a story . . .": MM's notations on the cover of the *Something's Got to Give* screenplay are reproduced in Christie's New York 1999, 47–48.

"Have you been trapped": MM, quoted in Rollyson 2014b, 225.

"We've got a dog": Christie's New York 1999, 78.

"Isn't it a terrible thing" (n. 6): quoted in Morgan 2007, 321.

Chapter 15

"A woman in crisis": Leaming 1998, 267.

Epilogue

"Please don't make me": MM to Richard Meryman, July 4, 1962. Audio recording played in the 1992 TV documentary *Marilyn: The Last Interview*.

Filmography

This list represents all the known, verified film appearances made by Marilyn Monroe. As noted in chapter 1, there may be additional, unbilled film work, particularly as part of her 1946–1947 contract with Twentieth Century-Fox.

Dangerous Years

Twentieth Century-Fox. Released December 7, 1947. 62 minutes.

Director: Arthur Pierson. *Producers:* Sol M. Wurtzel, Howard Sheehan. *Screenplay:* Arnold Belgard. *Cinematographer:* Benjamin H. Kline. *Editor:* William F. Claxton.

Cast: William [Billy] Halop, Scotty Beckett, Richard Gaines, Ann E. Todd, Jerome Cowan, Anabel Shaw, Darryl Hickman, Dickie Moore, Marilyn Monroe (Evie).

Scudda Hoo! Scudda Hay!

Twentieth Century-Fox. Released April 1948. 95 minutes.

Director: F. Hugh Herbert. *Producer:* Walter Morosco. *Screenplay:* F. Hugh Herbert, based on a novel by George Agnew Chamberlain. *Cinematographer:* Ernest Palmer (Technicolor). *Editor:* Harmon Jones.

Cast: June Haver, Lon McCallister, Walter Brennan, Anne Revere, Natalie Wood, Robert Karnes, Henry Hull, Tom Tully, Marilyn Monroe (Betty, uncredited).

Ladies of the Chorus

Columbia. Released February 10, 1949. 62 minutes.

Director: Phil Karlson. *Producer:* Harry A. Romm. *Screenplay:* Harry Sauber, Joseph Carole. *Cinematographer:* Frank Redman. *Editor:* Dick Fantl. *Songs:* Allan Roberts, Lester Lee.

Cast: Adele Jergens, Marilyn Monroe (Peggy Martin), Rand Brooks, Nana Bryant, Eddie Garr, Steven Geray.

Love Happy

An Artists Alliance production released by United Artists. Released March 3, 1950. 91 minutes.

Director: David Miller. *Producer:* Lester Cowan. *Screenplay:* Frank Tashlin, Mac Benoff. *Cinematographer:* William C. Mellor. *Editors:* Basil Wrangell, Al Joseph.

Cast: Groucho Marx, Harpo Marx, Chico Marx, Ilona Massey, Vera-Ellen, Marion Hutton, Raymond Burr, Melville Cooper, Eric Blore, Leon Belasco, Paul Valentine, Bruce Gordon, Marilyn Monroe (Grunion's client).

The Asphalt Jungle

MGM. Released May 12, 1950. 112 minutes.

Director: John Huston. *Producer:* Arthur Hornblow Jr. *Screenplay:* Ben Maddow, John Huston, based on a novel by W. R. Burnett. *Cinematographer:* Harold Rosson. *Editor:* George Boemler.

Cast: Sterling Hayden, Louis Calhern, Jean Hagen, James Whitmore, Sam Jaffe, John McIntire, Marc Lawrence, Anthony Caruso, Marilyn Monroe (Angela Phinlay).

A Ticket To Tomahawk

Twentieth Century-Fox. Released May 19, 1950. 90 minutes.

Director: Richard Sale. *Producer:* Robert Bassler. *Screenplay:* Mary Loos, Richard Sale. *Cinematographer:* Harry Jackson (Technicolor). *Editor:* Harmon Jones.

Cast: Dan Dailey, Anne Baxter, Rory Calhoun, Walter Brennan, Connie Gilchrist, Arthur Hunnicutt, Chief Yowlachie, Marilyn Monroe (Clara, uncredited).

Right Cross

MGM. Released October 6, 1950. 90 minutes.

Director: John Surges. *Producer:* Armand Deutsch. *Screenplay:* Charles Schnee. *Cinematographer:* Norbert Brodine. *Editor:* James E. Newcom.

Cast: June Allyson, Dick Powell, Ricardo Montalban, Lionel Barrymore, Teresa Celli, Tom Powers, Marilyn Monroe (Dusky Ledoux, uncredited).

The Fireball

A Thor Production released by Twentieth Century-Fox. Released October 1950. 84 minutes.

Director: Tay Garnett. *Producer:* Bert Friedlob. *Screenplay:* Horace McCoy, Tay Garnett. *Cinematographer:* Lester White. *Editor:* Frank Sullivan.

Cast: Mickey Rooney, Pat O'Brien, Beverly Tyler, James Brown, Ralph Dumke, Milburn Stone, Marilyn Monroe (Polly).

All about Eve

Twentieth Century-Fox. Released October 27, 1950. 138 minutes.

Director: Joseph L. Mankiewicz. *Producer:* Darryl F. Zanuck. *Screenplay:* Joseph L. Mankiewicz, based on a story by Mary Orr. *Cinematographer:* Milton Krasner. *Editor:* Barbara McLean.

Cast: Bette Davis, Anne Baxter, George Sanders, Celeste Holm, Gary Merrill, Hugh Marlowe, Gregory Ratoff, Thelma Ritter, Marilyn Monroe (Miss Caswell), Barbara Bates, Walter Hampden.

Home Town Story

A Wolverine Production released by MGM. Released May 18, 1951. 61 minutes.

Director, writer [and uncredited producer]: Arthur Pierson. *Cinematographer:* Lucien Andriot. *Editor:* William Claxton.

Cast: Jeffrey Lynn, Donald Crisp, Marjorie Reynolds, Alan Hale Jr., Marilyn Monroe (Iris Martin), Barbara Brown, Melinda Casey, Glenn Tryon.

As Young as You Feel

Twentieth Century-Fox. Released June 1951. 77 minutes.

Director: Harmon Jones. *Producer:* Lamar Trotti. *Screenplay:* Lamar Trotti, based on a story by Paddy Chayefsky. *Cinematographer:* Joe MacDonald. *Editor:* Robert Simpson.

Cast: Monty Woolley, Thelma Ritter, David Wayne, Jean Peters, Constance Bennett, Marilyn Monroe (Harriet), Allyn Joslyn, Albert Dekker, Russ Tamblyn.

Love Nest

Twentieth Century-Fox. Released October 10, 1951. 84 minutes.

Director: Joseph M. Newman. *Producer:* Jules Buck. *Screenplay:* I. A. L. Diamond, based on a novel by Scott Corbett. *Cinematographer:* Lloyd Ahern. *Editor:* J. Watson Webb Jr.

Cast: June Haver, William Lundigan, Frank Fay, Marilyn Monroe (Roberta "Bobbie" Stevens), Jack Paar, Leatrice Joy, Henry Kulky.

Let's Make It Legal

Twentieth Century-Fox. Released November 1951. 77 minutes.

Director: Richard B. Sale. *Producer:* Robert Bassler. *Screenplay:* F. Hugh Herbert, I. A. L. Diamond, based on a story by Martimer Braus. *Cinematographer:* Lucien Ballard. *Editor:* Robert Fritch.

Cast: Claudette Colbert, Macdonald Carey, Zachary Scott, Barbara Bates, Robert Wagner, Marilyn Monroe (Joyce Mannering), Frank Cady, Harry Harvey.

Clash By Night

A Wald/Krasna Production released by RKO Radio Pictures. Released June 6, 1952. 105 minutes.

Director: Fritz Lang. *Producer:* Harriet Parsons. *Screenplay:* Alfred Hayes, based on a play by Clifford Odets. *Cinematographer:* Nicholas Musuraca. *Editor:* George Amy.

Cast: Barbara Stanwyck, Paul Douglas, Robert Ryan, Marilyn Monroe (Peggy), J. Carrol Naish, Keith Andes, Silvio Minciotti.

We're Not Married

Twentieth Century-Fox. Released July 1952. 85 minutes.

Director: Edmund Goulding. *Producer:* Nunnally Johnson. *Screenplay:* Nunnally John, Dwight Taylor, from a story by Gina Kaus and Jay Dratler. *Cinematographer:* Leo Tover. *Editor:* Louis Loeffler.

Cast: Ginger Rogers, Fred Allen, Victor Moore, Marilyn Monroe (Annabel Norris), David Wayne, Eve Arden, Paul Douglas, Mitzi Gaynor, Eddie Bracken, Zsa Zsa Gabor, Louis Calhern, Jane Darwell.

Don't Bother To Knock

Twentieth Century-Fox, released August 1952. 76 minutes.

Director: Roy Baker. *Producer:* Julian Blaustein. *Screenplay:* Daniel Taradash, based on a novel by Charlotte Armstrong. *Cinematographer:* Lucien Ballard. *Editor:* George A. Gittens.

Cast: Richard Widmark, Marilyn Monroe (Nell Forbes), Anne Bancroft, Donna Corcoran, Jeanne Cagney, Lurene Tuttle, Elisha Cook Jr., Jim Backus, Verna Felton, Willis Bouchey, Don Beddoe.

Monkey Business

Twentieth Century-Fox. Released September 5, 1952. 97 minutes.

Director: Howard Hawks. *Producer:* Sol C. Siegel. *Screenplay:* Ben Hecht, Charles Lederer, I. A. L. Diamond, based on a story by Harry Segall. *Cinematographer:* Milton Krasner. *Editor:* William B. Murphy.

Cast: Cary Grant, Ginger Rogers, Charles Coburn, Marilyn Monroe (Lois Laurel), Hugh Marlowe, Henri Letondal, Robert Cornthwaite, Larry Keating.

O. Henry's Full House

Twentieth Century-Fox. Released October 16, 1952. 117 minutes.

Directors: Henry Koster ("The Cop and the Anthem"), Henry Hathaway, Jean Negulesco, Howard Hawks, Henry King. *Producer:* Andre Hakim. *Screenplay:* Lamar Trotti, Richard Breen, Ivan Goff, Ben Roberts, Walter Bullock, Philip Dunne, Ben Hecht, Nunnally Johnson, Charles Lederer, based on stories by O. Henry. *Cinematographers:* Lloyd Ahern, Lucien Ballard, Milton Krasner, Joe MacDonald. *Editors:* Dick DeMaggio, Barbara McLean, William B. Murphy.

Cast: John Steinbeck, Fred Allen, Anne Baxter, Jeanne Crain, Farley Granger, Charles Laughton, Oscar Levant, Marilyn Monroe (Streetwalker), Jean Peters, Gregory Ratoff, Dale Robertson, David Wayne.

Niagara

Twentieth Century-Fox. Released February 1953. 89 minutes.

Director: Henry Hathaway. *Producer:* Charles Brackett. *Screenplay:* Charles Brackett, Walter Reisch, Richard Breen. *Cinematographer:* Joe MacDonald (Technicolor). *Editor:* Barbara McLean.

Cast: Marilyn Monroe (Rose Loomis), Joseph Cotten, Jean Peters, Casey Adams, Denis O'Dea, Richard Allan, Don Wilson, Lurene Tuttle, Russell Collins, Will Wright.

Gentlemen Prefer Blondes

Twentieth Century-Fox. Released August 1953. 91 minutes.

Director: Howard Hawks. *Producer:* Sol C. Siegel. *Screenplay:* Charles Lederer, based on the novel by Anita Loos and the musical comedy by Loos and Joseph Fields. *Cinematographer:* Harry J. Wild (Technicolor). *Editor:* Hugh S. Fowler. *Songs:* Jule Styne, Leo Robin, Hoagy Carmichael, Harold Adamson.

Cast: Jane Russell, Marilyn Monroe (Lorelei Lee), Charles Coburn, Elliott Reid, Tommy Noonan, George Winslow, Marcel Dalio, Taylor Holmes, Norma Varden, Howard Wendell.

How to Marry a Millionaire

Twentieth Century-Fox. Released November 20, 1953. 95 minutes.

Director: Jean Negulesco. *Producer:* Nunnally Johnson. *Screenplay:* Nunnally Johnson, based on plays by Zoe Akins, Dale Eunson, Katherine Albert. *Cinematographer:* Joe MacDonald (Technicolor/CinemaScope). *Editor:* Louis Loeffler.

Cast: Betty Grable, Marilyn Monroe (Pola Debevoise), Lauren Bacall, David Wayne, Rory Calhoun, Cameron Mitchell, Alex D'Arcy, Fred Clark, William Powell.

River of No Return

Twentieth Century-Fox. Released May 1954. 91 minutes.

Director: Otto Preminger. *Producer:* Stanley Rubin. *Screenplay:* Frank Fenton, based on a story by Louis Lantz. *Cinematographer:* Joseph LaShelle (Technicolor/CinemaScope). *Editor:* Louis Loeffler. *Songs:* Lionel Newman, Ken Darby.

Cast: Robert Mitchum, Marilyn Monroe (Kay Weston), Rory Calhoun, Tommy Rettig, Murvyn Vye, Douglas Spencer.

There's No Business Like Show Business

Twentieth Century-Fox. Released December 1954. 117 minutes.

Director: Walter Lang. *Producer:* Sol C. Siegel. *Screenplay:* Phoebe Ephron, Henry Ephron, based on a story by Lamar Trotti. *Cinematographer:* Leon Shamroy (DeLuxe Color/CinemaScope). *Editor:* Robert Simpson. *Songs:* Irving Berlin.

Cast: Ethel Merman, Donald O'Connor, Marilyn Monroe (Victoria Hoffman/Vicky Parker), Dan Dailey, Johnnie Ray, Mitzi Gaynor, Richard Eastham, Hugh O'Brian, Frank McHugh, Rhys Williams, Lee Patrick.

The Seven Year Itch

A Charles K. Feldman Group Production released by Twentieth Century-Fox. Released June 3, 1955. 105 minutes.

Director: Billy Wilder. *Producers*: Charles K. Feldman, Billy Wilder. *Screenplay*: Billy Wilder, George Axelrod, based on the play by Axelrod. *Cinematographer*: Milton Krasner (DeLuxe Color/CinemaScope). *Editor*: Hugh Fowler.

Cast: Marilyn Monroe (The Girl Upstairs), Tom Ewell, Evelyn Keyes, Sonny Tufts, Robert Strauss, Oscar Homolka, Marguerite Chapman, Victor Moore, Roxanne, Donald MacBride, Carolyn Jones.

Bus Stop

Twentieth Century-Fox. Released August 1956. 96 minutes.

Director: Joshua Logan. *Producer*: Buddy Adler. *Screenplay*: George Axelrod, based on the play by William Inge. *Cinematographer*: Milton Krasner (DeLuxe Color, CinemaScope). *Editor*: William Reynolds.

Cast: Marilyn Monroe (Cherie), Don Murray, Arthur O'Connell, Betty Field, Eileen Heckart, Robert Bray, Hope Lange, Hans Conreid, Casey Adams.

The Prince and the Showgirl

A Marilyn Monroe Productions production released by Warner Bros. Released July 6, 1957. 115 minutes.

Director and producer: Laurence Olivier. *Screenplay*: Terence Rattigan, based on his play. *Cinematographer*: Jack Cardiff (Technicolor). *Editor*: Jack Harris.

Cast: Marilyn Monroe (Elsie Marina), Laurence Olivier, Sybil Thornike, Richard Wattis, Jeremy Spenser, Jean Kent, David Thorne, Gladys Henson, Harold Goodwin, Charles Victor.

Some Like It Hot

A Mirisch Company Picture presented by Ashton Productions and released by United Artists. Released March 19, 1959. 121 minutes.

Director and producer: Billy Wilder. *Screenplay:* Billy Wilder, I. A. L. Diamond, suggested by a story by Robert Thoeren and Michael Logan. *Cinematographer:* Charles Lang Jr. *Editor:* Arthur P. Schmidt.

Cast: Marilyn Monroe (Sugar Kane), Tony Curtis, Jack Lemmon, George Raft, Pat O'Brien, Joe E. Brown, Nehemiah Persoff, Joan Shawlee, Billy Gray, George E. Stone, Dave Barry, Mike Mazurki, Harry Wilson, Beverly Wills, Barbara Drew, Edward G. Robinson Jr.

Let's Make Love

A Company of Artists production released by Twentieth Century-Fox. Released September 8, 1960. 119 minutes.

Director: George Cukor. *Producer:* Jerry Wald. *Screenplay:* Norman Krasna, Hal Kanter, based (uncredited) on a screenplay by Gene Markey, William M. Conselman. *Cinematographer:* Daniel L. Fapp (DeLuxe Color, CinemaScope). *Editor:* David Bretherton. *Songs:* Jimmy Van Heusen, Sammy Cahn, Cole Porter.

Cast: Marilyn Monroe (Amanda Dell), Yves Montand, Tony Randall, Frankie Vaughan, Wilfrid Hyde-White, David Burns, Michael David, Mara Lynn, Dennis King Jr., Joe Besser, Milton Berle, Gene Kelly, Bing Crosby.

The Misfits

A Seven Arts Production released by United Artists. Released February 1, 1961. 125 minutes.

Director: John Huston. *Producer:* Frank E. Taylor. *Screenplay:* Arthur Miller, based on his story. *Cinematographer:* Russell Metty. *Editor:* George Tomasini.

Cast: Clark Gable, Marilyn Monroe (Roslyn Taber), Montgomery Clift, Thelma Ritter, Eli Wallach, James Barton, Kevin McCarthy, Estelle Winwood.

Something's Got to Give

Twentieth Century-Fox, 1962 (uncompleted).

Director: George Cukor. *Producer:* Henry Weinstein. *Screenplay:* Nunnally Johnson, Walter Bernstein, et al., based on the screenplay by Bella Spewack and Sam Spewack. *Cinematographer:* Franz Planer, Leo Tover (DeLuxe Color/CinemaScope).

Cast: Marilyn Monroe (Ellen Arden), Dean Martin, Cyd Charisse, Steve Allen, Tom Tryon, Phil Silvers, Wally Cox, John McGiver, Alexandra Heilweil, Robert Christopher Morley, Grady Sutton.

Annotated Discography

Even counting the soundtrack cuts from her musical films, Marilyn Monroe left only a small number of recordings. Aside from the soundtracks, very few of them were released in her lifetime. Since her death, it appears that every available recorded scrap of her singing has been released and rereleased on various compilations and anthologies (with one exception, the early "How Wrong Can I Be?"). This list covers only the original recordings or releases.

1948 (?)

"How Wrong Can I Be?" Unreleased private recording, with Fred Karger at the piano.

1953

"Kiss"/"Do It Again." Released posthumously.
Gentlemen Prefer Blondes. Soundtrack, MGM Records.
"A Fine Romance"/"She Acts Like a Woman Should." Released posthumously.

1954

"River of No Return"/"I'm Gonna File My Claim." Soundtrack cuts from *River of No Return*, RCA Victor.
"Heat Wave"/"Lazy"/"After You Get What You Want You Don't Want It"/ "You'd Be Surprised." RCA Victor. The first three are soundtrack cuts from *There's No Business Like Show Business*; "You'd Be Surprised" is a studio recording. Released on a 45-rpm "extended play" disc titled *Marilyn Monroe Sings Selections from the Soundtrack of Darryl F. Zanuck's Presentation of Irving Berlin's There's No Business Like Show Business*. (Due to her recording contract with RCA, Monroe's *Show Business* cuts were not included on the

Decca soundtrack album for the film. On that disc, her songs were performed by Dolores Gray.)

1959

Some Like It Hot. Soundtrack, United Artists.
Marilyn Monroe Sings! United Artists. A 45-rpm "extended play" disc that includes Monroe's three songs from the *Some Like It Hot* soundtrack—"Runnin' Wild," "I Wanna Be Loved by You," "I'm Through with Love"—plus her recording of the title song, not used on the LP or in the film.

1960

Let's Make Love. Soundtrack, Columbia.

Selected Radio and Television Appearances

Although Marilyn Monroe received extensive coverage on radio and television, particularly from 1950 onward, she is known to have given only a small number of performances in either medium, as opposed to short interviews or news-related appearances. Possible other early appearances on radio and television are unverified.

1947

February 24: *Lux Radio Theater* (CBS Radio). As part of a one-hour version of the 1945 film *Kitty*, Monroe appears as an "intermission guest" in a scripted interview with host William Keighley.

1950

Television commercial. Monroe endorses Royal Triton motor oil, a product of the Union Oil Company of California.

1952

August 31: *Hollywood Star Playhouse* episode "Statement in Full" (NBC Radio). Monroe played murderess June Cordell in her only known "dramatic" radio appearance; she had taped the program on August 21.

October 26: *The Edgar Bergen Show with Charlie McCarthy* (CBS Radio). In a sketch taped on October 18, Monroe and Charlie McCarthy announce their "engagement."

1953

September 13: *The Jack Benny Program* (CBS Television). In this live telecast, Monroe plays herself in a sketch titled "Honolulu Trip."

1955

April 8: *Person to Person* (CBS Television). A live interview by Edward R. Murrow. Milton Greene and Amy Greene also appear.

Selected Bibliography

As has been noted in the text and elsewhere, the books on Marilyn Monroe now number somewhere around one thousand. They range from sober, well-researched biographies to glorious picture volumes to outright fiction to, as you might expect, junk that should be labeled fiction and isn't. It goes without saying that many of those recall Arthur Miller's words about the *Let's Make Love* script: "Not worth the paper it's typed [or printed!] upon." Those aren't included in this list, and, it must be admitted, neither are some of the more worthy volumes. There's just so much, and so much an opinionated guide can take in.

The list that follows, then, includes some (not all) of the most worthwhile and informative literature about Monroe and her work. Many of these were vastly helpful, and all of them deserve a look by those who wish to investigate further.

Also listed are sources cited in the text.

Banner, Lois W. 2011. *MM—Personal: From the Private Archive of Marilyn Monroe*. New York: Abrams.

Banner, Lois W. 2012. *Marilyn: The Passion and the Paradox*. New York: Bloomsbury.

Brown, Harry, and Patte B. Barham. 1992. *Marilyn: The Last Take*. New York: Dutton.

Buchthal, Stanley F., and Bernard Comment, eds. 2010. *Marilyn Monroe: Fragments*. New York: Farrar, Straus & Giroux.

Buskin, Richard. 2001. *Blonde Heat: The Sizzling Screen Career of Marilyn Monroe*. New York: Billboard.

Carey, Gary, and Mankiewicz, Joseph L. 1974. *More about* All about Eve. New York: Bantam Books.

Castle, Alison, ed. 2001. *Billy Wilder's* Some Like It Hot: *The Funniest Film Ever Made, the Complete Book*. Cologne: Taschen.

Christie's New York. 1999. *The Personal Property of Marilyn Monroe*. New York: Christie's.

Clark, Colin. 1996. *The Prince, the Showgirl, and Me*. New York: St. Martin's.

Clark, Colin. 2011. *My Week with Marilyn*. New York: Hachette.

Curtis, Tony, and Mark A. Vieira. 2009. *The Making of "Some Like It Hot."* Hoboken: Wiley.

Davis, Ronald L. 2005. *Just Making Movies*. Jackson: University Press of Mississippi.

De La Hoz, Cindy. 2010. *Marilyn Monroe: The Personal Archives*. London: Carlton.

Glatzer, Jenna. 2008. *The Marilyn Monroe Treasures*. New York: Metro.

Goode, James. 1963. *The Story of* The Misfits. Indianapolis: Bobbs-Merrill.

Guiles, Fred Lawrence. 1969. *Norma Jean: The Life of Marilyn Monroe*. New York: McGraw-Hill.

Guiles, Fred Lawrence. 1984. *Legend: The Life and Death of Marilyn Monroe*. New York: Stein and Day.

Hansford, Andrew, and Karen Homer. 2011. *Dressing Marilyn: How a Hollywood Icon Was Styled by William Travilla*. Milwaukee: Applause.

Hoyt, Edwin. 1965. *Marilyn: The Tragic Venus*. New York: Chilton.

Hutchinson, Tom. 1982. *Marilyn Monroe*. London: Hamlyn.

Kael, Pauline. 1968. *Kiss Kiss Bang Bang*. Boston: Little, Brown.

Kobal, John. 1985. *People Will Talk*. New York: Knopf.

Kobal, John. 1986. *Marilyn Monroe: A Life on Film*. New York: Simon & Schuster.

Lambert, Gavin. 1972. *On Cukor*. New York: Putnam's.

Law, John William. 2019. *Goddess & the Girl Next Door: Marilyn Monroe, Doris Day & the Movie They Shared*. San Francisco: Aplomb.

Leaming, Barbara. 1998. *Marilyn Monroe*. New York: Crown.

Loos, Anita. 1925. *Gentlemen Prefer Blondes: The Illuminating Diary of a Professional Lady*. New York: Boni & Liveright.

Mailer, Norman. 1973. *Marilyn: A Biography*. New York: Grosset & Dunlap.

Martin, Pete. 1956. *Will Acting Spoil Marilyn Monroe?* Garden City: Doubleday.

Maslon, Laurence. 2009. *Some Like It Hot: The Official 50th Anniversary Companion*. New York: Harper Design.

McCann, Graham. 1987. *Marilyn Monroe*. New Brunswick, NJ: Rutgers University Press.

McCarthy, Todd. 1997. *Howard Hawks: The Grey Fox of Hollywood*. New York: Grove.

Mellen, Joan. 1974. *Marilyn Monroe*. New York: Pyramid.

Miller, Arthur. 1987. *Timebends: A Life*. New York: Grove.

Miracle, Berniece Baker, and Mona Rae Miracle. 1994. *My Sister Marilyn: A Memoir of Marilyn Monroe*. Chapel Hill: Algonquin.

Monroe, Marilyn, and Ben Hecht. 1974. *My Story*. New York: Stein & Day.

Morgan, Michelle. 2007. *Marilyn Monroe: Private and Undisclosed*. New York: Carroll & Graf.

Murray, Eunice, and Rose Shade. 1975. *Marilyn: The Last Months*. New York: Pyramid.

Riese, Randall, and Neal Hitchens. 1987. *The Unabridged Marilyn: Her Life from A to Z*. New York: Congdon & Weed.

Rollyson, Carl. 2014a. *Marilyn Monroe Day by Day*. Lanham, MD: Rowman & Littlefield.

Rollyson, Carl. 2014b. *Marilyn Monroe: A Life of the Actress*. Revised and updated. Jackson: University Press of Mississippi.

Rosten, Norman. 1973. *Marilyn: An Untold Story*. New York: Signet.

Schwarz, Ted. 2009. *Marilyn Revealed: The Ambitious Life of an American Icon*. Lanham, MD: Taylor Trade.

Smith, Pete. 1956. *Will Acting Spoil Marilyn Monroe?* New York: Doubleday.

Solomon, Aubrey. 2002. *Twentieth Century-Fox: A Corporate and Financial History*. Lanham, MD: Scarecrow.

Spoto, Donald. 1993, *Marilyn Monroe: The Biography*. New York: HarperCollins.

Steinem, Gloria, and George Barris. 1986. *Marilyn: Norma Jeane*. New York: Henry Holt.

Strasberg, Susan. 1992. *Marilyn and Me: Sisters, Rivals, Friends*. New York: Warner.

Summers, Anthony. 1985. *Goddess: The Secret Lives of Marilyn Monroe*. New York: Macmillan.

Taraborrelli, J. Randy. 2009. *The Secret Life of Marilyn Monroe*. New York: Grand Central.

Victor, Adam. 1999. *The Marilyn Encyclopedia*. New York: Overlook.

Vitacco-Robles, Gary. 2014a. *Icon: The Life, Times, and Films of Marilyn Monroe, Volume 1: 1926 to 1956*. Albany, GA: BearManor.

Vitacco-Robles, Gary. 2014b. *Icon: The Life, Times, and Films of Marilyn Monroe. Volume 2: 1956 to 1962 & Beyond*. Albany, GA: BearManor.

Wagenecht, Edward, ed. 1969. *Marilyn Monroe: A Composite View*. Philadelphia: Chilton.

Weatherby, W. J. 1976. *Conversations with Marilyn*. New York: Mason/Charter.

Wills, David, and Stephen Schmidt. 2011. *Marilyn Monroe: Metamorphosis*. New York: It.
Wolfe, Donald H. 1998. *The Last Days of Marilyn Monroe*. New York: William Morrow.
Zolotow, Maurice. 1960. *Marilyn Monroe*. New York: Harcourt Brace.
Zolotow, Maurice. 1997. *Billy Wilder in Hollywood*. New York: Putnam.

Index

For the benefit of digital users, indexed terms that span two pages (e.g., 52–53) may, on occasion, appear on only one of those pages.

Years given for films (in parentheses) denote release date. Names in parentheses after titles of literary works denote author.

Karger, Fred, 12, 56, 57–58, 59, 60, 118
Karlson, Phil, 57–58
Karnes, Robert, 52–53
Kazan, Elia, 15, 26–27, 31, 81, 93–94, 153–54, 186
Keighley, William, 10–11, 50–51, 55–56
Kelley, Tom, 13, 63
Kelly, Gene, 38, 194–95
Kelly, Grace, 148, 158n.4
Kelly, Nancy, 158n.4
Kennedy, John F., 34, 36, 217–18, 223–24
Kennedy, Robert F., 217–18
Keyes, Evelyn, 144–45
Khrushchev, Nikita, 31
King Lear, 77
King, Henry, 91
Kiss Me, Stupid (1964), 179n.4
Kiss of Death (1947), 93–94
Kitty (1945), 152
Koster, Henry, 21, 100–1, 121–22, 131
Krasna, Norman, 31, 88–89, 187–88

Ladies of the Chorus (1949), 12, 13, 19, 56–60, 62–63, 89, 96, 114, 118, 218n.5
Lady L [uncompleted, 1961], 216n.4
Lamarr, Hedy, 104–5
Lambert, Gavin, 108–9
Lancaster, Burt, 148–49, 163
Lang, Fritz, 89–90
Lang, Walter, 10, 23, 48–49, 134–35, 138
Lansing, Joi, 77–78, 226
Laughton, Charles, 53–54, 98, 100–1
Laura (1944), 52–53, 73–74, 125–26
Lawford, Peter, 6
Lean, David, 145–46
Leave Her to Heaven (1945), 91–92
Ledger, Heath, 204
Leigh, Vivien, 152, 154–55, 163–64, 169–70n.3, 172–73
Lemmon, Jack, 174, 177, 178–79, 180
Let's Make It Legal (1951), 16, 75, 84–86, 87–88, 99, 101, 102, 227n.4
Let's Make Love (1960), 3n.1, 31, 32–33, 34, 39, 42n.2, 88n.1, 123–24, 128–29, 166n.1, 171–72, 185–95, 200, 202–3, 205–6, 209, 211–12, 213–14, 215, 216, 221–22

Letter to Three Wives, A (1949), 73–74, 145n.3
Letter, The (1929), 210n.1
Levant, Oscar, 99–100
Levathes, Peter, 35, 37–38
Lieutenant Wore Skirts, The (1956), 187 n.2
Lili (1953), 141n.1
Lipton, Harry, 9, 53–54
Little Big Shot (1935), 41n.1
Loco (Albert/Eunson), 120
Logan, Joshua, 154, 155–56, 157–58, 159, 160–61, 164–65, 166–67
Lollobrigida, Gina, 216n.4
Loos, Anita, 113–14, 119–20
Lopat, ["Steady"] Eddie, 145–46
Louis, Jean, 217–18
Love Happy (1950), 10, 13, 61–62, 63–64, 72, 85–86, 98
Love Nest (1951), 16, 75–76, 82–84, 87, 101, 103–4, 106–7
Lower, Ana, 8–9
Lundigan, William, 82–84
Lux Radio Theatre, 10–11, 50–51
Lynn, Jeffrey, 69–70
Lyon, Ben, 9–10, 47–50
Lytess, Natasha, 12, 14, 19, 20, 21, 28, 55–56, 62–64, 66–68, 71–72, 76–77, 89, 92–93, 95, 107–8, 115–16, 118, 126–27, 132–33, 142–43, 150–51, 152–53, 156–57

MacLaine, Shirley, 39, 179n.4, 186n.1
Madonna, 2, 227
Mailer, Norman, 223–24
Malneck, Matty, 182–83
Mankiewicz, Joseph L., 70–71, 74, 149, 154
Mansfield, Jayne, 78–79, 108–9, 143n.2, 226
Marathon Man, The (1976), 167
March, Fredric, 29, 209–10
Marie Antoinette (1938), 42
Marilyn (1963), 39, 221–22
Marilyn (Mailer), 223–24
Marilyn Monroe Productions, 25, 26–27, 149–50, 153, 154–55, 163–65
Marley, Eve, 93n.3
Marriage-Go-Round, The (1961), 212
Martin, Dean, 37, 39, 215, 217, 218–19, 220